SO-AXJ-585

100 MOST

DANGEROUS

THINGS IN EVERYDAY LIFE

AND WHAT YOU CAN DO ABOUT THEM

LAURA LEE

APPLE

An EYE book

100 MOST DANGEROUS THINGS IN EVERYDAY LIFE AND WHAT YOU CAN DO ABOUT THEM
Copyright © 2004 EYE Quarto, Inc.

Conceived, designed and produced by
EYE
276 Fifth Avenue
Suite 205
New York, NY 10001

Editor: Michael Driscoll
Illustrations: SJI Associates, Inc.
Cover design: SJI Associates, Inc.
Interior design: SJI Associates, Inc. and Sheila Hart Design, Inc.
Copyeditor: Stephanie Finnegan
Proofreaders: Edwin Kiester Jr. and Adam Sommers

Publisher: William Kiester

First published in the United Kingdom by
Apple Press
Sheridan House, 4th Floor
112-116A Western Road
Hove, East Sussex BN3 1DD
United Kingdom
www.apple-press.com

MANUFACTURED IN CHINA.

ISBN 1-84092-442-x

10 9 8 7 6 5 4 3 2 1

Acknowledgments

To Valeri Lantratov, without whom this book would have been finished much sooner. "Don't worry. Easy." Thank you also to my publisher, and to Michael Driscoll and William Kiester at EYE for extreme patience when the author ran away to manage a ballet troupe in the middle of the writing process.

Contents

Introduction

The assertion on the opposite page defies conventional wisdom, but it's true nonetheless. Grizzlies may have knives for teeth and claws like razors, but they're seldom found in the bedroom. A teddy's primary habitat, on the other hand, is under the covers. Particularly sinister ones have been known to sneak in button eyes that can be swallowed, loose fur that can be choked upon and a host of debilitating viruses and bacteria that were picked up at nursery school. But when was the last time you read a bedtime story featuring a menacing Winnie or Paddington?

Human beings, in general, tend to overestimate the dangers of rare events while dismissing the dangers of everyday ones. In fact, everyday events are more likely to cause you harm if for no other reason than they happen every day. We're also much more likely to fear man-made problems than natural ones. Risk consultant Peter Sandman believes our level of fear tends to correspond more to our level of "outrage" than to our actual level of risk. This is why, for example, we're more worried about getting AIDS from a blood transfusion than by being struck by lightning—when, in fact, the latter is thirty times more likely to occur than the former.

We travel less by plane than we do by car, so we fear it more, even though we're much more likely to die in a car crash. We worry about engineered chemicals even though many foods contain far more natural carcinogens. We worry about being assaulted in the streets but not about being injured in the kitchen (where, in America, for example, 1 million people are seriously hurt

Fact:

More people are killed
each year by teddy bears
than by grizzly bears.

each year), the lounge (where 400,000 are injured annually) or the toilet (site of more than 150,000 serious accidents each year).

If you watch the news today, you may have a sense that the world is more fraught with danger than at any time in the past. Yet people in the developed world are healthier, safer and living longer than ever before. In the fourteen hundred years between the fall of the Roman Empire and the 1800s, the life span of an average person living in the most developed societies increased by just nine years, from 38 to 47 years. Since 1900, it has increased almost four times as fast, to nearly 80 years. In the poorer countries of Asia, the average life span has increased by 20 percent since 1950. In a recent study of Swedish national death records conducted at the University of California at Berkeley, the maximum age was found to have moved up slowly throughout the past century, and shows no sign of levelling off. The researchers wrote: "[We found] no scientific basis on which to estimate a fixed upper limit. We are changing the limits of the human life span over time." If you missed that story on the six o'clock news, you probably did not miss the many stories about "epidemics" that are supposedly making us less healthy than previous generations. In fact, in terms of overall life expectancy, the world is probably a safer place now than it was when you started reading this paragraph.

Each year around the holidays there is a story about the dangers of toys. While toys do pose dangers to children, other household objects receive much less attention while posing a much greater threat—a child is eight times as likely to be injured by home furnishings, three times as likely to be injured by stairs and twice as likely to be injured by a chair as by a toy.

The truth is, you can't create a risk-free environment no matter how hard you try. Protecting against one thing often leads to another unintended consequence. To cite one famous example, the masks issued to the British population in September 1938 to protect against the threat of deadly gases released by the Nazis had filters made of asbestos. When used properly, the safety devices sent microscopic fibres of damaging mineral silicates into the lungs.

So what's one to do? Never climb out of bed? (Not a good idea, page 20.) Take a holiday to get away from it all? (Better not, page 222.) Acquire every safety device imaginable? (Guess again, page 162.)

As it turns out, even avoiding risks is not risk-free, but one can take solace in this book's paradoxical purpose, which is not to increase the general paranoia but to diminish it. If you can look such deadly items as kitchen knives, bedding, vegetables and teddies in the face each day without fear, you should be able to stare down the much more statistically unlikely threats that now haunt our collective consciousness. In the words of Helen Keller, "Security is mostly a superstition. It does not exist in nature. Life is either a daring adventure or nothing."

Don't worry. You're safe.

Art Supplies

I f the pen is mightier than the sword, it should come as no surprise that the paintbrush is more dangerous than the rifle. Dr. Stephen Roberts, an Oxford University scholar, compiled a list of the thirty most dangerous occupations by studying government workplace fatality records between 1976 and 1995. The results were published in the British medical journal the *Lancet*. Painters and decorators ranked twenty-seventh on the list, military personnel twenty-eighth.

Why are so many people suffering for their art? Visual arts involve the use of many chemicals, solvents and materials. Painters can slowly poison themselves by putting paintbrushes in their mouths or accidentally swallowing small amounts of emulsion and other art materials.

Exposure to solvents like turpentine can cause nerve damage. Stained-glass artists are regularly exposed to lead, which can damage the brain, nerves, red blood cells, reproductive system and digestive system. Ceramic artists are often felled by what they call "potter's rot," another name for silicosis, a lung disease. They get it by breathing in too much silica dust.

These problems are often exacerbated by the nature of the artist's life. Many artists are famously fond of clutter—dangerous clutter. A study of university art departments conducted by the state of Maryland's Department of Labor and Industry in the mid-1980s found that art studios often improperly stored volatile solvents and didn't clean up leftover materials like wood and metal shavings.

"Often there was total disregard for personal safety, health and well-being in the guise of keeping an environment that is nonrestrictive and conducive to 'free expression,'" wrote C. Donald Schott of Johns Hopkins University, one of the authors of the study.

A number of studies since the 1970s have furthermore established a link between mental illness, particularly bipolar disorder, and artistic creativity. A new study by psychologists at the University of Toronto and Harvard University found that creative people as a group are poor at shutting out irrelevant information, a process called "latent inhibition." Such a wide focus may be useful for creating original art, but it is also associated with mental illnesses like schizophrenia.

"It appears likely that low levels of latent inhibition and exceptional flexibility in thought might predispose to mental illness under some conditions and to creative accomplishment under others," writes Shelley Carson, one of the authors of the study.

All of this is made worse by the fact that, as a rule, artists do not make huge sums of money nor are they employed by large firms. Therefore, a large percentage of U.S. artists do not have health insurance. The Arts-Medicine Project at the University of Illinois at Chicago specialises in treating artists. Roughly half of the patients at the clinic have no medical insurance.

What You Can Do
Become an accountant.

Assuming you're not interested in that option, here are some suggestions for making an artist's life a little less hazardous, courtesy of the University of Ottawa's Department of Visual Arts:

Learn about the hazards of the materials and processes you use. Always keep your studio clean and well ventilated and do your best to avoid breathing vapours from solvents and emulsions. Solvents are often flammable, so do what you can to avoid static electricity discharges while using them. After working with pigments or solvents, wash your hands before eating. Sculptors should always wear dust masks, eye protection and hearing protection.

Autumn Leaves

In certain parts of the world, nature unleashes a spectacular display of natural beauty every autumn as leaves change from universal green to vibrant shades of red, orange and gold. Meanwhile, nature is unleashing something else—a wide variety of health and safety hazards. The leaves do not simply disappear. They accumulate in waterways and in gardens. Their decomposition and the side effects of their disposal put people's eyes, lungs and immune systems at risk.

As the colourful foliage floats lazily down a chilling stream, it fills the waterway with poison. This, according to a 2000 study by Steven J. Balogh and his colleagues at Metropolitan Council Environmental Services in St. Paul, Minnesota. The scientists monitored concentrations of mercury and methylmercury (the organic form of mercury) at sites on two southern Minnesota waterways and found that concentrations of methylmercury were highest in late fall. Drew Bodaly of Fisheries and Oceans Canada in Winnipeg, Manitoba, told Science News that the concentrations of methylmercury found in the tested rivers were as high as those near industrial pollution sources.

Methylmercury gets into the human food supply when people eat tainted fish. Enough mercury in the system can cause neurological deficiencies in children who have been exposed to it in the womb.

But be careful in your rush to rid yourself of leaves. Burning them causes yet another health problem. The American Lung Association warns that leaf burning produces carbon monoxide, which is a potentially lethal gas that deprives the body of oxygen. The association is currently studying the long-term health effects of the practice.

What You Can Do

Instead of burning leaves, the American Lung Association recommends mulching. Before you begin, however, you should know that not even this is entirely risk free. In 1991, a New Jersey man was burned over 40 percent of his body while mulching leaves. A spark from the petrol-operated mulcher ignited the leaves around the man's feet, and his trousers caught fire. Use caution.

A more creative solution would be to put an end to autumn altogether, or at least to the deluge of leaves. Richard Amasino and Susheng Gan of the University of Wisconsin-Madison in 1996 isolated a genetic marker that starts the process that makes the leaves change colour and eventually fall. They also found a way to create a synthetic promoter of a hormone that blocks the process. The result? No falling leaves. Genetically engineering that blocker into all the deciduous trees in the world might be a little impractical, however.

Bagels

It will probably come as no surprise to learn that knives are dangerous. Each year in the United States an estimated 386,352 people are hurt by them. Before you conjure up images of street fights or the shower scene from *Psycho*, however, you should know that most knife wounds are made in a much more mundane way. Blame the bagel.

Bagels, with their hard outer crusts, are an accident waiting to happen. A man with a carbohydrate craving grabs a bagel and places it in his hand. With the other hand he grabs a knife. He starts slicing into the bagel toward his own palm and somehow forgets to stop once the knife makes it through the other side of the bread. Just such an injury threatened to end the career of golfer Skip Kendall. As he told the *Washington Times*, "One moment I'm cutting a bagel, and the next blood is spurting everywhere. ...I see I've basically amputated my left index finger [forefinger]. It's safe to say I was pretty stirred up." Fortunately, doctors were able to mend his finger, and he was able to golf again three weeks later.

News articles have reported that bagel slips are the most common complaint in American casualty wards. The *International Herald Tribune* looked into this assertion and found only a shred of truth in it. People who have sliced their own palms are some of the most common patients in the accident ward, but "bagel-slicing cuts are common at some of them, rare at others, as few as one case a month." Apples, scones, cheese, oysters, frozen foods and vegetables can all inspire unfortunate knife accidents.

Does this mean that you can relax around bagels? Not necessarily. The magazine *Environmental Nutrition* dubbed the bagel an "oesophageal terrorist" after a woman was sent to hospital by one. She swallowed a piece that was a bit too large and it ripped a hole in her upper oesophagus. Fortunately, she recovered with treatment.

Shortly thereafter, a couple from Panama City Beach, Florida, sued a McDonald's restaurant. The couple claimed a hard bagel damaged the man's dental work and caused his wife to lose "the care, comfort, consortium and society of her husband."

What is more, a single poppy-seed bagel is enough to produce a false positive in a drug test for opiates. So bagels could potentially tear up your insides, ruin your marriage and land you in jail. Don't say you weren't warned.

What You Can Do
For those who favour technical solutions, there are special kitchen devices available for slicing bagels without resting them in the palm of your hand. A less expensive solution suggested by the *International Herald Tribune* is to place the bagel flat on the counter with one hand on top. Cut parallel to the counter, and don't curl your fingers around the bagel as you do so.

Environmental Nutrition suggests that when you are eating bagels and other potentially sharp foods (tortilla chips, crackers, vegetables), take small bites and chew thoroughly.

Finally, don't feed bagels to black bears. The only human to be injured by a black bear in the state of New Jersey since 1953, when the state began keeping records, was a 5-year-old boy named Billy Jacobs. Billy made the mistake, in 2001, of offering a bagel to a 130-lb/58.97-kg bear. The bear gobbled up the bagel and apparently liked it so much that he came back for more. He swiped at young Billy and left him with four long scratches across his shoulder. The boy was treated in hospital and suffered no lasting damage. Would the same thing have happened if the boy had offered the bear beetroots?

Ballet

Which is more violent—boxing or ballet dancing? Boxing, of course. Which is more genteel and delicate? Ballet, no question. Which produces more injuries? That would be ballet.

Professional ballet dancers get hurt more often than boxers or hockey players, and their injuries are as serious as are those to athletes in any of the major contact sports. In fact, if you look at injury statistics alone, ballet is more dangerous than boxing and ice hockey combined. Dance results in about 45,000 accident ward visits a year in the United States, while boxing accounts for only 11,506 and ice hockey 16,854.

Steve Targett, a sports doctor who has worked with both professional rugby players and professional ballet dancers in New Zealand, says the two are not so different. "In a way ballet dancers are pretty similar to the rugby guys," he told the newspaper *Dominion*. "They are pretty determined and don't want to stop. They want to keep on dancing and will dance through injuries."

Ballet may be graceful and beautiful, but some of the movements are, let's face it, a little unnatural. How often do you lift a woman over your head with one hand, or walk down the street on the very point of your toe? Ballet dancers routinely perform such feats. They must also do "the turnout." This is the main feature of ballet, and involves rotating their lower extremities, from the feet up to the hips, outward as far as possible to allow for quick changes in movement in different directions. Unfortunately, this may cause stress on the dancers' lower backs and lower extremities, putting them at risk for injury. Repeated strain to joints has also been implicated in an increase in arthritis among retired dancers.

Not surprisingly, injuries to the foot and ankle are common, particularly among female dancers, who are called upon to balance all their weight on the tip of a single toe. Dancing *en pointe* requires a woman to balance on a spot only slightly larger than 1 square inch/2.5 square cm. One of the most difficult feats a ballerina performs is when she appears to stand still on the tip of her toe. In fact, she is constantly shifting, making tiny adjustments of her weight over her foot. One study revealed that 80 percent of professional ballet dancers suffer an injury to one or both ankles sometime in their careers. In fact, fractures of the metatarsal bones (in the foot) are common enough that doctors sometimes refer to them as "dancer's fractures." A Canadian study examined the length of dancers' second toes and found that, among female dancers who dance *en pointe*, those with second toes that protruded out beyond the big toe experienced more pain and more foot injuries than those with shorter second toes.

Professional dancers are also prone to groin strains, stress fractures of the vertebrae, inflammation of the Achilles tendon, muscle strains and knee problems. And, yes, sometimes ballerinas do get dropped. That's called a *pas de "doh!"*

What You Can Do
You can dance if you want to. You can leave your friends behind—because the best Safety Dance tips follow:

Dance medicine experts believe most injuries can be prevented with proper training and warm-up techniques. It is important for young dancers to pace themselves and not try to become a prima ballerina in a single day. Be sure to warm up sufficiently each time you dance, and, as anxious as you may be to get *en pointe*, wait until your teacher tells you you're ready.

If something hurts for more than three days, stop doing it and see a doctor. Don't try to dull the pain by medicating yourself. Dancers have been known to develop ulcers or kidney damage by taking too much aspirin.

The Bath

When the stress of the workday gets to be too much, what could be better than a nice, hot bath? People take long baths to relax and unwind, but sometimes the experience is more stressful than planned.

Baths and showers produce 150,000 serious injuries per year in the United States. In the United Kingdom, there are 104 domestic drowning incidents a year and an estimated 30,855 injuries related to baths. (Another 8,377 get hurt in the shower, and 238 are bashed by bidets.)

How do people drown in their bathtubs? Generally, they lose consciousness first. This may be from another medical condition or because of the relaxing combination of a warm bath and a couple of glasses of wine.

When it comes to the hazards of bathing, drowning is only part of the picture. Each year in the United States, between seventy and eighty children are killed in baths and showers. Fewer than a third of those deaths are caused by drowning. Most are caused by scalds, and nowhere are more people scalded by bathwater than in Japan, where long, hot baths are part of the culture. The most common type of bath in Japan has a built-in boiler and a hot-water supply system. In newer baths, the water temperature from the hot-water supply system is adjustable, or an instrument regulating the temperature of the bath is attached to the boiler. Older baths, however, do not have these thermostats, and the water can get very hot. Because they like to soak for a long time, Japanese bathers will frequently refill the bath with more hot water, providing new opportunities for scalding.

What You Can Do

You could outfit your bath with all the safety devices hotels use—industrial-strength skid guards and handrails. On the other hand, hotel baths are not accident free. In one case, a woman got her arm caught between the wall and the handrail while she was bathing and got stuck for three days before someone finally found her. Her arm had become swollen and gangrened due to the compression of her artery. She was found conscious, but when freed, she went into a coma and later died. The lesson here is to be careful using hand bars and not to use anything that is not a grab rail—say, a soap dish or towel rack—to help you out of the tub.

Another smart course of action is to make sure your immersion heater is set properly. Studies show that less than 3 percent of North American parents know the temperature of their immersion heater. Safety experts say it should never be set at a temperature of more than 120 Fahrenheit/49 Celsius. Anything above 125°F/52°C can cause serious burns. Be sure to adjust the temperature before you get in, always supervise children in the bath, and stay awake while you enjoy your restful soak.

Nowhere are more people scalded by bathwater than in Japan.

Your Bed, and Staying In It

After reading about the many dangers lurking around you, you may have decided that it is best to avoid them all by staying in bed. Sorry—you're not safe there either. The British Department of Trade and Industry estimates that 50,426 people are injured by beds each year, while an additional 7,170 people are hurt on a "part of a bed." In fact, 96,000 people visited the casualty ward after an accident that occurred while they were "sleeping, relaxing, sitting or lying down." This means that a bed is, statistically, three times more hazardous than a knife. (An average of 28,000 Britons each year suffer knife wounds.)

The Hell's Angels may have a safer time of it than Sleeping Beauty. In the United States, 411,689 people a year experience injuries related to beds, mattresses and pillows, significantly higher than the number of people injured in motorcycle accidents (50,000 injuries and 2,100 deaths a year). Yet the hazards of sleeping command very little media attention. Most of the news stories on bed safety focus on one type of bed—the bunk bed. Bunk beds, so high off the floor, are a source of bed injury, but not the greatest source. They account for about 27,750 of those 411,689 accidents and about 11 deaths a year. Believe it or not, few of those accidents are the result of falling. In most of the cases, children become trapped between parts of the bed, for example, the slats of a headboard.

Meanwhile, mattresses are second only to upholstered furniture as the source of home fires. According to the United States Consumer Product Safety Commission, in 1998, 18,100 fires began with burning bedding. Most of the fires were caused by a small open flame, like a bedside candle or a cigarette, that ignited the fabric on the bed.

Folding beds have their own risks. In the United Kingdom, sofa beds hurt 896 residents a year. Most folding-bed injuries are cuts on the hands that occur when fingers get stuck in folding mechanisms. One German man, however, made international headlines when he inadvertently folded himself into his sofa bed. As he was removing the sheets, the bed sprang shut. He was trapped for four hours before his neighbours heard his cries for help. The man was treated at the hospital, but was not seriously injured despite his ordeal.

What You Can Do
Those films where two people, fresh from the act of love, immediately light up a cigarette … ignore them. Never smoke in bed.

If you use an electric blanket, be sure that it is of fairly recent vintage. As blankets age, the wiring can become pinched and damaged, creating a fire risk.

Make sure that your mattress is the appropriate size for the bed frame. Also, be sure that it is not positioned in such a way that the sleeper can be pinned between the bed and the wall, the headboard and the mattress, or the bed and any nearby furniture.

If you want extra security, you could trade in your bed for a safety model with side rails, the kind used at hospitals and nursing homes. But be forewarned: From 1985 to 2001, the U.S. Food and Drug Administration received 479 reports of patients becoming trapped in hospital beds; 297 of them died. They'd been trapped in openings within or between side rails, between side rails and the mattress, or between side rails and the headboard or footboard.

CAUTION

Bees

It's a lazy summer afternoon and you are relaxing on a beach. Suddenly a deadly creature appears on the horizon, ready to claim the life of its unsuspecting victim. No *Jaws* theme here, however. This menace flies rather than swims. Statistically speaking, you have much more to fear from a humble bumblebee than from a killer shark.

There hasn't been a fatal shark attack in Sydney Harbour since 1963, and on average, sharks only kill 1 person a year along the entire Australian coast. Twice as many Australians (1.8 to 2.2, depending on the source) are felled by bees every year. In Britain, wasp and bee stings cause about 30 deaths annually. Severe allergic reactions can cause the throat to swell and cut off breathing. They can even cause heart failure.

In 2000, a Sydney woman was killed as she tried to protect her 12-month-old daughter from a swarm of bees. The daughter suffered more than fifty stings, but survived. Also that year, two pedigree show dogs were killed by a swarm of bees at a New South Wales cattle station. The dogs had been tied to a tree next to a beehive. The more the dogs struggled, the more bees attacked, and the dogs were stung thousands of times.

In 2001, two bee sting deaths in a single day prompted Australian health officials to issue a bee warning. On 30 January of that year, a motorcyclist had a severe allergic reaction and died minutes after being stung by a bee. The same day a contractor at St. Peter's School in Adelaide was removing the top of a chimney when he uncovered a bee's nest. He was stung about fifty times.

A particularly dramatic bee event happened in Milwaukee, Wisconsin, in 1998. An articulated lorry that was transporting beehives overturned, releasing between 4 and 5 million bees. A special team of beekeepers had to be assembled to herd the bees. Fortunately, although a few people were stung, no one was killed.

"We're used to tactical situations … dealing with people," Police Captain Craig Evans told CNN. "But the possible injury of multiple stings from bees is something strange to us."

Wasp and bee stings are most likely to happen in late summer, when adult insects are on the hunt for food. In Australia, the most dangerous month is February, when roughly a quarter of bee attack deaths have historically taken place. According to Dr. Ken Winkel of the Australian Venom Research Unit, men are more often the victims of bee sting deaths than women. He believes that this is because more men than women work outdoors in the summer.

What You Can Do

Most people do not have a severe reaction to bee or wasp stings and can be stung without suffering any major consequences. But if you are allergic, be sure to carry Adrenalin with you, which can be used to treat allergic reactions to stings. Researchers at the Australian Venom Research Unit in Melbourne conducted a study of deaths by wasp and bee stings and found that five out of seven of the wasp sting fatalities knew they had allergies but did not carry Adrenalin. If you are not sure if you're sensitive to stings, you can find out with a simple blood test.

Birds

The Israel Defense Force has been fairly powerless against one particular threat. In August 1995, a $50 million F-15 fighter jet collided with one and burst into flames, killing the pilot. Two years later, an Israeli Air Force F-16 was downed, and the pilot and copilot were seriously injured when they bailed out at 500 mph/800 kph. What's more, these flying menaces can spread radiation as they travel through the sky. What are they? Birds.

Let's say you have a large bird, like an eagle. It can fly as fast as 31 mph/50 kph. It collides with a small plane moving at 160 mph/257 kph. The combined force of impact can be as much as 15.1 tons (short tons)/13.7 tonnes (metric tons).

During migration season, Israel has the highest concentration of birds per square kilometre of any country in the world. Every spring and autumn, more than half a billion birds from three continents and 280 species cross the tiny nation. Combine this high concentration of bird life with a relative abundance of fighter jets, and you've got an especially volatile combination. Between 1972 and 1998, there were 1,282 bird strikes with Israeli fighters, 696 with helicopters and 637 with transport planes and light aircraft.

The problem is not limited to Israel. More than 70 percent of the collisions between birds and planes are not reported. From those that are, we know that over the past thirty years, bird strikes have killed at least 41 pilots and caused more than 130 fighter jets from ten

Western air forces to crash. In all, bird strikes cost the aviation industry $3 billion a year, mainly due to the cost of flight cancellations and repairs to aircraft.

In truth, "bird strike" is something of a misnomer. Birds aren't really dive-bombing planes. Planes are flying into birds. When it comes down to a battle of which creature is more dangerous to the other, humans win every time.

But what about the radioactivity? Scientists from the Norwegian Radiation Protection Authority in Tromsö found droppings from seabirds with high concentrations of radioactive isotopes like uranium-238, radium-226 and cesium-137, which does not occur naturally. They suspect that the birds eat fish and crustaceans contaminated with radioactive material that seeps into the ocean floor through natural geological processes. They theorise that the fish and shellfish pick up the cesium-137 from the fallout from atmospheric nuclear tests and accidents like the one at Chernobyl in 1986. The birds' radioactive stool is a great fertiliser for plants, especially in the Arctic. The plants further concentrate the radioactive material, then are eaten by mammals, like reindeer.

A similar study of pigeons roosting in contaminated buildings on the site of British Nuclear Fuels' Sellafield complex found that the birds contained forty times the European Union's safe limit of cesium-137.

What You Can Do
In the United Kingdom, the Civil Aviation Authority is working to change jet engine standards so that they can withstand impacts with larger birds. The U.S. Federal Aviation Administration is working on similar standards. Some engineers, however, argue that the solution lies not in the strength of the engine but in the sharpness of the fan blades. Bird lovers may not want to read this next sentence: sharp engine blades quickly mince a big bird into little pieces, which cause less damage.

Of course, the best way to avoid a bird strike is to avoid flying in the path of birds. The only aircraft the Israeli Air Force permits to fly wherever the pilot wishes is a glider belonging to a scientist who follows birds and tracks their flight paths and behaviour. This effort has saved an estimated $400 million in downed jets. The U.S. Air Force, which reports around three thousand bird strikes a year at a cost of $50 million, has also instituted an Avian Hazard Advisory System to warn pilots about large concentrations of birds.

Books

If you think you can avoid injury by shunning sports and curling up with a good book, think again. If there were a manual on the proper use of books, quite a few people would cut their fingers on its pages, then trip over the cover on the way to get an Elastoplast. Books are an often overlooked hazard, sending more people to emergency rooms than many common sports. In case you were looking for an excuse to put down that copy of Tolstoy's *War and Peace*, here it is: in the United Kingdom more people are hurt by books (2,707 a year) than by training weights (1,884), trampolines (1,902) or cricket balls and bats (1,174). Lest you think only British books are hazardous, you should know that 10,683 U.S. citizens lose their battles with what the U.S. Consumer Product Safety Commission's National Electronic Injury Surveillance System (NEISS) categorises as "books, magazines, albums or scrapbooks" in an average year, and another 1,490 are clobbered by magazine racks or bookends. What are so many people doing wrong?

"From working with books for many years," said Karen Miller of the American Library Association, "I could offer up things like broken toes when books fall, losing one's balance when reaching for books, and repetitive stress from shelving them. Magazines could also be dangerous if the staples are loose and scrape the skin."

The heft of books is a special problem. Back injuries from moving overloaded boxes of books are common. Heavy schoolbags are also a concern.

In 2003, a Hong Kong schoolboy was killed when his heavy book bag pulled him over the railing of his high-rise flat. The 9-year-old's bag weighed about 20 lb/9 kg. Although fatalities like these are rare, heavy rucksacks are still a health risk because most spinal growth occurs during childhood. According to the U.S. Consumer Product Safety Commission, casualty wards treated more than 13,260 injuries from rucksacks in 2000.

Secondhand book use can also be hazardous to your health. Researchers in Bogotá, Colombia, tested the book dust in twelve libraries and ran skin tests on fifty-seven librarians. About 12 percent of the librarians had allergic reactions to the book dust, but the doctors found no evidence of common allergens. This led the researchers to conclude that new respiratory allergens may be lurking and evolving in the shelves.

Book exposure may even get you high. Mycologist (fungus doctor) Dr R. J. Hay, of Guy's Hospital in London, reported to a British medical journal, the *Lancet*, that various fungi that feed on the pages of old books could be a source of hallucinogenic spores.

"The source of inspiration for many great literary figures may have been nothing more than a quick sniff of the bouquet of moldy books," wrote Hay.

What You Can Do
Before you vow to watch more telly, you should consult the entry on injuries by TVs (page 219).

Be sure your bookshelves are substantial enough to hold all your books. If you're moving them from one place to another, lift with your knees, not your back. When moving, be sure to pack books in small boxes. If you're lugging them around in a rucksack, look for one with compartments. Pack the heaviest books closest to your back, and make sure you use the straps on both shoulders. Some students have been swamped with so much homework that they've taken to using bags with wheels, the kind air hostesses use.

If that novel is making your heart race and you feel light-headed, make sure the story is really that good. If it's not, put down the book and open a window.

Boredom

Which job is more likely to give you a coronary and send you to an early grave—air traffic controller or phone book proofreader? The answer is the phone book proofreader. (You didn't think those things proofread themselves, did you?)

If you left your high-stress job for something calmer because you thought you might avoid a heart attack, you might want to ask the boss to take you back. Recent studies show that boring, mindless jobs are more likely to send your soul skyward than their more exciting counterparts. A dull, repetitive job, where you have little opportunity to make decisions, will give you a 50 percent greater chance of dying early than working in a high-stress job, where you must make decisions.

Dr Benjamin C. Amick III of the University of Texas in Houston studied twenty-five thousand subjects and found that building-site workers, assembly line workers and waiters were more likely to die than doctors and politicians. Other research has shown that uninteresting work triggers the release of stress hormones, which can aggravate heart disease and a number of other illnesses.

Boredom takes its toll in other ways. Monotony is one of the most frequently cited reasons students give for dropping out of school—more than two thousand young Americans drop out of school each day. Some of the bored will land in gaol—fully 80 percent of the prison population is made up of school dropouts.

Persistent boredom could be a sign of clinical depression. The symptoms of depression include a loss of interest in hobbies and things that a person once enjoyed. Right now, 10 million Americans are suffering from depression, and 10 percent will take their own lives.

Alan Caruba, the founder of the Boring Institute, a clearinghouse on information about boredom, put it this way in an interview with *USA Today*: "The next time someone tells you they're bored to death, take it seriously."

What You Can Do
Pretend you're the boss. The good news is that you do not really need to have control in your job to relieve the stress. You only have to *believe* you have control. A recently published study analysed the stress associated with control issues. Researchers measured the heart rate and blood pressure of people as they played video games while being distracted by blasts of noise in headphones. Half of the subjects were told they controlled the blasts with their game performance. Half were told the blasts were random, which, in fact, they were. Those who believed they were in control, however, experienced less stress than those who believed they were not. While you're pretending to be the boss, go ahead, give yourself a pay rise.

Meanwhile, as you're surfing the Web at work, visit the Boring Institute's Web page for more information on this riveting topic: www.boringinstitute.com.

Bras

It may seem like a simple undergarment, but the brassiere is a dangerous thing ... to men. Or so says plastic surgeon Andrew Fleming of London's St. George's Hospital. In his study in the *British Journal of Plastic Surgery*, Fleming cites the case of a 27-year-old man whose enjoyable evening with a female companion ended in hospital. The patient twisted his left middle finger in the bra strap and sustained a fracture and ligament damage.

While there are few reliable worldwide statistics on the incidence of bra-related hand injuries, surveys show as many as 40 percent of men in their 30s and 40s have problems removing a bra.

In one recent test, it took men an average of twenty-seven seconds to remove a bra using both hands. Right-handed men using their left hand took an average of fifty-eight seconds, while one unfortunate volunteer took twenty minutes. If such a lack of skill does not injure the practitioner, it does, at the very least, run the risk of killing the passion.

But are bras a hazard to women? Dr Dimitri Trichopoulos, a lecturer in cancer prevention and epidemiology, has done research on the link between bras and breast cancer. In a study published in the *European Journal of Cancer* in 1991, he discovered that premenopausal women who never wore bras had half the risk of breast cancer of those who did.

It's a snap!

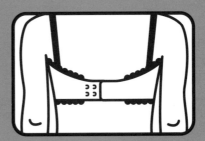

1. Delicately grasp the hook.

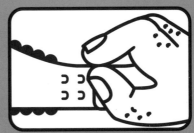

2. Gingerly pull forward.

3. Expertly unhook...

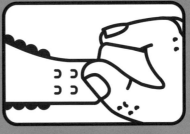

4. ...and release!

The husband-and-wife research team of Sydney Ross Singer and Soma Grismaijer are the authors of the book *Dressed to Kill*. They interviewed forty-seven hundred women and found that those who wore ill-fitting bras or wore one for unusually long periods had a higher incidence of breast cancer. The researchers speculate that the constriction of lymph nodes in the area of the bra causes a buildup of toxins.

Before you burn your bra, you should know that the National Cancer Institute and the National Institutes of Health do not agree with Singer and Grismaijer's findings, and that Dr. Trichopoulos does not believe it is the bra itself that causes cancer. Because women who do not wear bras tended to have smaller breasts, he concluded breast size was the determining factor.

Whether or not they cause disease, bras certainly cause injuries. In Britain, more than four hundred underwear-related injuries a year are catalogued by the Department of Trade and Industry, including a bizarre 1999 incident in which two London women were killed by a massive bolt of lightning after the metal wiring in one of their bras acted as a conductor.

What You Can Do
Be thankful that women are no longer wearing corsets. Corsets were not only time-consuming to get on and off, they were often laced so tightly that they squeezed vital organs literally out of shape.

If you're a man, practise, practise, practise. "[We] advocate patient self-education (during the adolescent years) on the mechanism of external female mammary support, and postulate that it may be important in reducing the incidence of other such injuries," writes Dr Fleming.

HAZARDOUS

CANDLES

Candles

W hat could be more romantic than the glow of candles on the table or beside the bath? Ah ... the fresh aromatherapy scent, the particulates, the risk of fire, the lead.

The use of candles in the home has seen a steady rise of late, and the candle industry has grown to $2.3 billion/£1.25 billion annually in the U.S. Seven out of ten American homes burn candles on a regular basis. As candle use has grown, so have candle-related fires. In 1997, candle fires hit an eighteen-year high of 11,600 in the United States, according to the National Fire Protection Association. In the United Kingdom, candle consumption has risen by 50 percent in recent years. UK fire brigades reported over two thousand house fires started by candles in 2000, causing ten fatalities and nine hundred injuries. The number of injured has increased consistently from 452 in 1994. Candles are the third leading cause of home fires in Australia and Denmark. A recent survey of candles purchased from local shops found that 41 percent did not have adequate safety instructions and only half burned in a satisfactory manner.

You probably do not give it much thought, but the open flame of a candle is caused by a complex chemical reaction. The base of the candle, usually wax but sometimes mineral oil or vegetable oil gel, is the fuel source. Most candles are made of the type of wax known as paraffin. In its solid state, paraffin wax does not burn. If you

33

tried to light the base of the candle instead of the wick, you'd have a very hard time. When the wick is set on fire, however, it stays burning long enough to heat up the wax, liquify it, and pull up the wick by capillary action. The wax then vapourises, and it is the vapour that actually burns. If you look carefully (don't get too close when you do this), you'll see that the bluest, and hottest, part of the flame is actually located a slight distance from the wick.

If that candle is tipped over, if the wind blows the curtains over the flame, if the flame burns too hot and high, or if the candle holder gets too hot, the results can be disastrous. Spilled wax has also been known to result in a trip to the casualty ward.

Even when a candle burns as it should, your aromatherapy could actually be causing indoor pollution. Testing has shown that candles can emit acetone, benzene, soot and other particles into the air. If the wick doesn't burn at the same rate at which the wax diminishes, the wick gets longer by comparison and burns with a dark smoke that releases more particulates.

The biggest health threat from wick soot is in the form of lead. Wicks with metal cores can spread dangerous levels of lead throughout the home. Lead poisoning can lead to behavioural changes and damage internal organs, especially the kidneys. Most North American candle makers voluntarily stopped using metal-core wicks some time ago, but candles imported from other countries, especially China and Taiwan, may still contain wicks with lead. In 2001, the U.S. Consumer Product Safety Commission voted to ban the import and sale of candlewicks containing lead, but a 2002 study conducted by the University of Michigan found fourteen different brands of candles with metal-core wicks sold in the state. In 2002, a team of researchers from the Air Pollution and Control Division of the U.S. Environmental Protection Agency bought one hundred sets of candles in North Carolina and found that 8 percent contained lead wicks. Canada, meanwhile, has issued an advisory on metal-wick dangers, but has not banned their sale. Burning two lead-wicked candles can raise the concentration of lead in a room beyond the limits allowed by the U.S. Occupational Safety and Health Administration.

What You Can Do

Two words: dimmer switch.

If you're a candle maker, don't put lead in your candles, please. If you're a candle buyer, throw out the ones you suspect might have lead in them. How do you know? Health Canada says you can test them by separating the wick fibers. If you see metal, rub the core of the wick on a piece of white paper. If the mark left on the paper is grey, the metallic core is probably lead.

The most common cause of a candle-related house fire is leaving a burning candle unattended. Don't do that. The second most common cause is putting a lit candle too close to fabric, like upholstered furniture or curtains. Don't do that either. Follow the instructions that come with your candle and trim the wick to $1/4$ in/.635 cm before burning.

Some candle injuries have nothing to do with fire. Use care removing melted and dried wax from candleholders and other surfaces. Many people use knives for this purpose, and cut themselves in the process.

Use caution with candles in glass containers, and do not set new candles inside glass jars without first removing the wax from the previous candle. If the old wax begins to melt, the new candle can tip and superheat the glass jar. The hot glass can burn tables, or become unstable and shatter when touched. In general, it's a bad idea to let the flame get too close to the container. Stop burning a candle when there are 2 in/5.08 cm of wax left.

Ceiling Fans

In January 2004, 7-year-old Aditi Mukhi headed to her class at Villa Theresa Convent High School in Mumbai, India. She sat quietly studying beneath a gently spinning ceiling fan. Her day continued uneventfully until about 1:30 P.M., the last period of the day. That's when the fan suddenly came crashing down on her head. One blade cut deep into her forehead and penetrated the bone. She was treated in a nearby hospital for a skull fracture. Two other students were also injured.

This is not an isolated occurrence. Newspapers contain numerous reports of injuries by what amounts to a contraption of swiftly spinning blades mounted above the head. Each year in the United States more than 19,700 people are hurt by them. This is slightly more than the population of the Republic of Palau.*

One hospital in North Queensland, Australia, alone treated fifty patients in 1998 and 1999 for ceiling fan injuries, many of which arose from failing to turn the fan off before painting the ceiling or while fixing the fan. Injuries ranged from grazes to compound skull fractures, and seven patients required admission to hospitals.

Ceiling fans, in the words of the *Saturday Evening Post*, are "bought in the wrong sizes and mounted improperly in the wrong places. After that, they're run at the wrong times, the wrong speeds—and even in the wrong direction."

Here are but a few of the tales of terror:

- September 2000: Four-year-old twins from California were injured, one critically, when a ceiling fan weighing approximately 35 lb/15.88 kg fell 5 ft/1.52 m and crashed onto their heads as they were watching television.
- October 2000: Two students in Alor Star, Malaysia, were studying mathematics when the blades and cover of the ceiling fan above their heads came falling down. One student needed stitches on her chin, another on her forehead.
- May 2001: One of the oldest homes in Florida's Siesta Key Beach was destroyed by fire after sparks from a ceiling fan started the blaze. The house was being renovated, and the spark ignited fumes from a paint stripper.
- March 2002: A 25-year-old Florida man was electrocuted as he tried to install a ceiling fan in his fiancée's attic. He was pounding a nail into the ceiling when he struck a live wire.
- June 1999: Five hundred people were evacuated from the Denver Tech Center in Greenwood Village, Colorado, when a ceiling fan motor overheated and began to smoke. Fortunately, the building did not catch fire and employees were allowed back in.

What You Can Do

Do you ever inspect your ceiling fan to make sure it's still in good shape? You should.

If it is not, or if you simply decide to install a new one, be sure that you turn the fan off before you start work. Also, be sure to turn the power supply off. Don't rely on the light switch—sometimes the power enters at the mains even when the switch is located in the circuit beyond it. Turn off the circuit you are working on by switching off the circuit breaker or by removing the fuse. Less current than it takes to light a 60-watt bulb can be lethal.

Be sure the fan is mounted high enough that people can't accidentally raise their hands into the spinning blades.

* Located in the Pacific Ocean, the island nation of Palau has an average rainfall of 120 to 160 in/304.80 to 406.40 cm per year and an average temperature of 81°F/27°C. Palau has more species of marine life than any other area of similar size in the world. The U.S. military employs more Palauans than does any other industry. Reef fishing comes in second.

Chairs

The Texas Chair Massacre. Okay, so it doesn't have quite the ring to it that *The Texas Chainsaw Massacre* has, but the fact of the matter is, chairs are more than *thirteen* times as likely to cause injuries as chain saws.

In the United Kingdom, more than 285,000 people have seating mishaps each year, as do about 410,000 Americans. Most of these injuries come from falls. You lean back too far in that office chair and *whooo—aaaa—ahhhh!* There are other risks as well. In Australia, parents were warned not to let small children play on recliners after a toddler was asphyxiated in one. A child's head can become trapped in the gap between the chair and the footrest, and the chair can then close.

The most dangerous forms of seating, according to the Royal Society for the Prevention of Accidents, are couches and ottomans. Not even beanbag chairs are safe, however. The U.S. Consumer Product Safety Commission recently announced the voluntary recall of 142,000 zipped beanbag chairs because children can unzip the bags, then crawl inside and suffocate. At least five children have met their deaths this way.

Meanwhile, according to the *Wall Street Journal*, most of the lower-back pain in America is caused by long stretches of chair sitting. Bad backs cost the U.S. economy $70 billion a year.

It's even possible that there is a correlation between bad chairs and poor academic performance. A recent study published in the *Journal of Adolescent Health* found that 80 percent of students are forced to sit in chairs with seats that are too high or too deep for their bodies. This mismatch created an environment that was not conducive to learning, the researchers concluded.

What You Can Do

As ubiquitous as they are in Western society, a raised platform for sitting with feet dangling below is not actually a universal fact of life. Until fairly recent times, the majority of the world's people never saw a chair. The king's throne was a sign of status not because it was the most ornately decorated chair, but because it was a chair at all. In China, the characters for "chair" translate into "barbarian bed," which attests to its foreign status. In many countries, chairs are still a rarity.

That said, a sudden switch to Japanese tatami (or straw floor mats) is not recommended. Your seating habits have been deeply ingrained, not only in your psyche, but also in your body. Your ligaments, tendons and joints have become accustomed to chairs after a lifetime of chair sitting. Switching late in life to kneeling and cross-legged sitting can cause knee damage.

Instead, make sure your chairs are comfortable, fit well to your body, and are in good shape. Broken wheels and loose backs on office chairs can lead to dangerous falls. Chairs in hospital waiting rooms and other institutions that are open twenty-four hours a day get three times the use of normal chairs and need regular safety inspection.

Be extra careful when buying secondhand furniture. Older furniture may be in bad shape and may not comply with current safety standards.

Finally, it is best to avoid metal folding chairs when sitting under a tree in an electrical storm. This tragic oversight has led to a handful of deaths over the years, including that of a Salt Lake City, Utah, couple in June 2003. When a storm hit, the couple and their three children took cover under trees. The parents sat in metal chairs, which conducted the electricity very efficiently when lightning struck. Both died.

HAZARDOUS

Cheerleading

Give me an *I*! Give me an *N*! Give me a *J*! Give me a *U*! Give me an *R*! Give me a *Y*! What does it spell? *Injury!*

The smiling, fluffy image of the peppy, pigtailed pom-pom girl is deceptive. Cheerleaders put themselves at risk for paralysis with their prodigious pyramids. If a secondary school or college athlete is seriously injured—paralysed, permanently disabled or killed—there is a very good chance that she was cheering when it happened. Cheerleading is responsible for fully half of the cases of catastrophic injuries to female secondary school and college athletes. In 2001, 24,860 American cheerleaders were rushed to hospital, up from 11,700 in 1991. While this is much lower than the number of American football injuries, cheerleading accidents are more likely to be severe. The average cheerleader loses twenty-eight to thirty-five practice days per injury—more than any other sport. American football players, on average, lose only seven to ten days per injury.

One of the most tragic cases was the 1986 injury of Janis Thompson, a 21-year-old senior at North Dakota State University. Scheduled to be named the top cheerleader in America by the National Cheerleading Association later that week, Thompson was practicing and fell from the top of a two-tier human pyramid. She smacked her head on a hard gymnasium floor and was rushed to hospital, where she was pronounced brain-dead.

The story illustrates two of the great risks to cheerleaders—challenging stunts with a risk of falls, and performing and practicing the stunts on hard surfaces rather than mats.

Historically, cheerleading has been viewed as an extracurricular activity rather than a sport. That means it is not regulated like other sports and doesn't receive the same oversight. But whatever it's termed, cheerleading has evolved, and today it incorporates more stunts and gymnastics than in days gone by.

Squads often practice in school hallways with concrete surfaces. They typically perform on gymnasium floors. These hard surfaces can cause injuries even to ground-bound squads (that is, squads that do not allow stunts like pyramids, back flips and tosses). The most common cheering injury is an ankle sprain. Broken bones are also common.

Cheerleading squads are often supervised by an educational advisor rather than an athletic coach. And ironically, the younger, less experienced junior team often receives less training and supervision than the more experienced senior team. In 2001, a junior cheerleader suffered permanent brain damage and other injuries after a fall onto a wooden floor. In the lawsuit that followed, it was revealed that there had been no coach for the cheerleading squad, only a part-time academic advisor responsible for discipline, travel plans and uniforms. The advisor worked with the senior squad on its routines, but the junior squad was left to its own devices. The junior members taught themselves how to perform stunts and decided on their own when they were ready to perform them, a recipe for disaster.

What You Can Do
Get your schools to accord cheerleading the same status they do other sports. This should greatly reduce the number and severity of cheering accidents, say the experts. A simple thing like making sure coaches require cheerleaders to stretch and do proper warm-ups would help them condition their ligaments and make them less likely to tear. Coaches should also ensure that cheerleaders don't move on to difficult stunts before they are fully trained.

Already, many organisations are taking steps to change some of the riskiest cheering practices. The Atlantic Coast Conference of American colleges has

Go!   Team!   Go!

forbidden high-flying stunts by cheerleaders at the league's basketball tournaments, although the same types of feats can still be performed at cheerleading competitions that fall outside the conference's jurisdiction.

The American Association of Cheerleading Coaches and Advisers publishes a safety manual and administers a safety certification program for coaches. The organisation's guidelines prohibit pyramids more than "two persons" high. Minitrampolines, once used to create spectacular flying feats, were banned in 1986.

Finally, don't be too aggressive in your training, and don't have your squad try pyramids or back flips without fully mastering the basics.

Chips, Fish and

It is Britain's most famous dish, as much a symbol of England as the royal family, red phone boxes or Big Ben. And in an era when the queen rarely says, "Off with your head," a plate of fish and chips is by far the most likely item on that list to cause an untimely death.

It is not the chips themselves (although they do contain enough fat to result in a slow, artery-clogging death) but the pans they are fried in. Chip pans are the leading cause of fires in the United Kingdom. A full quarter of fires result from attempts to fry up a tasty, high-fat meal. In the year 2000, an estimated 447 people died and 14,400 were injured in this way. That's far more people than were injured by open flames from gas fires (457), by coal or wood fires in grates (677), or by blowtorches (128). Even axes (2,268), chain saws (1,116) and power drills (3,036) harm fewer people.

If you live outside the United Kingdom, fish and chips with a side of mushy peas is fairly easy to avoid. In Britain, however, chip shops outnumber McDonald's fast-food restaurants by an eight-to-one margin. Half of the British population eats fish and chips once a month, and 14 percent twice a week. Ten percent of all the potatoes in Britain end up as chips, which Winston Churchill once declared "the good companion." During World War II, Lord Woolton, the minister of food, allowed mobile frying vans to carry fish and chips to evacuees around the country.

Fish and chips are easy to prepare: just drop them into the deep fryer, wait about five minutes, and presto—you have a meal. This is why there is something of a British tradition of coming home from a night in the pub and frying up a late-night snack. But that is a big part of the problem. Drunken chip frying is believed to account for forty deaths a year. After a few drinks, it's easy to fall asleep at the chip pan, or to forget that it was ever turned on. Nearly a third of injuries from chip-pan fires occur between 10:00 P.M. and 4:00 A.M. Men are twice as likely to be victims as women. A recent study in southern England showed that half of all the people who died in house fires were over the legal blood-alcohol limit for driving a car.

What You Can Do

Take the advice of the professors at the Public Health Intervention Research Unit at the London School of Hygiene & Tropical Medicine. In a report for the journal *Injury Prevention* entitled "Potential Public Health Importance of the Oven Ready Chip," they suggest that microwaving your fries will not only result in fewer fires, but also will improve cardiovascular health. Oven-made chips contain 4.2 grams of fat per 100 grams, as opposed to 6.7 grams of fat from deep-fried chips.

Should you decide to deep-fry, be sure to use only a small amount of oil, never leave pans unattended, don't cook while intoxicated, and don't put food into a pan that is smoking.

Or you may soon be able to buy a safer chip fryer. Scottish sewing machine repairman and sometime inventor Jim McConkey has designed a pan that puts out a fire within six seconds if the contents go up in flames. A metal lid is hinged above the pan with a plastic strip. The flash point of oil is around 340°F/171°C, but the flame can burn to around 500°F/260°C. At 400°F/204°C, the plastic strip melts and the lid closes tight, starving the fire of oxygen.

Finally, be sure to have a pair of underpants handy. A pair of damp underpants recently helped save ten people from a chip-pan fire in Walsall, England. When a fire broke out, the quick-thinking residents used damp clothing, including underwear, to smother the flames. The family had seen fire-safety television adverts that encouraged people to use damp cloths to put out fryer fires.

Coins

Pennies may come from heaven, but they can send someone there too. In recent years, aggrieved football fans in Europe have acted as loose cannons, and their loose change has become the cannonballs. Victims of coin peltings include Arsenal football club striker Thierry Henry (cut on the side of his head), referee Hugh Dallas (head wound), Hoops goalkeeper Rob Douglas (hit on the back of the head), French referee Gilles Veissiere (hit in the eye) and the teenage daughter of Coventry City FA Cup champion Dave Bennett (hit in the eye and partially blinded).

Such ill-advised use of coinage gets most of the money-hazard headlines, but there are dangers to the nonsporting public as well. Coins are an attractive menace to children who like to examine small, shiny things by taste. In 1996, 21,000 children ended up in U.S. casualty wards after swallowing coins. Hospitals report that coins are the most frequently ingested foreign objects by children. In the United Kingdom, where they do not separate paper and metal money in their injury stats, the Royal Society for the Prevention of Accidents (RoSPA) estimates that about 10,206 people a year are injured by some form of money.

Your change is also dangerous to animals. Recently, the *Grand Rapids Press* reported the story of Eddy the dog, who became dangerously ill with zinc poisoning after swallowing twelve coins. Eddy needed a blood transfusion and consultations with

Michigan State University experts to recover. His owners renamed him Money in honor of his $1,580/£870.40 medical bill.

Milwaukee County Zoo officials put up signs saying COINS KILL, but they don't seem to stop visitors from throwing the shiny things into pools of water inside animal habitats. Zinc poisoning from coins killed a wattled curassow (a South American bird) and a Humboldt penguin at the zoo in 1997.

If you think it's dangerous handling coins, just try making them. In 2002, the U.S. Occupational Safety and Health Administration (OSHA) identified the Philadelphia and Denver mints (the only two places in America where coins are made) as two of the most dangerous places to work in the federal government. (Admittedly, it should not be surprising that the mint, where massive stamping machines press metal sheets into coins, would be more dangerous than other federal offices, where pieces of paper are put into folders in alphabetical order.)

What You Can Do
The best medical wisdom once prescribed that if your child swallows a coin, wait—it too shall pass, and usually within twelve hours. Since 1981, however, things have got a bit more complicated. Although most coins will pass through a child's system, recently minted U.S. pennies might cause problems. Pediatric radiologist Sara M. O'Hara treated a 2-year-old boy at Duke University Medical Centre. Four days after swallowing a penny he was unwilling to eat, had a terrible tummy ache and was vomiting blood. O'Hara took X rays and discovered that a rough-edged penny was causing an ulcer. Pennies, it turns out, are no longer made of mostly copper. Instead, they're made of zinc with a copper coating. Inside the acid wash of the stomach, the copper can crack and the zinc can begin to dissolve. Mixed with stomach acid, the zinc can cause a reaction that is harmful to the stomach lining. Other U.S. coins, made of mostly nickel, don't have the same problems.

You should check with your doctor to be sure the coin is passing through as it should. There can be complications if it gets lodged in the esophagus. Over the past couple of years, casualty ward doctors have come up with a simple way to find out where a swallowed coin has gone, according to the medical journal *Pediatric Emergency Care*: they're using metal detectors.

Collectible Toys

Over the past half century, the lovable (if anatomically prepos-terous) Barbie doll has become ubiquitous. She is marketed in more than 140 countries, and it is estimated that, worldwide, two Barbie dolls are sold every second. So odds are none too long that you, or someone you know, may just have an old Barbie doll in the loft. What you may not know is that your old fashion doll could be oozing a sticky and dangerous chemical.

When Barbie was invented in 1957, plastics were seen as an indus-trial breakthrough. Plastic toys from the era were made with polyvinyl chloride (PVC), and archivists today say such toys are deteriorating rapidly. Studies in Europe have shown that about fifteen years after they were made, some PVC products started to exude a chemical that was used in the plastic moulding process. The chemical can mimic oestrogen and disrupt development in the very young, according to Yvonne Shashoua of the National Museum of Denmark, who discussed the problem at the 2000 meeting of the American Chemical Society. One sign that your beloved doll may be doing this is if it feels sticky to the touch. Children who play with sticky toys tend to clean their fingers by putting them in their mouths, thus ingesting the chemical.

Mattel, the maker of Barbie, announced it was phasing out petro-leum-based plastic from its products in 2000. Most European toy makers had already begun the process, shifting to plant-based plastics. The toy makers altered their formulae based on concerns that dibutyl phthalates in soft plastics could be harmful to children's health. Dibutyl phthalates make hard plastics soft and studies have shown that in large doses they can cause liver and kidney damage, and cancer, in laboratory animals.

"It's outrageous that a scientist who buys a bottle of phthalate chemicals receives a full hazard warning, but a consumer buying a mouthing toy with phthalates often finds it labeled non-toxic," Jessica Tritsch of the Wisconsin Public Interest Research Group told the *Capital Times* in 2000.

Old dolls and eroding plastics are only a symptom of a larger problem. Collectible toys and products can still be floating around long after safety guidelines have changed and even after they have been recalled. One study cited by the U.S. Consumer Product Safety Commission (CPSC) found items that were considered hazardous by current guidelines in two-thirds of American thrift shops. Each year the organisation holds a press conference to get the word out about potentially hazardous products that remain in people's homes because they are unaware of product recalls.

"People should do some spring cleaning and check their lofts and other storage areas for old products that could be hazardous," said CPSC chairwoman Ann Brown.

It's not just dolls, either. One toy the CPSC specifically urges consumers to look for is metal lawn darts, which were banned by the CPSC in 1988. They have been responsible for the deaths of three children since they were taken off the market, including that of a 7-year-old boy who suffered a fatal brain injury when a dart pierced his skull.

What You Can Do
The disintegration of old plastic is a problem not just for children, but for archivists like Shashoua, who hopes to develop a plastic spray to stabilise older plastic toys so they can be kept on display for future generations. In the meantime, you can make your old plastic toys safe by wrapping them in cling film and not touching the original plastic directly.

If you're concerned about the safety of any of your old toys, the CPSC keeps an archive of its past announcements and recall notices. You can visit its Web page at www.cpsc.gov.

Cotton Buds

With their soft cushions of cotton at either end, cotton buds appear perfectly safe. But don't let them fool you. Those simple little lavatory tools send more people to hospital than razor blades or electric razors—more than twice as many. In the United Kingdom in 1999, for example, sixty-five hundred people were sent to hospital after misusing cotton buds, while only twenty-eight hundred were hospitalised after hurting themselves with electric razors.

Why are so many people walking into hospital after bouts with these soft, white swabbers? For the most part, it is because they do not follow the directions. Boxes of these fearsome items contain stern warnings in many countries. Do not, under any circumstances, put cotton buds into your ears, they advise. Sure, they may *look* like they were designed to clean out your ears, but the people who make them insist they were not. Clean your ears at your own risk.

In fact, the experts say, using cotton buds to remove earwax is a bit like using a broom on an earthen floor. It just moves things around. Instead of making your ears cleaner, it pushes the stuff farther down the ear canal, where it makes things worse. Sometimes a person, faced with this deeply compacted earwax, gets a little overly enthusiastic with a cotton bud and probes so deep that he hits the eardrum and creates a small tear. This sounds like a cannon being fired inside the head. Between 1992 and 1997, more than a hundred people in the United States experienced a serious eardrum injury as a result of cleaning their ears with buds. Some sources estimate that as many as twenty thousand people worldwide are so injured each year.

This injury, however, is mild compared with the damage that can be done by the hapless swabber who gets distracted and trips or bumps his arm, forcing the stick so far into the ear canal that it hits the small bones in the middle ear. If these bones are damaged, the result can be hearing loss.

What You Can Do
The ear canals are self-cleaning. Actions of the jaw, such as talking and chewing, help to "massage" the wax out of the ear canal. Instead of swabbing, then, simply have a conversation. Here's a starter: "What does the *Q* in Q-Tip stand for, anyway?" (The answer, by the way, is "quality.") Another: Q-Tips were originally marketed as Baby Gays. Discuss.

Keep cotton buds out of your ears and use them for the many other tasks for which you buy them.

DANGER

Crutches and Wheelchairs

Crutches can put you on crutches. Just ask any of the estimated 73,615 people each year who are injured by, as the National Electronic Injury Surveillance System categorises it, "crutches, canes or walkers [frames]." It's about the same number of people as are injured doing such risky activities as in-line skating or riding a horse. Even more people are injured by wheelchairs each year, an estimated 95,228 in the United States.

There is, of course, a difference between your average in-line skater and your average crutch-walker. The person on crutches already has some problems with balance and health. This means that a fall from a frame is often much more deadly than a fall from a pair of skates. A young, athletic person who falls as she glides around a rink will probably pick herself right back up and keep going. A 90-year-old who slips with a frame can end up with serious, sometimes fatal, injuries.

One problem with crutches and frames, according to Kris Schmidt of St. Mary's Hospital Medical Center in Wisconsin, is human stubbornness. People are often reluctant to use a frame because they fear it makes them appear weak or old. Instead, they ask for crutches.

"With crutches, you get more fatigued," said Schmidt. "Another thing about crutches is that people tend to lean on them, damaging all those nerves under the arms and causing numbness in the hands."

Uneven surfaces that would pose little problem to a pedestrian can bring a wheelchair to an abrupt stop—or worse, tip it. Wheelchair riders are particularly vulnerable to the elements, and snow, ice or plain water can turn a ramp into a slide. When a ramp or lift isn't available, wheelchair users must be carried up stairs and risk being dropped.

Wheelchairs and cars can be a particularly deadly combination. Researchers at the University of Pittsburgh School of Health and Rehabilitation Sciences evaluated the crashworthiness of wheelchair seating in vans and other large vehicles in four different studies. In almost all the studies, standard wheelchairs failed to withstand simulated crashes, placing wheelchair users at a greater risk of injury than non-wheelchair-bound riders.

What You Can Do

If you need to use crutches, walking frames or wheelchairs for any period of time, spend some time learning to use them safely. The Children's Hospital in Westmead, Australia, offers the following tips for safe use of crutches: Be sure your crutches are the proper length—about 2 in/5 cm shorter than the distance from your armpit to the floor. Make sure all the nuts and bolts are fastened properly, that the stoppers at the bottoms are not worn, and that the handgrips are adjusted so there is a slight bend at the elbow when standing in a relaxed position.

In 1996, the Sister Kenny Institute in Minneapolis, Minnesota, opened the first "virtual reality" wheelchair-training programme. Patients use their own chairs, which sit on stationary platforms wired into computers. They then watch a television screen or wear a virtual-reality helmet that shows a variety of obstacles and terrains, and are instructed to manoeuvre the chairs accordingly. The programme allows wheelchair users to practise navigating through the various scenarios, and has proved to be realistic and compelling enough to keep them from getting bored and abandoning the lessons.

Cute Guys

G osh, he's cute. Those big eyes, that cherubic grin. Makes you want to pinch his cheeks.

A mug like that immediately puts a woman at ease. Women find these baby-faced males most attractive and view them as kinder and more trustworthy, even as better potential fathers. But be afraid. Be very afraid. A series of studies by researchers at Brandeis University in Massachusetts show that baby-faced boys dislike their cutesy image and compensate for it by engaging in crimes and delinquent behaviour.

Strike up a chorus of Joe Jackson's "Is She Really Going Out with Him?" here. If it seems like perfectly nice women are always going out with twits, you can put the blame on deeply ingrained psychology. It may seem as though women are drawn to tough, square-jawed macho men, and that these blokes are more prone to behave badly. In fact, scientists from the University of St. Andrews in Scotland believe the opposite is true. Their study of male and female preferences for facial characteristics of the opposite sex reveal that while men find women with the most feminine features attractive, women do not look for the most masculine of men. They also find femininity in men's faces appealing. (Ask a woman in your life: Arnold Schwarzenegger or Jude Law?)

The researchers speculate that women prefer such faces because they make their owners seem more gentle and nurturing. Good "dad material." Another study on attractiveness, this one conducted at the University of California, revealed that when a woman meets a man she considers attractive, she is more likely to assume that he shares her attitudes and beliefs. The more attractive she thinks he is, the more she assumes he thinks like her.

So women are drawn to men with delicate, feminine features, and such men are more likely to behave badly to compensate for the view that they are childlike or weak. Because women go into a relationship with so many assumptions about the man's inherent goodness and agreeability, they are more likely to be disappointed later on.

The consequences of our stereotypes go further than broken hearts. They affect our decisions in all areas of life, including criminal trials. A 1981 study of the effect of attractiveness on the judgments in rape cases showed that jurors convicted 57 percent of male defendants rated attractive, while those thought to be unattractive were convicted 82 percent of the time.

What You Can Do
The good news for men who have, let's say, "ordinary" mugs is that you'll probably win out in the end. A 1984 study at the University of North Carolina, Chapel Hill, revealed that young men who are less facially blessed tend to concentrate more on academics, go further in school, and end up with a more highly educated woman and a job of greater-than-average prestige.

It's not all genetics. You can make yourself more attractive by simply smiling. Studies show that both men and women find smiling faces more attractive than gloomy mugs. Studies also show that if you don't consider yourself to be good-looking, it's likely other people won't either. You can also make yourself more appealing by hanging out with the beautiful people. You might think you'll look like the ugly duckling in comparison, but studies show that we are, in fact, judged by the company we keep. Stand next to Tom Cruise, and you'll look cool too. If you have lost touch with Tom, any reasonably attractive, smiling friend will do.

As for what women can do to avoid the charms of baby-faced blokes, well, we'll get back to you on that.

Debt

It may seem like a good idea to buy that cubic zirconium sparkler from the Home Shopping Network with your triple-platinum Visa card, but beware. That hasty decision could be the death of you.

Consumer debt has reached an all-time high in many parts of the world. In the consumer-oriented United States, in the 1980s, households had 70 cents of debt for every dollar they spent in a year. Today Americans carry almost 99 cents of debt for every dollar they spend. To the north, where Canadians once boasted, "Americans spend, Canadians save," the story is not much different. In 2000, Canadian household debt reached 97.4 percent of disposable income. The average household in 2000 owed $52,690 Can ($40,912 US/£22,332). Meanwhile, personal savings plummeted to the lowest rate in Canadian history.

With this has come an increase in bankruptcies, suicides, health problems and feelings of despair. Psychological studies have shown that there is a cross-cultural rule of reciprocity. Human beings hate to be in a state of obligation. Reciprocal arrangements are vital to human culture. If a person does something kind for us, we feel obligated to do something kind in return. It is so universal that sociologists have identified it in all human societies. A person who accepts goodness without attempting to return it is disliked by the members of his society and shunned.

If a person finds himself, because of economic hardship, in a position in which he is forced to receive without being able to reciprocate, this state of affairs can be psychologically devastating. He may avoid asking for help. He may withdraw from friends rather than put himself in the position of being unable to repay. Meanwhile, heavy debt can leave an individual with less access to preventative health care, medicine and medical visits. In 1997, a team of Ohio State University researchers came to the shocking conclusion that all of this is bad for your health. In a survey of 1,036 Ohioans, they found that those who claimed the highest levels of stress about their debt reported worse health than those with lower levels of debt-related stress.

This combination of stress, health problems, feeling like a worthless member of society and social isolation creates the perfect climate for depression and suicide. This is especially true, at least one study has shown, when a person is hounded by debt collectors. Being all alone, except for calls from one's creditors, is enough to push a lot of people over the edge.

Studies in Finland and England both found a correlation between suicide and indebtedness.

In Sri Lanka, there has been a rash of suicides in four major paddy-farming districts because of poverty and debt. Farmers there often borrow against their future crop successes. Unfortunately, the yields sometimes cannot be sold for enough to cover the debt. In the period before harvest, traditionally a time of celebration, financially hard-pressed farmers swallow pesticides. In 1997, one region, Kurunegala, had 6,858 cases of poisoning and 436 deaths.

But nowhere is this issue more pressing than in Japan, where there is a prevailing stigma against asking for help for mental-health issues. This, and an especially strong sense of social obligation, can create an overwhelming burden for a man who finds himself unemployed or in debt. Japan's suicide tally is now more than thirty thousand a year, roughly three times the number of people killed in traffic accidents and double the per capita suicide rate in the United States. Most of the victims are men, and nearly a third of the suicide notes cite economic hardship.

What You Can Do
Never a borrower or a lender be. On second thought, never a borrower be. The lenders seem to come out okay, especially at 18 percent interest compounded monthly.

MENACE

DEER

Deer

"All I could see was blood," a witness told the *Washington Times*. "It was like someone had dumped gallons of blood."

What creature could be responsible for such carnage? The beast must be one with bristling fur and snarling fangs. Surely not a deer, whose mention evokes visions of a Disney-animated fawn lazily munching grass as butterflies drift on the breeze.

It is all propaganda. The witness was describing the aftermath of an encounter with one of Bambi's relatives. The deer was struck in a head-on collision, and flew across the road and through the windscreen of a coach in the opposite lane. The animal shattered the window and was sliced into three parts. The largest ended up in the third row of the bus, injuring five passengers.

At least 200 Americans are killed each year when their vehicles collide with deer. Some experts put the number at closer to 300, because often motorists swerve to avoid deer and are instead killed by collisions with trees or posts. In all, about 1.9 million people have car-vs.-deer accidents each year, and 40,000 people are injured in them. In the state of Michigan alone there were 67,669 deer-car crashes in 1999. The Wisconsin Department of Natural Resources spent $557,322/£304,216 that year to remove dead deer from roads. And the number of people killed by wolves that year? Exactly nil. In fact, there are no conclusively documented cases of humans ever being killed by wolves in U.S. history.

Fairy tales like *Little Red Riding Hood* cast them as villains, but wolves, though often big, are not really that bad. In fact, the *Canadian Encyclopedia* describes them as "shy." They're more of a threat to deer, which make up a large part of their diet, than they are to people. This is not to say you should go up to a wolf and pat it.

What You Can Do
There is an ongoing debate between hunters and animal rights organisations as to how to solve the problem of deer accidents. Some favour thinning out herds with longer hunting seasons and more hunting licences. Animal-rights activists say the problem is not the deer but the people. As the suburbs take up more and more of the deer's former habitat, the animals are forced into the streets. These advocates argue that road accidents actually increase during hunting season as deer run away from gunfire and into oncoming traffic.

Some roadworks are installing devices called wildlife reflectors. These reflect the light from oncoming car's headlamps to create a low-intensity red beam directed into the nearby woods. The lights are not seen by drivers, but when the deer see the strange light patterns they're stopped in their tracks until the car has passed.

As a driver, the best thing to do is to drive cautiously and pay attention, especially when it is dark out.

Desk Germs

Chances are you would never even consider eating lunch off your office toilet seat. Well, maybe you should. There are an estimated 5 million trillion bacteria living on Earth, and a surprising number of them are hanging out on your desk. According to researcher Chuck Gerba, a professor of microbiology at the University of Arizona, your office desktop is four hundred times dirtier than a toilet seat. By taking samples of germs from workstations in New York City, San Francisco, California, Tucson, Arizona, and Tampa, Florida, Dr Gerba discovered that the average desk is home to 21,000 bacteria per square inch, or 8,400 per square centimeter, whereas the average toilet seat has only fifty.

"People spill coffee and eat their meals [at their desks] and nobody cleans it," Dr Gerba told *BusinessWeek*. Meanwhile, people use disinfectant to clean their toilets.

They apparently don't use disinfectant on their telephones. Your office phone receiver probably is home to more bacteria than the desktop or the toilet seat—about twenty-five thousand per square inch or ten thousand per square centimetre—and most office coffee cups are swimming in bacteria. In Gerba's study, about 40 percent of the cups had coliforms in them, including Escherichia coli, or E. coli, a common family of bacteria that generally does not cause human disease. There is one strain to look out for, however. E. coli 0157:H7 lives in the innards of cattle and can cause bloody diarrhoea in humans who eat contaminated meat products. If any meat products are prepared in your office kitchen, it is possible to transfer these bacteria to other parts of your office.

Perhaps receptionists should be entitled to hazard pay. According to Gerba's research, their desks are the filthiest of all because so many people stop and put their hands (and germs) on the welcoming space.

What You Can Do
Some observers chalk this up to a lifestyle problem. Take a little time away from the office and don't eat at your desk.

Dr Gerba's research is largely funded by Clorox bleach, and, not surprisingly, his suggestions for combating the rampant spread of office bacteria are largely bleach-related. Scrub everything you touch with bleach and there will be fewer bacteria lurking next time a scientist shows up with a swab.

On the other hand, you could try the "single bloke's flat" solution—don't clean at all. This avoids spreading bacteria around your work space. It turns out that much of the dangerous bacteria in the office travel on cleaning rags and sponges. Wiping up doesn't harm the bacteria—it just moves them around.

Then again, there is another solution that is even easier to implement, and that's not to worry about it. Germs may be transferred from hard surfaces to hands, but according to some microbiologists, there is no scientific proof that this mode of transmission causes infection. In fact, some scientists argue that trying to kill off the bacteria in your environment does more harm than good. It weakens the body's ability to fight off germs and allows resistant strains of bacteria to develop that may pack even more of a wallop.

If you're worried that you'll get a cold or flu from those bacteria, don't be. Colds and flus are caused by viruses, not bacteria.

DISHWASHERS

Dishwashers

E ach year in the United States an estimated 7,477 people suffer dishwasher-related injuries. Not to be outdone, another
1,353 British citizens have dishwasher mishaps, and that's not
even counting the 219 people who do themselves harm with
Brillo pads and the 91 who are injured with drying racks.

The dishwasher was invented by Josephine Garis Cochrane, an
Illinois housewife who was always chipping her china during the
washing up. She rigged a copper boiler with wire racks so that it
sprayed soapy water through a hand pump. To rinse the dishes,
she poured on boiling water from a teakettle, then let the dishes dry in the open air. Her creation took the top medal for "best
mechanical construction, durability and adaptation to the line
of work" at Chicago's 1893 Columbian Exposition.

Since then, dishwashers have become somewhat less cumber-
some, but they still employ the same basic principle: very hot
water poured over soapy dishes. Many dishwasher accidents are
related to heat and steam. The heating element can inflict a serious burn if you touch it before it has had a chance to cool down,
and if you open the machine while it's running, beware the
release of steam. The most common dishwasher accidents, however, involve the dishes themselves. People reach in to get plates
and cut themselves on the forks and knives.

Dishwasher/knife injuries are some of the most dramatic, and the most apt to be fatal. In 2003, a Scottish woman died after she slipped and fell into her dishwasher. She landed, full force, on a knife. In 1997, there were reports from Denmark and the United Kingdom of similar accidents. In Denmark, a small girl who tripped and fell into a dishwasher ended up with a long, though not fatal, cut across her neck. A 12-year-old British schoolboy was not so lucky. He was reaching across an open dishwasher and fell onto a knife. It severed an artery in his heart. He did not survive.

What You Can Do

The magazine *Consumer Reports* suggests that you load the cutlery in your dishwasher with the pointy bits downward. Keep children away from the dishwasher while it's running. Door vents are often at a toddler's eye level and can emit steam.

Also, keep dishwashing detergent out of the reach of children. While it is corrosive and poisonous, many brands have an appealing smell that entices children to taste it. A study by doctors at Royal Children's Hospital in Melbourne, Australia, of dishwashing-detergent poisonings found that few children are poisoned by detergent in the box. Most scoop out the leftover detergent residue when the dishwasher door is open—it's at just the right height for tots. The researchers suggest that altering detergent so that it doesn't cake in the dispenser might prevent some of the accidental poisonings. Education on the dangers of detergent is also a key. In their study, the doctors found that only 38 percent of parents were aware that the detergents were poisonous.

Dogs

They're man's best friends. They are cuddly, fun to play with and occasionally cause explosions.

In 2001, a Willenhall, United Kingdom, family was left homeless after its dog bit through a can of hairspray. The aerosol was ignited by heat from a gas fire and exploded into a giant fireball that damaged the house and killed two cats.

And explosion is not the only danger posed by our canine companions. In 2003, the Royal Society for the Prevention of Accidents warned that in a car accident a dog could become "a canine cannonball." At 30 mph/48.28 kph, a 50-lb/22.68-kg dog could be hurled forward with a force equivalent to nine 170-lb/77.11-kg men.

Meanwhile, veterinarians are warning BBC viewers about the "hidden dangers of dog stroking." Stroking a dog could infect a child with a parasitic worm that leads to blindness, according to veterinarians Alan Wolfe and Ian Wright. They examined 60 dogs and found that 25 percent had Toxocara Canis, or roundworm eggs in their fur. It had previously been assumed that the parasite could only be picked up by contact with dog feces, but a quarter of the eggs in Wolfe and Wright's study were mature enough to infect humans and could easily be picked up by patting a dog. The parasites can cause anything from a stomachache to eye damage. Still, the risk is relatively low: there are only about twenty cases a year in Britain.

In 2003, the United Kingdom's Health Protection Agency warned that pets were carrying antibiotic-resistant "superbugs." The British Veterinary Association found a dozen pets that tested positive for methicillin-resistant staphylococcus aureus, or MRSA, which kills five thousand British hospital patients a year.

Finally, having a pet can be hazardous in a fire or natural disaster. Various studies have shown that people with pets are less likely to evacuate their homes in an emergency, that they may refuse medical care until they know their pet is safe, and that they may put themselves at risk by running back into burning buildings to save their four-legged friends.

What You Can Do
Wash your hands. When Dr Alistair Gibson of the British Veterinary Association was asked about the risks from MRSA-carrying pets, he told the *Observer*: "We don't want to see a massive scare that will make people get rid of their pets. Owners should take a sensible approach, wash their hands regularly and not panic."

Be careful with veterinary medicines. According to the American Association of Poison Control Centres, 3,702 Americans were poisoned by veterinary drugs in 1998. The medicines are rarely packaged in childproof containers. In 2000, a U.S. toddler died after taking a drug prescribed for the family Doberman. Not all veterinary medical use is accidental, however. CNN recently featured a story on a growing trend in the United States—humans buying veterinary medications to reduce their costs and avoid restrictions. The American Pet Products Manufacturers Association has reported that annual sales of all pet products jumped 35 percent between 1995 and 2000, too much to be caused by pets alone. Don't jump on this bandwagon. Medications sold for animal use are not created in the same concentrations as they are for people. You could suffer serious consequences.

Before you ship your pet off, it is worth noting that numerous studies tout the benefits of pet ownership. Children with pets have better school attendance. Old age pensioners are less lonely and pet ownership can lower blood pressure.

Doors

They appear to be simple dividers separating one room from another, but doors do damage. The dreaded doorway has done its dirty work to many, including such luminaries as England's Prince Harry, who needed stitches in 2001 after he stuck his foot out to stop a glass door from slamming shut.

Doors are a threat to us commoners as well. The totals are staggering. In the United Kingdom, an estimated 92,620 people are injured annually by interior doors and another 41,674 are hurt by doors that lead to the outside. These figures do not include automatic doors and revolving doors in public places.

Automatic-door accidents are rare, but when they occur, they can be very violent, and can result in more serious injuries than the typical home-door accident. Automatic-door accidents usually involve elderly individuals who can't move fast enough to get away from a closing door, or who, after getting their signs mixed up, try to go out through the entrance door and are struck when another customer enters.

One of the most unusual doorway-related deaths to make recent headlines was that of an 18-year-old Cincinnati, Ohio, woman who was electrocuted as she tried to enter her hotel room. The victim was barefoot and soaking wet from a rainstorm when she slid the electronic key into the door's lock and received a fatal shock.

(Authorities blamed a charge from a faulty air conditioner, not the electronic key device, which is powered by a handful of tiny batteries.)

So much for the uncommon accidents. Doorway accidents are usually injuries to the hands from slams or from fingers getting stuck in hinges. Although they sound insignificant, such accidents can sometimes be fairly serious, ending in amputations. Glass doors have their own special dangers. Hospital casualty wards often play host to homeowners who have accidentally put limbs through them.

What You Can Do
When you're about to walk into a room, shout, "I'm here and I'm opening the door!" This will prevent someone on the other side from opening the door at the same moment and hitting you in the head. It may also cause your housemates to move away, thus permanently eliminating that particular risk.

One easily avoidable accident is common enough that some ladder manufacturers have put a label on their products: "Warning: Do Not Use Ladder in Front of Unlocked Doors." Enough said.

If you have glass doors, you might want to have a glazier check to see if the glass meets current safety standards. There are two main types of safety glass: laminated, which consists of two panes with a layer of plastic in between, making the glass very difficult to shatter, and tempered glass, which is heat-treated so it is more break-resistant and more likely to shatter into relatively harmless pieces. Newer homes are built with break-resistant glass, but most older homes were not.

Dust

It seems like nothing more than an insignificant speck, but that dust particle, and a million or so of his friends, may cause more premature deaths than highway accidents do. The Natural Resources Defense Council estimates that as many as sixty thousand Americans die each year from lung diseases, heart conditions and other problems brought on by inhaling dust. Worldwide, that number could be as high as 2.8 million deaths, according to the World Health Organization.

Did you ever wonder what the dust on your mantle shelf is made of? Most indoor dust is made of stuff that used to be you—shed skin and hair. You'll also find bits of food, carpet fibres, dead insects and clothing lint.

Researchers at the California Institute of Technology went along Southern California's highways with a hoover to check the contents of the state's dust. They discovered that outdoor dust is made up largely of dirt, motor vehicle exhaust, pollens, particles from brake linings and tyres, heavy metals and animal dander. Tests have shown that dust on farms typically consists of animal feed, animal skin, excrement, bacteria and fungi.

This tiny stuff is bad for your heart. Researchers at the Harvard School of Public Health in Boston, Massachusetts, found that when the level of airborne particulates was high, heart rates fell, which is a known risk for heart attack. According to one estimate, dust may be responsible for 1 percent of all heart disease fatalities in the United States—that's about ten thousand deaths a year.

In 1991, an epidemiologist with the U.S. Environmental Protection Agency measured daily levels of particles in the air in Detroit, Michigan, and compared them to the number of deaths each day. When particle levels were high, more people died. Around the same time, scientists at the Johns Hopkins University School of Public Health found that, for every cubic metre of air, an increase of 20 microgrammes of airborne particulate matter (about 70 millionths of an ounce) led to a 1 percent rise in the death rate.

Oh, yes—and dust sometimes explodes, because it consists of organic matter that can emit flammable gases as it decays. In November 2002, three men were severely burned in an explosion that occurred while the men were welding a metal chute inside a grain silo in New London, North Carolina. One man was left with burns over 40 percent of his body. Six people were killed and dozens injured at the West Pharmaceutical Services plant in Kinston, North Carolina, in January 2003 when a volatile mixture of air and suspended dust caused an explosion. Fine powder from the manufacture of rubber products became trapped above a suspended ceiling. When mixed with air, the polyethylene powder needed only a small spark to ignite it.

What You Can Do
Your feather duster is not likely to help you much—the dust on your television screen and your side table is not the kind that is likely to kill you. As a general rule, if household dust is big enough for you to see, it will probably be trapped in your nose and eliminated before it can cause major health problems.

Health magazine offers the following suggestions: If you live in a city that is smoggy enough to air particulate alerts on the morning news, pay close attention. When particulate levels are high, keep windows and doors closed, and definitely do not go out jogging. Vigorous workouts can quadruple the amount of air, and dust, you take in. On the other hand, when the air is clear, open your doors and windows so you can let that indoor dust out.

Install a fan in your kitchen that vents to the outside. Cooking is a major cause of indoor air pollution. A major cause of outdoor dust is your car's emissions. You can help your neighbours by walking more and driving less. Use the car pool lane.

DANGER

Elevators/Lifts

A simple lift ride turned fatal when, on 16, August 2003, Dr Hitoshi Nikaidoh, a surgical resident at Christus St. Joseph Hospital in Houston, Texas, went to step into a lift that he had summoned. The doors suddenly snapped shut while he was in midstride, pinning his shoulders, and the car moved upward, severing his head as it passed the floor above. Inside the car was another hospital employee, who was treated for shock after spending twenty minutes trapped in the confined space with her coworker's skull.

According to data from the U.S. Bureau of Labor Statistics and the Consumer Product Safety Commission, lifts and escalators kill about thirty and injure about 17,100 people each year in the United States. Usually victims are trapped in doors, or trip getting in or out of a lift that is not quite aligned with the floor. Sometimes, however, the accidents are dramatic.

In 2002, an 11-year-old Hong Kong boy was caught halfway inside a lift as it continued to move upward even though its doors were not fully shut. He died in the hospital from abdominal injuries.

In 2003, an 8-year-old boy on vacation at a hotel in Maine was crushed when he was trapped in the doors of an antique lift that featured a hinged door and a collapsible gate inside. He became caught in a gap between the two doors just as a maid on the second floor rang for service. Following the accident, the Associated Press reviewed its coverage and found that at least nine children had been killed in similar fashion in the previous five years.

Also in 2003, a 32-year-old Polish woman living and working in London, England, was walking out of a lift at a gym in the city's financial district when it suddenly fell between the ground floor and basement. She became trapped between the elevator and the shaft. Fellow passengers tried to pull her out, but she was pronounced dead shortly after the fire brigade arrived.

In the United States, there is no national agency responsible for inspecting lifts. The rules vary by state. Some require no inspection at all. In 1998, ABC News did a survey of lifts in major U.S. cities and found lifts overdue for inspection in all of them. New York City had the worst record, with lifts as much as three and a half years behind on their inspections.

What You Can Do
Don't roughhouse. Young people have been killed by jumping and trying to rock lifts. In 2002, for example, a boy fell three floors down a lift shaft at Harry S. Truman High School in New York. He and a friend were wrestling in the car and jarred the door open by knocking it out of its bottom track.

Whatever you do, don't ride on top of lifts. A number of students have died in the past few years while engaging in a stunt called "lift surfing." They break into the shaft and take a joyride on the top of the lift. What can happen? You could end up like one 15-year-old lift surfer from Jersey City, New Jersey, who was flipped and dragged into the cables and left dangling upside down for an hour. He died.

There's an urban legend that if you are in a lift plunging earthward and you jump just before the crash, you won't be hurt. Not true. Even if you knew when you were going to hit bottom (which would be quite difficult to ascertain), a leap would not slow you down enough to keep you from being hurt. A better strategy would be to lie on the floor so the force of impact spreads over your entire body.

Whatever you do to quell your lift fears, don't take the stairs. You're statistically much more likely to be injured there. (See page 190.)

English Winters

The icy breath of the wind chills the skin, and its frosty effects change the very functioning of the circulatory system. Thousands meet their deaths after venturing out into this frigid environment. Siberia? No. London, Engalnd. The winter may be milder, but more people die from the effects of cold weather in Britain than in any other European country, including Russia and Finland.

The United Kingdom has between forty thousand and fifty thousand more deaths during the winter months than in summer months. Even Yakutsk, Siberia, the coldest city on Earth, sees a smaller rise in excess deaths in winter. Temperatures in Yakutsk routinely dip to -40°F/-40°C with average temperatures of only -15.8°F/-26.6°C from October to March. Britain has relatively mild temperatures for its latitude because it is influenced by the Gulf Stream, a warm ocean current that originates in the Gulf of Mexico. The coldest part of the United Kingdom, northern Scotland, has average winter temperatures of 37.4°F/3°C, while Gulf Stream-affected southwest England has mild winters with average temperatures around 62.6°F/17°C.

So why does the winter claim more lives in the United Kingdom than in Siberia? Because no Siberian has ever been shocked to discover it was cold outside. Siberia has cold like Bill Gates has money. People who live there take care (and a certain pride) in their ability to withstand their infamously cold winters. Russians, like Finns and northern Canadians, have become some of the world's experts on how to keep warm.

Britons aren't of a like mind, explains William Keatinge of London's Queen Mary and Westfield College, an expert on the effects of climate on health: "Those in very cold climates are very careful at avoiding exposure to cold. Those in London or Athens do not take it seriously."

One reason they don't is that the effects are not always immediately apparent. Very few winter deaths in Britain are from hypothermia, or low body temperature. Extreme cold strains the body, weakens the immune system, and causes a series of changes in the blood. These changes increase the chances of blood clots forming, which can lead to heart attacks and strokes. Deaths from heart disease occur a day or two after exposure, those from stroke about five days later, and those from immune suppression and respiratory distress as much as two weeks later. Therefore, people fail to see the connection between the weather and the illness, and tend to assume they can get through the cold just fine in their short skirts and lightweight jackets.

What You Can Do
Dress in warm layers. When Keatinge and his peers studied the community of Yakutsk, they found that residents wore an average of 4.26 layers of clothes, with an outer layer of fur or similarly thick material. Yakuts wear fur hats that cover the ears, and often the sides of the face too. In fact, researchers found that throughout mainland Europe, when the temperatures dip, most people wear hats, gloves, mufflers and thermal attire. The British, meanwhile, often add little more than a coat in winter, and sometimes only a jacket.

The British government is taking a small step toward raising awareness of the problem. It recently awarded a $2,377,296/£1,400,000 grant to the Met Office (Meteorological Office) to develop a Health Forecast Unit, which correlates hospital admissions and health conditions with temperature, humidity and air pressure. The unit is expected to provide valuable data on how all types of weather phenomena affect the nation's health.

Escalators

You see it again and again in dramatic movies—the hero is in the wilds of a tropical rain forest and finds himself sinking uncontrollably into quicksand. A leading man desperately trying to free himself from sinking into an escalator, on the other hand, is something you are more likely to see in a comedy. In the real world, however, things are quite different.

Quicksand might be more appropriately called "slowsand." It is simply a tract of loose sand and clay mixed with water. It appears solid, but contains a surprising amount of liquid. It is often no more than a few inches deep, and is not likely to reach above your knees. The best news about quicksand is that it is actually more buoyant than water. If you find yourself in deep, you can float, or swim, out.

Getting stuck in an escalator is far more dangerous. All over the world, passengers have found themselves trapped in escalator mechanisms. The results have been amputation, strangulation and death. One of the worst escalator tragedies occurred in Moscow, Russia, in 1982, when eight people were killed and thirty injured at the Aviamotornaya railway station. The motor broke and the escalator band that comprises the "stairs" came sliding down, throwing passengers into a heap at the bottom. As panicked passengers climbed onto the guardrails, these gave way under their weight, plunging more people into the mangled escalator works.

Another major escalator accident occurred in Boston, Massachusetts, in 1996, when a crowded escalator at the city's Back Bay train station malfunctioned, pitching dozens of people down the incline and injuring twenty-three. In this case, there were no fatalities.

Common culprits in escalator injuries are shopping trolleys (in shops and shopping centres) and luggage (in tubes and airports). The trolleys can put the riders off balance or cause other mishaps. In 2002, two passengers at the Kievskaya station in Moscow had their toes crushed when their feet got caught at the top of the escalator. The accident was blamed on a heavy trolley that got jammed between the moving steps and the comb plate at the top of the escalator. The gap between the band and the plate widened, and the two victims could not pull their feet out in time.

Clothing is another escalator hazard, as a Washington, DC, Metro passenger tragically learned in 1998. The woman's clothes became caught in the steps of the machinery and she was fatally strangled. In 1997, another Washington, DC, Metro rider died when his T-shirt became caught in the works of a station's escalator.

In all, in the United States more than five thousand people are sent to the casualty ward for injuries related to escalators each year, and three, on average, do not live to tell the tale.

What You Can Do
Stairs are an option. Mind you, most escalator riders do get to their destinations without any problems. Schindler, one of the largest manufacturers of escalators, estimates that about 70 billion escalator rides take place each year in the United States alone.

To ensure that yours is one of the uneventful trips, keep your feet away from the side of the escalator. Shoelaces and straps can sometimes get sucked into the works, so be sure your laces are tied and mufflers and loose clothes are not close to any moving parts. Children should hold a parent's hand rather than the handrail because as children stretch, they tend to put their feet very close to the edge. If you have luggage, prams or trolleys to transport, see if there is a lift nearby.

DEADLY

Falling Objects

A coconut falls from a palm tree and bops a man on the head. It could be a moment from a cartoon, or it could be the trag-ic ending of a beautiful holiday. Chicken Little was right—the sky sometimes *is* falling. Or at least things are falling from it.

It all depends on where you live. Injuries from being hit on the head by falling coconuts (and from climbing trees in order to get at them) are as common as traffic- and sports-related injuries in the Solomon Islands. A coconut that falls 82 ft/25 m has an impact velocity of 49.7 mph/80 kph, with a 2.2 to 8.2 lb/1 to 4 kg nut exerting a force of more than a metric ton. That's enough to cause some serious damage. After a young boy was admitted to hospital with severe brain damage from a falling coconut, an injury audit was conducted and published in the *Journal of Trauma*. The audit uncovered 105 coconut-related injures in the Pacific Islands that year. A four-year review of trauma admis-sions to a Papua New Guinea hospital revealed 2.5 percent of admissions were related to falling coconuts.

"It may seem funny from our perspective," said Dr Peter Barss, the author of the study, "but when you're treating these injuries daily, it's not funny at all."

Don't think that the absence of palm trees means it's safe to look up. In Moscow, Russia, there is an entirely different danger—icicles. Moscow's winters feature an average of fifty snowstorms.

The city has nine thousand buildings with iron roofs, coupled with narrow streets. This means there is a great danger of giant ice spears landing on people and property, so much so that in a typical winter, authorities stretch 125 m/201.17 km of warning ribbon to cordon off the walkways beneath particularly menacing icicles. The city of Moscow employs five hundred teams of icicle-busters—trained mountaineers—to remove shafts that can stretch to 9.84 ft/3 m long and weigh upwards of 132.28 lb/60 kg. By January of a given winter season, a half-dozen Muscovites will have been wounded by falling ice. (Twice as many will have filed false claims for compensation after pretending to have been hit.)

Urban landscapes with tall buildings have their own hazards. Over the years, residents of tall cities—like Hong Kong, Chicago and New York—have been struck by a number of falling objects, including pieces of ornamental facades, bricks, construction debris, security fences, flowerpots, buckets and even a pole with a "Walk/Don't walk" signal. In 2000, a window fell twenty-nine floors from a bank building in Chicago, killing Ana Flores, aged 37, as she walked with her 4-year-old daughter.

"This is not an unusual event," Alderman Bernard Stone, of the Chicago City Council's Buildings Committee, told the *Washington Post*, "and as these 80- and 90-year-old buildings get older, it's going to happen even more."

Then there is space junk, which can land anywhere on the planet. Human beings have been leaving their rubbish in space for decades. Since *Sputnik I* and *II* in 1957, about forty-five hundred satellites have been launched. The European Space Agency's Space Debris Observation System tracks about eight thousand large objects in orbit and a huge amount of other debris that measures less than 3.94 in/10 cm in diameter. Occasionally some of it makes it to Earth. Shards have landed in Zambia, Finland and Nepal. In 1962, a 21-lb/9.53-kg metal cylinder landed in an intersection in Manitowoc, Wisconsin. It was later identified as a fragment of the Soviet's *Sputnik IV*, launched two years earlier, in May 1960. In 1963 a charred metal sphere with a 15-in/38.10-cm diameter turned up on a sheep station in New South Wales, Australia. It was also believed to be a piece of a Soviet craft. In 1978, Cosmos 954, a 5-ton, nuclear-powered Soviet ocean-surveillance satellite, came down. Bits of it were scattered over hundreds of square miles in northern Canada. The following year, the remains of NASA's Skylab were strewn across the Indian Ocean and Australian outback.

What You Can Do
You could move to an underground city. The Berbers of Matmata, Tunisia, dug their villages underground to escape the extreme heat of the surface. (You may have seen the landscape before as the home of Luke Skywalker in *Star Wars*.) In Turkey, in the region of Cappadocia, there are five underground cities. Ancient volcanic eruptions created soft, conical rocks, some ten stories tall. The Hittites began carving out homes, and eventually created underground cities, some eight levels deep and once home to up to ten thousand inhabitants. You can still visit these cities today, and stay in underground hotels.

Coconut catchers: A young Queensland, Australia inventor, Tim Straatman, won the 2002 Australian Design Award Invention of the Year for a tree-mounted coconut catcher—a sort of upside-down brolly that wraps around a coconut tree like an inverted skirt. He hopes to market his "Coconet" to tropical resorts.

Don't worry too much about space debris. Sure, there's a lot of it out there, and theoretically it could come crashing down on you. The vast majority, however, burns up in the atmosphere before it gets anywhere near a human head. The probability of being clocked by a falling piece of Sputnik is so small that Lloyds of London considers the odds impossible to calculate. The only confirmed victims of falling space junk were struck in 1969, when a Japanese freighter in the Sea of Japan was hit with wreckage from a Soviet spacecraft. Five crewmen were seriously injured. So far, there are no recorded cases of human deaths from space debris on planet Earth—though in 1961, Fidel Castro claimed that a piece of a U.S. rocket killed a Cuban cow.

Finally, don't wear birdseed on your head. No, really. According to the *Evening Telegraph*, part-time inventor Mike Madden of West Yorkshire, England, was trying out his latest creation, a bird-feeding hat, when he was struck by a falling squirrel. The rodent sprang for the morsels and landed on Madden's head with so much force that the inventor was knocked to the ground. He wound up in a neck brace. Don't try this at home.

Farming

Many a city dweller has dreamed of leaving the urban land-scape behind for the simple pleasures of the country life. What could be safer than planting things and harvesting them? The answer, as it happens, is nearly everything. Farming is one of the world's most dangerous occupations, outpacing other industries in injuries and deaths.

A farm may appear calm and serene, but danger lurks around every corner. There are tractors waiting to tip or to collide. There are large threshers and milkers, plus machines with any number of moving parts that can as easily suck in a farmer's ear as an ear of maize. Of course, there are also the animals. As a representa-tive of New Zealand's Department of Occupational Safety and Health (OSH) put it: "Cattle are so strong, and they just lash out instantly."

In New Zealand, an average of eleven farmers are seriously injured every day, and one is killed each week. These are the injuries that the government knows about—because of fear of investigations and penalties, OSH officials believe farm accidents are greatly underreported. In Australia, there are an estimated 150 farm deaths and 6,500 hospital admissions a year. Each year more than 2,000 Canadians are hospitalised because of farmwork and 135 die.

While machinery accidents are the major cause of injury and death on farms, they are not the only hazard. Less obvious dangers come from things that float on that famous "fresh" country air. Farmers who work closely with livestock can catch diseases from their animals. These illnesses that can be passed from livestock to people are called zoonoses.

Another cause of concern is farmer's lung, an allergic disease usually caused by breathing the dust from mouldy hay and other crops. Doctors call it "extrinsic allergic alveolitis." The reaction, if untreated, can cause permanent lung damage, physical disability or even death. Canada's Centre for Occupational Health and Safety estimates that the disease occurs in about 2 to 10 percent of farmworkers, depending on the region.

Another danger, believe it or not, is dung. Large collections of animals produce large amounts of waste. Hydrogen sulfide, a by-product of decomposing hog waste, is as lethal as hydrogen cyanide, a gas that has been used to execute convicted criminals. During the 1980s, nineteen farmers in the United States died from hydrogen sulfide poisoning.

What You Can Do
Change careers to something safer, say, manufacturing explosives. According to the U.S. Bureau of Labor Statistics, in a given year there are roughly six injuries and fatalities for every one hundred employees of explosives manufacturers. In agriculture, there are more than ten per 100. If you decide, however, that the benefits of a farmer's lifestyle outweigh the risks of being mangled by a threshing machine, attacked by a raging bull, or overwhelmed by toxic dung fumes, here are a few safety tips:

Raise poultry. You're less likely to be seriously injured by a chicken than a cow. Dairy farming, according to New Zealand's Accident Compensation Corporation, is the segment of the farm industry with the greatest number of accidents, about fifty-four hundred over the course of five years. Sheep-raising came in second with just over thirty-two hundred claims.

Keep farming machinery well maintained and be extra careful if you venture out onto the road with it. Traffic accidents play a substantial factor in farming injuries.

CAUTION

FASHION

Fashion

It hangs in your closet, and lurks in your chest of drawers. Next thing you know, it is wrapped around your body, where it can maim or kill. Yes, your clothing can be the death of you. The toll of fashion violence is staggering. In the U.S. each year, an estimated 110,463 people are hurt by clothes and accessories. This is about 100,000 more people than are injured each year by fireworks, and almost 96,000 more than are hurt by nail guns. It gives a whole new meaning to the expression "fashion victim."

In England, 9,635 people are injured in an average year by socks, 3,695 by trousers, 1,573 by coats, 1,353 by shirts, 1,353 by jumpers and 311 by underwear.

Clothing accidents can be brutal. In October 1998, a 9-year-old died when his anorak toggle got caught in the closing door of a London Underground train. He was dragged to his death when the train moved off. The automatic switches designed to disable a train when the door is obstructed could not sense something as small as the toggle.

The U.S. Consumer Product Safety Commission recently reported the case of a 22-year-old building site worker who was killed when his oversize, wide-legged trousers got tangled in a moving tractor. On the other hand, tight jeans can also be a problem. They can cause skin inflammation and groin rashes—doctors call it "jean folliculitis." Fertility specialists also caution that too much time in tight jeans can make men sterile.

Vanity knows pain in other ways as well. If you've put on a bit of weight but are unwilling to expand into the next size of jeans, the constriction of your waist could be causing you indigestion. The stomach doesn't have room to expand, and acid comes up into the gullet, causing heartburn. Corsets can cause similar problems, and some studies suggest that corsets may actually make you flabbier because they weaken abdominal muscles through lack of exercise.

Tight neckties could lead to damage of the optic nerve and loss of vision, according to research reported in the British *Journal of Ophthalmology*. The researchers' tests showed that 70 percent of healthy volunteers had increased eye pressure when wearing a tight tie. If you're going to be taking an eye exam, shun the tie. It could lead to a false diagnosis of glaucoma.

One German expert, a professor Helmut Ippen, argues that short skirts cause cellulite. The body reacts to exposure to cold air, he says, by building a protective layer of fat.

What You Can Do

Become a nudist. You will not be alone. The combined membership of the American Association for Nude Recreation (AANR) and the Naturist Society in 2003 was seventy-five thousand. You might start with a visit to Cap d'Agde, France's largest nudist colony. It attracts forty thousand European tourists each year.

Make safety gear sexy by holding a fashion show. Angie Lee, a bike helmet specialist from Redding, England, regularly stages bike helmet fashion shows. Meanwhile, in Canada, *Injury Prevention News*, a magazine published by Alberta's Injury Prevention Centre, held an "injury prevention fashion show" at Sir George Simpson Junior High School in St. Albert, Alberta. Students and staff modeled helmets and sports padding. The organisers said the students thought the event was "fun, interesting, creative and got the point across." No word directly from the kids.

Make sure children's clothes, in particular, do not have any hanging parts like hood pulls or drawstrings. Velcro fasteners are recommended. Be especially careful to keep mufflers, sleeves, skirts or other bits of clothing away from moving machine parts and sliding doors.

Finland

Its unspoiled natural beauty, charming towns, thick forests and crystalline lakes make it the perfect setting for a holiday getaway, or an accident. Humble Finland leads the European Union in scars, bruises, broken bones and stitches, according to the national newspaper *Helsingin Sanomat*.

Each year, about 1 million accidents occur in Finland, a country of only 5 million people. In other words, 1 out of every 5 Finns will be in an accident this year. Meanwhile, Austria, with a population of 8 million, averages only 800,000 accidents. Only the countries of Eastern Europe best Finland when it comes to accident frequency, according to Markku Heiskanen of Statistics Finland.

What dangerous activity are the Finns engaged in that they so often manage to mangle their bodies? Walking. The leading cause of accidents amongst all age groups in Finland is falling down. This could be explained by the fact that there is plenty of ice and snow to slip on. Finnish winters are cold, very cold— temperatures of -4°F/-20°C are not uncommon in many areas. Then again, it could be the darkness. In winter, the sun remains below the horizon for fifty-one days in the far north.

The problem with these theories is that far more accidents occur in summer than in winter. That's when people get out and about, fix their cottage roofs, build campfires, and generally put themselves in harm's way.

What You Can Do

You could, of course, avoid Finland, but you would miss out on some beautiful views, including the aurora borealis, Europe's largest archipelago and dense forests interspersed with countless lakes, ponds and rivers. Avoiding Finland is also highly impractical if you happen to be Finnish.

The best way to avoid accidents in Finland is to avoid drinking alcohol while enjoying the great outdoors, or even the great indoors (as with most countries, most of Finland's accidents happen at home). "Finns still have a strong belief that a drunkard's luck protects him from accidents," said Merja Söderholm of the Ministry of Health and Social Welfare.

But believing it doesn't make it so. Alcohol is a factor in a large number of Finnish accidents, including five hundred to six hundred poisonings annually and half of all drownings and fires. So, for best results, enjoy the scenery of Finland while drinking a nice cup of tea. (Just be careful with it—see *Tea*, page 204.)

LETHAL

Fishing

It is a heartwarming picture. Father and son heading off together to the river on a brilliant afternoon, fishing gear in hand, prepared to engage in a highly dangerous sporting activity. In the United States and United Kingdom, fishing reels in more injuries than boxing and ice hockey combined—a grand total of 79,369 American and 1,339 British wounded. Fishing simply provides many more ways to get hurt: there is drowning, electrocution, lost fingers and limbs from being wrapped in fishing lines, and hooks embedded in muscles and eyes. If you live in the right (or wrong) part of the world, you may also be putting yourself at risk of shark attacks or stings by poisonous fish. Recently, two Australian fishermen were thrown overboard when their boat was attacked by a whale.

Professional fishermen also have a high death toll. The International Labour Organization puts the figure at twenty-four thousand, but the U.N. Food and Agriculture Organization believes the true figure is much higher, because 97 percent of fishermen work on vessels that are too small to be within the scope of international guidelines. A study by Oxford University that reviewed death statistics from 1976 to 1995 ranked trawler fishing as the riskiest occupation in Britain, far ahead of fire fighting and police work, which ranked twenty-third and twenty-fourth, respectively.

Fishermen have somehow not acquired the same image of daring that bull-fighters have. Yet they're performing essentially the same task—fighting an animal to its death. The fish fight for their lives. If a fisherman, or the fisherman's friends, get caught in the line, the force can be surprisingly strong. It has been known to choke unsuspecting boat mates and to lop off pinched digits. Sometimes the fish wins the tug-of-war and pulls the fisherman overboard. A competitor in the 1994 Big Rock Tournament met his end this way when his hand got tangled in a leader attached to a blue marlin.

If the fish manages to free itself, the line can suddenly fly back, flinging that barbed hook right at the fisherman. The hooks are designed to pierce fish flesh, and they'll do just as well with the human kind. The danger doesn't end when the fish is out of the water. Fish don't like to be out of the water. Sometimes a fish with a treble hook in its mouth will thrash around and lodge an exposed barb into a fisherman.

One Brazilian fish apparently decided to make a preemptive strike against a fisherman on the Maguari River in the Amazon. According to the syndicated newspaper column "Earthweek," the fisherman was yawning when a 6-in/15.24-cm fish leaped out of the water and became lodged in his throat. He suffocated.

Not all fishing injuries, however, are caused by the fish. If a fisherman does not pay careful attention when he casts his line, he can catch something, like a friend, on his backswing. Then there are the injuries caused by the elements—graphite fishing rods are excellent conductors of electricity. Recently

a competitor in a Florida bass-fishing tournament discovered this as he and a fishing partner were taking advantage of a thunderstorm to improve their catch. (The drop in barometric pressure brings the fish out.) Perhaps he did not know that Florida leads the world in thunderstorms, lightning strikes and lightning deaths. Before he knew what hit him, his rod exploded into shards and he was lying prone in a boat in which all the wiring had melted.

Researchers in China reported on eight patients between 1991 and 1995 who were electrocuted while holding fishing rods. Some were struck by lightning, others hit overhead electrical wires with the rods. One of the most unusual fishing/electrocution cases on record comes from Australia. A deckhand on a fishing boat was electrocuted when a huge wave swamped him as he played a computer game in his cabin.

What You Can Do

If you're on a boat, wear your life vest. One professional fisherman's drowning death in Scotland in 1999 was widely attributed to "the culture on the vessel," which reportedly made him "feel a sissy for taking seriously his own safety." Although life vests were available, none of the crew would wear them. The fisherman drowned. Life jackets are orange, they're puffy, they're not the least bit sexy. Wear them anyway.

It is also important to wear wellies with nonskid soles. They should be at least one size larger than normal street shoes. This way, you can wear extra socks to keep your feet warm, and if you do get pulled overboard, you can kick them off easily and swim.

At least there's one cool accessory you can sport in the name of safety—sunglasses, which reduce the risk of getting a hook in the eye.

If you're at a stream or river and your fishing line gets snagged beneath the surface, resist the urge to jerk on the line until it snaps—you're liable to dislodge the hook from whatever has caught it and send it hurtling back toward you. If you need to break the line, point the rod directly at the snag, turn your back, and walk away until it snaps.

Finally, take a bolt or wire cutter with you, so if a hook does get lodged in your skin, you can cut the barb off and remove it.

The Flu

It's not anthrax. It's not AIDS. It's just the flu. But "just the flu" is nothing to sneeze at—it outpaces AIDS as a killer. Anthrax and SARS combined end the lives of far fewer people. Even traffic accidents take a backseat to the flu.

Flu epidemics kill more than 40,000 people across the European Union in a normal year, which is more than the number lost in car accidents. Each year, about 20 percent of Australians contract flu and as many as 3,000 die from complications. In the United States, 36,000 people a year die from the flu, compared with about 15,000 AIDS deaths. Even worse, the number of flu deaths is rising dramatically. Flu fatalities quadrupled from 1976 to 1998, according to the U.S. Centers for Disease Control and Prevention. In all, influenza outbreaks kill between 250,000 and 500,000 people each year across the world, according to World Health Organization estimates. Predictions of which strains are going to be prevalent in the upcoming flu season are about as accurate as six-month weather forecasts.

One of the reasons the flu is so difficult to eradicate is that it mutates as it travels around the planet and from year to year. The World Health Organization global-surveillance system analyses about six thousand different flu samples. That is only a fraction of the variety of flu life that circles the globe. Some strains cause little damage to the body, while others are deadly.

Researchers in Hong Kong believe the key factor in killer strains may be the human immune system itself. Something in the genetic makeup of a particular flu strain triggers a very strong immune response. The body creates cytokines, which attack harmful cells. The immune response is so strong and there are so many cytokines that they start to attack the body's own cells and cause organ failures.

One of the most devastating outbreaks of the flu occurred in 1918. That flu pandemic killed as many as 40 million people throughout the world. Scientists say we're overdue for another.

What You Can Do

You know the old adage, "Starve a fever and feed a cold"? Ignore it. It doesn't work. You'll just end up hungry with the flu, or full with a cold.

Flu vaccines are a great help in stemming the spread of the virus, but you have to actually take the vaccine for it to be effective. Researchers from the National Institute of Infectious Diseases in Japan reported that while U.S. flu death rates remained the same or increased, Japan saw a dramatic decrease in influenza death rates between 1962 and 1994. The reduction coincided with a mandatory vaccination programme for schoolchildren. Since children are considered to be the fastest spreaders of the flu, the vaccination programme was credited with reducing mortality rates from influenza among older adults as well. When the mandatory programme was dropped in 1994, death rates began to shoot up again. This can serve as a lesson to people in the United States who fail to heed the call to get their voluntary flu injections. Among older Americans (those most at risk from the flu), only 65 percent get vaccinated. Among those with high-risk conditions like diabetes and heart disease, only 30 percent get flu injections.

Don't take your leftover antibiotics when you have the flu. Antibiotics do not work on the flu, which is caused by a virus. (Besides, you should always take the full course of antibiotics anyway.) They only work on bacterial infections. All the same, a study published in the *Journal of the American Medical Association* reported that doctors wrote 12 million antibiotic prescriptions in 1992 for colds and flu. Overuse of antibiotics is contributing to the emergence of drug-resistant strains of bacteria. A category of drugs called antivirals can reduce some flu symptoms, but only those of influenza type A, not type B.

If you've got an extra $50 million, you can help scientists from the Department of Epidemiology at the University of California at Los Angeles. They want to build a high-tech global laboratory that will increase the number of flu strains currently being analysed from six thousand to a hundred thousand. The nonprofit centre will take around two years to build and five years to become fully operational—that is, if the scientists get their funding.

Oh, and that statistic about the increase in flu deaths? It's not as bad as you think. It means that we're healthier and living longer. Deaths from the flu are most common in older people—those over age 85 are most susceptible. One of the reasons there are so many more deaths from the flu is that there are so many more people over the age of 85.

The Full Moon

On a dreary night the clouds part to reveal a glowing, full moon. Animals begin to howl and bite, psychopaths go on the prowl, casualty wards fill with cardiac emergencies, and the crime rate skyrockets … maybe. It depends on what study you trust.

Robert A. Millikan, a Nobel Prize winner and former chairman of the California Institute of Technology, is credited with stating: "If man is not affected in some way by the planets, sun and moon, he is the only thing on Earth that isn't."

Indeed, numerous studies have shown a link between violence and the lunar cycle. C. P. Thakur and D. Sharma published the results of their study of crime reports from 1978 to 1982 in the *British Medical Journal*. They found that the incidence of crimes committed on full-moon days was much higher than on other days. They suggested the increase might be due to "human tidal waves" caused by the gravitational pull of the moon. Dr Glenn Wilson of King's College in London, England, poetically suggested that the moon's glow created "an aura of unreality which seems to transport people from the mundane … not because of any astronomical force, but because it creates the optimum lighting conditions."

In December 2000, Chanchal Bhattacharjee, a staff grade practitioner at Great Britain's Bradford Royal Infirmary, analysed the records of 1,621 patients admitted to the casualty ward between 1997 and 1999 for animal bites. He and his team found that the number of bites rose from an average of 40 to 60 bites on the day before the full moon to just under 120 on the day of the full moon itself.

As for heart attacks, studies published in the *Journal of the Indian Medical Association* and the *European Journal of Emergency Medicine* both concluded that there was no increase in the incidence of heart attacks during the full moon. Does this mean there is no connection between the moon and the heart? Maybe not. The Indian study found an increase in heart problems when there was a new moon. The European study, on the other hand, found that there were 6.5 percent fewer heart attacks when there was a new moon compared with other moon phases.

What You Can Do
Move to Mercury or Venus. Neither one has a moon. (This is not to say that the extreme heat, lack of oxygen and toxic atmosphere won't be an inconvenience.)

Should you find yourself Earthbound, you might take solace in the knowledge that not all researchers agree that the moon affects personality. In 1989, a team of researchers from Allegheny General Hospital in Pittsburgh, Pennsylvania, looked at the records of 1,444 trauma victims and found that 3.6 patients on average were admitted when there was a full moon, and about 4 a day during other lunar phases. In 1998 a team from the Northern Sydney Area Health Service studied the records of mental-health hospitals and reviewed incidents of violent behaviour to see if they had been more frequent when the moon was full. They found no significant difference in the incidence of violence on full-moon days and non-full-moon days.

Similarly, researchers at the Department of Public Health and Community Medicine at the University of Sydney, Australia, found no full-moon increase when they reviewed dog bite admissions against the lunar calendar. "Dog bites are no more frequent on full moons than at any other time of the month. Skeptics rejoice," they wrote in the *British Medical Journal*.

And there's another reason to be grateful we have a moon, full or otherwise: If it weren't for our lone satellite, we would not have tides. Without tides, the life we see around us would have evolved differently, or not at all. People might not exist. Without the moon, the Earth's axis would wobble and conditions would probably be too unstable to support life. Surely, all of that is a fair trade-off for a little lunacy every twenty-eight days.

Garbage/Rubbish

When you think of hazardous occupations, you probably think of things like firefighter, lion tamer, bomb squad employee, policeman, dustbin man, race car driver ... Wait, go back one. You don't think of dustbin man? Why not? The people who take away our rubbish are some of the bravest of them all.

Once we put our rubbish on the kerb, we don't think too much about it—it just goes away. Well, not really. Someone has to pick up those thin plastic bin bags full of broken jars and discarded hypodermic needles. They have to deal with the raccoons and snakes that creep into the cans in search of yummy food scraps. Even worse, rubbish collectors have to deal with impatient drivers who try to overtake stopped bin lorries—and run over their crews in the process.

How dangerous is rubbish collecting? Solid waste hauliers rank third on the list of deadliest jobs in the U.S. It is the most dangerous job in the state of Florida, where dustmen are killed at twice the national average. With an average of ninety deaths per hundred thousand workers, dustmen there have twice the rate of job-related deaths than firefighters or police officers, according to a recent University of Miami study. They also have an incredible injury rate, with dustmen injured five to seven times more than the average worker. Most are back injuries and lacerations from sharp castoffs.

Of course, spending all day moving and crushing rotting food, other people's used facial tissues and packets from cleansers and household chemicals can't be good for one's health either. A 1975 study of domestic waste collectors in Geneva, Switzerland, and data from the Danish Registry of Occupational Accidents and Diseases both showed an increased risk of pulmonary problems among rubbish haulers. A 1990 survey by the Washington State Department of Ecology of 940 Washington state waste industry workers found that although only 26 percent were trained specifically to deal with hazardous or medical waste, 22 percent reported having had contact with waste blood, and 6 percent had been stuck by hypodermic needles.

In case you were wondering—U.S. citizens, stand up and cheer. You're number one ... in the production of rubbish. In 1999, the 281,421,906 people of the United States produced about 230 million tons of municipal solid waste. (That's about 4.47 lb/2.03 kg per person, per day.) Meanwhile, China's 1,260,000,000 people produced 113 million tons, or .49 lb/.22 kg per person per day. Canada is number two in the per capita creation of municipal solid waste with 3.75 lb/1.70 kg per person per day, and Norway is number three with 3 lb/1.36 kg. Germany and Sweden generate the least amount of waste per capita for industrialised nations, with just under 2 lb/.91 kg per person per day.

What You Can Do
There are many things you can do to help protect the people who have such an important and largely thankless job. Most important, never speed around bin lorries that are stopped to pick up refuse. Traffic accidents are the main cause of on-the-job fatalities among waste hauliers. If you must pass, do it slowly, and watch out for workers.

For their health, be sure you refrain from putting into the rubbish things you should not. The following are classified as household hazardous waste: emulsion, cleaners, oils, batteries, pesticides, medical supplies. Instead of throwing these things in the rubbish, consult your local government agencies to see what types of household hazardous waste programmes are available. You can find more information on household waste at the U.S. Environmental Protection Agency's Web page: www.epa.gov.

Gardening

The scene: A white-haired woman is cheerfully pulling weeds and casting them aside. The sun shines and butterflies flutter about the petunias. Cue violins: the theme from *Psycho*. This woman doesn't know it, but she has entered a landscape that is as dangerous as any jungle—her garden.

Artists like Monet may have created idyllic visions of garden serenity, but don't be fooled. It may look and smell inviting, but the garden is teeming with dangerous creatures (very small ones, but still deadly), treacherous weapons (when used the wrong way), and abundant opportunities for illness, injury and even death.

In the United States, more than 400,000 people are treated for injuries from lawn and garden tools every year. In the United Kingdom, 69,000 people are injured while working in the garden, including an estimated 4,000 flowerpot injuries alone.

Most gardening injuries are cuts to the hands or feet from hedge clippers or poorly placed spades. Gardening also causes muscle injuries and strains, as people emerge from their homes after a long winter and go straight from sitting to shovelling. If you think you can brave the shovels and rakes and implements of destruction, be advised:

"If you live in a modern city, your garden is a dilute solution of cat stools." That according to Graham Rook, professor of medical microbiology at University College, London, England.

Yes, pets and wild animals use your garden as a toilet. They deposit parasites and germs like toxoplasma, which is found in cat feces and is especially dangerous to pregnant women.

Other small creatures live in the garden and are poised to cause a reaction in the human immune system. Aspergillus is a fungus that grows on decaying plants. It can cause lung infections and asthma. Tetanus, which kills twenty-five thousand people worldwide each year, can also be transferred through small cuts from garden thorns.

What You Can Do
If you're still intending to brave the garden wilderness, there are a few precautions you can take. First, do some warm-up exercises before you start pulling up weeds. Keep an eye out for rusty nails, broken glass and broken bits of tools.

Coil up your garden hose and get it out of the way so you don't trip over it. Wear a broad-rimmed hat to protect you from the sun and hard-toed shoes (not sandals) to protect you from your own digging.

Wear gardening gloves, especially if you are not pregnant, and make sure your injections are up-to-date. You should have a tetanus booster injection every ten years, and another if you get a dirty injury.

Finally, don't sniff the compost. Readers in other parts of the world may never have considered it, but in New Zealand, one of the nation's top gardening gurus, Professor T. W. Walker, inhales deeply of the fine earth by sniffing a handful of compost in a *Living Earth* telly commercial. This has prompted a Canterbury medical officer to send out press releases encouraging Kiwis not to follow his example—you could risk Legionnaires' disease.

Getting Fit

You start to notice that the pair of jeans you looked so great in last year don't quite button properly. You're afraid of the scale, and walking up a flight of stairs leaves you huffing and puffing for air. So you make a New Year's resolution, "I'm going to get fit, and I'm going to get fit now!" You buy that piece of fitness equipment that you saw on late-night telly and start working out immediately at full force. You think you're doing something good for yourself, and maybe you are. But then again, you may be courting disaster.

In the United Kingdom, an estimated 1,884 people are injured by weights, and 1,591 by exercise machines each year. (That's not even counting the 128 who are hurt on step machines.) Nearly one million Americans head to hospital after bad experiences with weight-training equipment annually. In the past twenty years, injuries from weight-training equipment in the United States have risen 35 percent. According to the Toronto-based Society of Weight-Training Injury Specialists, figures are similar in Canada.

How does a goal of getting fit end with a result of getting hurt? The experts say that inexperience and ambition play big roles. When people decide to get fit, they want to see instant results, and they often go from no physical activity to strenuous physical activity without anything in between. The result? Pulled muscles and other injuries. Another reason the experts say these types of accidents are on the rise is because more people are buying exercise devices for use in their own homes. They often lift weights without warm-ups or spotters. The most common injuries are sprained wrists, mangled hands from contact with chains and moving machine parts, and broken toes from dropping heavy things on them.

What You Can Do
First, what not to do: don't use the risk of injury as yet another excuse to sit in front of the telly instead of exercising.

You've heard the expression, "No pain, no gain." A better saying might be, "No pain, no pain." If you are a 33-year-old office worker and your workout partner is a 23-year-old triathlete, expect your regimen to be a little less ambitious. When you start to feel pain, rest. Pain is your body's way of saying that you've gone too far. Keep going and you're likely to get hurt. A good rule of thumb is to increase your activity by 10 percent every few weeks until you reach your goal. Also, rest between workouts. If you run on Monday, try something else on Tuesday—weight lifting perhaps.

Drink lots of water. If you begin your workout in a dehydrated state, you'll get tired, weak and even dizzy. Fatigue is a major contributor to acute injuries like sprains.

If you buy fitness equipment from the "good intentions" section of the thrift shop, be sure to check it carefully. Every year, close to two hundred exercisers in America fall victim to metal-seat posts when the seats on their stationary bikes collapse. Once you get the machine home, keep it where children cannot play on it without supervision. Remember, also, that whenever you lift weights, at home or at the gym, you should have a spotter.

Golf

If you thought the greatest danger in taking up golf was that you'd look silly in those plaid trousers, think again. When it comes to injury, golf outpaces even ice hockey. Only 16,854 people a year are injured on the ice in the United States, while 56,201 head to hospitals after teeing off.

There's a reason golfers shout, "Fore!" They know that they're about to strike a hard ball with great force, sending it hurtling at speeds of up to 140 mph/225.31 kph. It's a bit like throwing a rock as hard as you can, and then some. The term "fore," incidentally, dates back to 1878. Prior to that, golf balls were not quite the hard things they are today. They were made of a spherical leather pouch filled with wet goose feathers and then dried. When harder balls came into play, so did the warning: "Before!" which meant, basically, "Hey, buddy, you're in front of the ball!" Golfers eventually got tired of the first syllable.

The danger associated with stray golf balls remained. In 2003, police were summoned to help a group of frightened schoolchildren aboard a bus whose windscreen had been cracked by what the driver assumed was a bullet. After a few minutes of investigation, someone pointed out that the hole in the windshield matched the size and shape of a golf ball. And so it was.

Being hit in the head by a golf ball can cause serious trauma, even death. A report in the *Journal of Neurology, Neurosurgery and*

Psychiatry chronicled some of these cases. An 11-year-old boy hit on the right temple seemed to be fine at first, but three hours later he lost consciousness and suffered two seizures from a blood clot on the brain. Another boy, aged 16, started to have seizures four hours after being struck by a golf ball, also from a neural blood clot. Two children continued to have seizures up to four years after being hit. In Japan, a 50-year-old man was struck in the neck by a speeding golf ball and died from a ruptured artery before he arrived at hospital. Golf injuries to the eyes are relatively rare, but when they do happen, the result is often blindness.

Then there are golf clubs and golf carts. Golf club injuries almost always involve children, either because they stand too close to someone who is swinging, or because a child uses a golf club as a weapon against another child who is winning the game. Occasionally adults behave badly too, and with dangerous results. A casualty ward doctor wrote the editors of *Golf Digest* to tell the story of a California golfer who became frustrated with his game and bashed the cart with his club. The shaft snapped and flew into the neck of his golfing partner. The jagged end of the broken shaft, nearly 7 in/17.78 cm long, could be felt all the way through the skin of his back. Believe it or not, the man suffered no permanent disability from the incident.

Golf cart accidents affect all ages. *The Singapore Medical Journal* recently reported on three cases of serious injuries resulting from falls from golf carts. One of the three victims was injured so badly that he was left in a vegetative state. The greatest danger from the carts, however, may be that they take away what exercise there is in the game of golf.

Which brings us to the final danger from golfing—health strains—which do not even figure into the statistic of fifty-six thousand injured by golf equipment. Most golfers do not do any kind of warm-up before teeing off, according to an Australian study published in a 2001 issue of the *British Journal of Sports Medicine*. When they do any warm-up at all, it's usually a few air swings. This, combined with the twisting motion of the swing, can cause back injuries, and the repetitive stress of the golf swing can actually deform the bones in the lower back.

The number one cause of death on the golf course has nothing to do with golf balls or clubs. It is sudden cardiac arrest. You get middle-aged and retired people walking the long course without warming up first, and when heart attacks strike, they are far from help.

What You Can Do

Take up a safer sport—say, fencing. Only six Americans were injured by fencing equipment in 2001.

Abandon the plaid trousers and adopt a new form of golf attire. Helmets could reduce the risk of serious injury from misfired golf balls.

Warm up. Rowing and abdominal exercises can help reduce the risk of back injuries. Golfers can also work with professional trainers, who can offer tips on mechanics and injury prevention.

Finally, *Golf Digest* recommends having automated external defibrillators and people trained to operate them at major golf courses.

Health Warnings

Warning: The contents of this entry have not been reviewed by the American Medical Association. Do not read while operating heavy machinery. As with all advice, consult your doctor, educator or religious advisor to find out what is right for you. Edges of the page may cause paper cuts.

A recent study of the content of U.S. daily newspapers showed that 35 percent of all stories (and about 47 percent of front-page ones) in the "Home of the Brave" deal with the risks of modern life. The largely American obsession with ridding life of all potential risk, no matter how statistically insignificant, has—like the expressions "le weekend" and "les blue jeans"—been exported to much of the world. In the United Kingdom, usage of the term "at risk" in newspapers increased ninefold between 1994 and 2000.

Every year, hundreds of research studies are published in medical journals and are then picked up by the popular press. The studies that get the most attention are those that warn of a potential risk. The stories are often contradictory. One week, there's a story about caffeine raising cholesterol levels; the next week, another researcher finds no link between coffee and heart disease. What is a coffee lover to do?

"Science is the continual averaging of points of view until you get something of a consensus," *Health* magazine editor Sheridan Warrick told the *Record* news. "To journalists, on the other hand, consensus is the most boring and least newsworthy of all the things we could write about. Journalism loves conflict and contradiction."

In the United States, the Western fear of risk is coupled with a particularly American love of litigation. The United States has thirty times more lawsuits per person than does Japan. There are seventy thousand product-liability lawsuits filed in the United States each year, compared with only two hundred in the United Kingdom. Litigation adds an estimated 2.5 percent to the average cost of a new product in America, more if it is related to medicine, health or technology.

Born out of a legitimate desire to protect the public, political pressure to act on a hot safety issue and the fear of litigation, warnings are posted everywhere from medicine bottles to coffee cups, from orange-drink labels to toys. Michigan Lawsuit Abuse Watch (www.mlaw.org), an American citizens group, gives out an annual award for the most ridiculous product warning. Some examples of past winners include a warning label found on a pram that cautions the user to "remove child before folding"; a household iron that warns users to "never iron clothes while they are being worn"; a cardboard car sunshield to keep the sun off the dash that warns, "Do not drive with sunshield in place"; and a manufac-tured fireplace log that advises: "Caution—Risk of Fire."

Many experts now believe that the glut of warnings is becoming counterpro-ductive. In a *New York Times* article, "Amid Inconclusive Health Studies, Some Experts Advise Less Advice," doctors claim that consumers are now suffering from health and safety advice overload—to the point that they don't listen to any of it. As the American Tort Reform Association likes to put it, "He who warns of everything warns of nothing."

In a recent study involving two highly toxic products—a liquid drain opener and a wood cleanser—88 percent of consumers saw the warning labels, but only 46 percent read them, and only 27 percent actually followed the safety advice. A recent survey by the American Consumer Product Safety Commission concluded that the effectiveness of warning labels varies "from 0 to 100 percent" depend-ing on consumers' preexisting perceptions of the danger of a product.

What You Can Do
Legislators around the world are scrambling to create even more visible and attention-grabbing warning labels for products like cigarettes, alcohol and med-

icines. They are suggesting warnings that take up 45 percent of the packaging, red letters and skull-and-crossbones icons just to make people take notice.

The American Law Institute, an organisation of scholars that promotes legal reforms, suggests the creation of a standardised "warnings vocabulary" with easy-to-read labels that not only present risks but put them in perspective. For example, one label might indicate a 5 percent risk of injury, while another would show a .005 percent risk.

Many people place the blame for our health-warning apathy on media that give greater play to a story about a woman who claims the sound of a television newsreader's voice gave her epileptic seizures than to the health care plans of political candidates. Here's the deal: If you want the media to run the serious stories, you have to buy them. When a detailed analysis of the pros and cons of pasteurising orange drink grabs the public attention and sells more papers than a headline reading FRESH SQUEEZED ORANGE DRINK CAN KILL! the paper will surely print it.

In the meantime, there are a few ways you can better analyse health and safety news. Research stories should include an outside point of view to corroborate the evidence. Be more skeptical of news accounts about studies presented at conferences, rather than in professional journals, as conference papers are not necessarily subject to peer review. Finally, wait for a confirmation of a study before you change your habits. A new study in a few months should further confirm (or may debunk) the previous findings.

High Heels

If a friend were to say to you, "From now on, I've decided to walk to work on stilts," you would probably be concerned for her safety, not to mention her sanity. Yet when that same friend straps on a pair of shoes with a 3-in/7.62-cm heel, you don't worry at all. You should.

According to the U.S. National Floor Safety Institute, which devotes most of its time and energy to the study of slip-and-fall accidents, each year about 2 million Americans are admitted to hospital because of falls. Of those, 40 percent, or eight hundred thousand people, fell because of accidents involving their footwear. Half of those, or four hundred thousand injuries, are related to slips from the heights of tall heels. Most often, the women (and a few men) are treated for broken feet and ankles, or lacerations on the hands and arms that result from trying to brace their falls.

In Japan, platform shoes—the kind worn by '70s glam rock stars—are all the rage, and they have been blamed for at least two deaths. In one case, a 25-year-old schoolteacher fell from her shoes and died of complications from a skull fracture. In another case, the victim was not even the woman wearing the shoes but a passenger in her car. The driver, a 25-year-old office worker from Tokyo, was unable to hit her brakes in time because her 3.15-in/8-cm heels got in the way and she crashed into a pole. In New Zealand, authorities warn stiletto-wearing women to stay clear of railway tracks after a woman narrowly averted being run over by a train when her heel got caught in the rails. The approaching train stopped just metres from where she was stuck.

Sometimes high-heel accidents involve bystanders. For example, a well-dressed woman on the dance floor may pound that heel into someone else's foot. Even if she only weighs 120 lb/54.43 kg, with all her weight on ¼ to 1 in/.64 to 2.54 cm of heel, it is like being stepped on by an elephant. Top shoe designer Manolo Blahnik recently withdrew a pair of shoes from the market for that very reason. The heels, made of titanium, were 3.4 in/9 cm high and only .12 in/3 mm wide, so skinny that even the lightest wearer could cut through carpet or leave pockmarks in a wooden floor.

When people walk on stilts, they know they're doing something that is potentially hazardous, so they are careful. "It is actually very easy to walk quite safely on 2-to-3-ft/.61-to-.91-m stilts if they are properly constructed," says Sue Greene of the Dell'Arte International School of Physical Theatre. "It takes about two hours' practise to be able to negotiate confidently just about any terrain a person in high heels would attempt, which is more training time than the average high-heeled person gets, now that I think of it."

Even if you manage to walk for years on high heels without an accident, you probably have not escaped danger.

Unlike Barbie dolls, human feet were not constructed with high heels in mind. Stilettos push heels up at angles of 60 to 70 degrees and shorten the calf muscles, or the Achilles tendon, which runs from the back of the heel through the calf. Walking at such angles puts a disproportionate amount of weight on the ball of the foot, creating extra stress. Women who wear high heels are more prone to developing bunions. Twenty-nine women of every one thousand develop bunions, compared with a mere six men in one thousand, according to a 1990 study by the U.S. Public Health Service.

High heels also throw the lower body forward. The upper body stays on its natural alignment, which can cause lower-back pain. They have also been found to contribute to osteoarthritis of the knees. They increase the pressure inside the knee joint. The higher the heel, the greater the pressure, and the greater the risk of osteoarthritis.

Start a fashion trend for flat shoes.
Buy shoes that fit your feet.

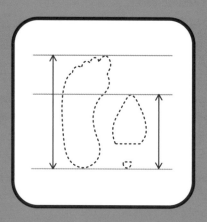

What You Can Do

Become a movie star, rock star, women's magazine editor or designer and single-handedly start a fashion trend for flat shoes.

If this option isn't open to you, there are a few other things you can try. If you must wear high heels, look for one with a slightly lower heel. The higher the heel, the more danger to your foot health and balance. Only wear them for a few hours a day, and make sure your longest toe is one finger's width away from the end of the shoe.

Finally, buy shoes that fit your feet. Believe it or not, studies show that 90 percent of women wear shoes that are a size and a half too small. Here's a simple test to see if you're one of them. Trace your feet without shoes. Next, trace the outline of your shoes. Which one's bigger? Hint, the correct answer should be "the shoes." To get the best foot fit, shop in the evening. Your feet swell a bit during the day, and you want your shoes to conform to your evening foot size.

Of course, if none of this works, you can always try stilts.

Holidays

Chestnuts roasting on an open fire. Jack Frost socks you in the nose. The most wonderful time of the year can also be the most deadly, say safety experts. When the holiday season arrives, make sure you deck the halls and that the halls do not deck you. The Royal Society for the Prevention of Accidents estimates that 80,000 UK residents each year end up in hospital following Christmas accidents. Each year in the United States, 1,344 people are injured by artificial Christmas trees alone. Another 3,038 are injured by Christmas tree lights and 4,542 by nonelectric Christmas decorations.

One of the most common risks associated with the holidays is fire. Contrary to popular belief, most holiday fires do not start with Christmas trees. The majority are caused by candles, shorts in the wiring for holiday lights, or from gifts and decorations that are placed too close to heaters or fireplaces.

According to the National Fire Prevention Association, little more than one-tenth of 1 percent of residential fires involved Christmas trees. In 1998, more than 32 million real trees were used in the United States, and of those, only .00093 percent ignited in-home fires.

Fire risk is not reserved exclusively for the Christian faith. The "season of light" can pose risks for Hanukkah celebrants as well. In 2003, Crate & Barrel stores recalled eight hundred menorahs because they could catch fire if the candles were left to burn down completely.

William Boissonnault, president of the American Physical Therapy Association's Orthopedic Section, warned CNN viewers that back, shoulder and neck injuries are common during the holiday gift-giving season as folks lug heavy packages and Father Christmas-like sacks.

Holiday plants can be hazardous, too. If you consume them, you could have medical problems as mild as diarrhoea or as serious as convulsions and comas. Mistletoe, for example, is a poisonous parasite. It's actually a family of plants, thirteen hundred species strong. All mistletoe is toxic to humans, as are holly and poinsettias. And according to legend, it is bad luck to let mistletoe touch the ground.

What You Can Do
The American Physical Therapy Association suggests that before you lift heavy packages or cases, you test their weight by pushing them with your feet. If they seem too heavy, take smaller loads, which are less likely to strain your back. When you lift, bend at the knees. Keep your lower back in its normal, arched position and bring the load as close to the body as possible. Lift with your legs, not your back.

The Ohio Christmas Tree Association suggests that you select the freshest tree available, remove any brown needles and keep it watered. When you take that old string of lights out of storage, check it carefully to make sure it is not frayed or damaged.

RoSPA adds that you should never place cards or decorations above the fire or near heat sources like lights.

Finally, be sure to keep an eye on your pets when they approach the Christmas tree. As the American Society for the Prevention of Cruelty to Animals (ASPCA) points out, tinsel and other glittery, dangly things are practically irresistible to cats. If swallowed, these items can get twisted in a cat's intestines, and you end up with what British writer Douglas Adams referred to as "a nonworking cat." Dogs and cats, for some reason, also love to chew on the insulation of flexes. They can electrocute themselves, cause dangerous frays, and bring the tree crashing down. The ASPCA suggests bundling the cords up in duct tape or polyvinyl chloride (PVC) pipe.

Holy Water

To believers, it is a balm for the body and soul, but to scientists, it is often a home for dangerous microbes. In 1998, student researchers competing in the Irish Young Scientist Contest twice examined holy water from local churches. Three girls grew bacterial cultures and discovered coliforms, staphylococcis, yeasts and moulds. Around the same time, some churches in Dublin removed fonts from their vestibules after they discovered that drug addicts were using them to rinse out their syringes. Two years later, three girls decided to examine church fonts after one of them developed a rash on her forehead after blessing herself with holy water. The young scientists' experiment was designed to compare outdoor with indoor fonts, but they found that water from both types contained dirt. In one font, they found green worms and worm eggs.

The threat of disease-causing agents in holy water is by no means limited to Irish churches. A 1995 article, "Amebiasis from the Miraculous Water of Tlacote," published in the *New England Journal of Medicine*, warned believers not to drink holy water from the shrine in Tlacote, Mexico, because of the risk of amoebic infection.

The following year, after a burn patient at Whiston Hospital in Prescot, England, acquired an infection from holy water splashed on the wound, a team of doctors analysed thirteen samples of holy water and found E. coli and other dangerous bacteria present. Often, concerned family members of patients travel to faraway shrines and bring back water containing foreign microbes, the team told the *Catholic Herald* newspaper. The contamination may not come from the water itself but from the hands of the people who collect it or from the bottles they use.

More recently, in response to the threat of SARS in Toronto, the Canadian government requested that Catholic churches temporarily suspend such practices as having the congregation dip fingers into communal holy water and sip from a communal cup at mass.

What You Can Do

You could convert to another religion, but it might not help. In no religion are holy water and health issues more in conflict than in Hinduism. The Ganges River flows with waters that will wash away sins and that can be offered in prayers. A "holy dip" in the Ganges includes bathing and sipping the water. Every day, some 60,000 people come to touch and bathe in the waters. Varanasi, on the banks of the Ganges, is one of India's holiest cities. Hindus believe that dying there frees the soul of sin and ends the cycle of life, death and rebirth. Unfortunately, something else flows from Varanasi, a city of 1.5 million—sewage. The city pumps 80 million gallons of sewage into the Ganges each day, and Varanasi is just one of 114 cities that dump sewage into the river. Meanwhile, despite a ban on the practice, many Hindus continue to dump the corpses and ashes of the dead into the holy river. India's most sacred river is also its most polluted. It is estimated that the concentration of pollutants is 340,000 times the permissible level. According to state and government health officials, as many as 45 percent of the pilgrims who dip in the river go away with skin or stomach ailments.

In the end, religious rituals are a matter of faith. By abandoning them, the faithful are likely to lose more than the antibacterial protection they gain. The only answer, therefore, is to take steps to ensure the water is clean and safe. This is a daunting challenge in the case of the Ganges, but for Catholic holy-water fonts, it should be somewhat easier. As the entrants in the Irish Young Scientist contest wrote in their report, at the very least "there should be someone there to clean the water and to take out anything that is big enough to be seen."

Home Improvement

A little home improvement can go a long way. All the way to hospital, in fact. In the United States, 365,799 people ended up in the casualty ward in 2002 after attempting home improvements. In the United Kingdom, another 195,260 a year were treated in the hospital, and 70 were killed, after their do-it-yourself projects went horribly awry, according to 1998 figures from the Royal Society for the Prevention of Accidents. The Welsh, for reasons unknown, are the most likely residents of the United Kingdom to end up being treated for home improvement injuries, according to a survey by home insurers AXA.

It should not come as a great surprise that attempts at improving the home so often end in disaster. Your home is just about the most deadly place you can be. In 2000, more than 7 *million* Americans were sent to the casualty ward as a result of accidents at home sweet home. Home accidents account for nearly 30 per-cent of all unintentional fatalities in the United States. That's more than in the workplace and all other public areas combined.

Since we spend so much time in our dwellings, it makes perfect sense that we try to spruce them up from time to time by adding a new lamp, changing the carpeting or painting a wall or two. It can't be that difficult, can it? Well, actually, it can. Power tools, ladders, electrical wires, and flying dust and debris can lead to a host of injuries. The most common are hand and eye injuries, followed by falls from ladders and electric shocks. The most likely months for injury are April and June, during holidays, and on Saturday and Sunday afternoons, when people are home from work.

The experts at RoSPA warn that DIY accidents are on the rise. They blame the increase on popular home-decorating programmes like *Changing Rooms* and *Trading Spaces*. Contestants on the programs redecorate rooms under tight deadlines. "Makeover programmes can encourage people to take on projects beyond their capabilities," David Jenkins of RoSPA told the *Sunday Telegraph*. "They portray how easy it is to transform your home and garden by using what can be very complex and dangerous equipment."

Critics of the programmes say that the designers are often shown disregarding safety precautions. In 2000, the *Changing Rooms* team remodelled a Scottish dormitory. The stylish new room featured beds on a scaffolding. When the university's health and safety experts examined it, they ordered it dismantled.

What You Can Do
RoSPA dispenses the following advice: If you're unsure about how to complete a home-improvement project, ask an expert. Don't be afraid to admit you need help.

It may seem like there is little risk from painting, but beware: falls from ladders while painting account for a large percentage of DIY accidents.

Always use proper safety equipment, like goggles, when sawing or drilling. And never perform work on electric appliances or light fixtures with the power on.

Hospitals

Q: What kills the most Americans each year?
A. Car accidents
B. Murder
C. Hospital visits

A: *C. Hospital visits.* In fact, deaths attributable to hospital-acquired infections kill more people each year than car accidents and homicides combined. One out of every 20 people who enters hospital leaves with an infection he did not have when he arrived. Hospital infections are common enough to have their own name: nosocomials. They affect nearly 2 million people each year; between 20,000 and 90,000 people die from them.

Hospitals are big, often poorly ventilated buildings filled with people who have germs of every description. Patients share close quarters and often come into contact with the same hospital equipment. This gives microbes ample opportunity to travel. Meanwhile, new medical technologies are increasing the risk of serious infection because the various catheters and implants probe ever deeper into the body and stay there longer.

Yet one of the most common ways that germs travel from patient to patient is also the most preventable. Germs like to hitch a ride on your doctor. Hand washing is the simplest line of defence against this type of microbial travel. According to the American Medical News Service, however, thirty-four separate studies have shown that doctors are not washing their hands regularly between patients. The Hospital of Saint Raphael's hand hygiene resource center, in New Haven, Connecticut, estimates that professionals only wash their hands thoroughly about 40 percent of the time.

"Experts in infection ... coax, cajole, threaten, and plead," wrote the *New England Journal of Medicine*. "And still their colleagues neglect to wash their hands."

Why? Hectic hospital schedules. "Health care personnel are always on the go," said Steve Solomon, MD, of the Centers for Disease Control and Prevention (CDC) in *American Medical News*. "This sometimes makes hand washing with soap and water difficult."

If you do manage to survive your hospital stay without acquiring an infection, beware the cure itself. You will probably not be surprised to know that side effects of medication are so common that there is an entire medical speciality devoted to them. Its name is iatrogenics. About one in two hundred hospital patients develops a *fatal* reaction to his medication. In all fairness, however, most of the patients who are killed by adverse reactions to medicine were suffering from severe terminal illnesses, and their doctors used medicines known to have serious side effects as a last resort—usually to relieve extreme pain. When it comes to *preventable* deaths by side effects, the number is about one in ten thousand.

What You Can Do
As a patient, probably not a lot. The solution lies in the (clean) hands of your doctor. You'll be pleased to know that the medical establishment is working to spread the word about washing up. In October 2002, the CDC issued new guidelines that urge doctors to use alcohol-based hand rubs, which take fifteen seconds compared with sixty using soap and water.

Meanwhile, many hospitals and pharmaceutical companies are seeking technological solutions like new medicines to fight antibiotic-resistant bacteria and advanced air-handling equipment. The new Helford Clinical Research Hospital, Duarte, California, for example, is seven stories tall, but only four floors are available to patients and staff. Two floors are devoted to an environmental control system that recycles the air in a room fifteen times an hour.

Kittens

Which are you more afraid of encountering—a playful kitten batting a thimble about, or a mad dog foaming at the mouth? The fact of the matter is you're much more likely to suffer a serious injury from an encounter with Fluffy than you are to ever come into contact with a rabid dog.

Rabies today is mostly found in wild animals. The fear of rabid dogs dates back to before the 1950s, when vaccination and animal control programmes brought the cases of rabies among household animals to a very low level. According to the Wilderness Medical Society, no human being in the United States has contracted rabies from a dog or cat since 1979. If you really fear rabies, stay away from undomesticated creatures. There have been twenty-two rabies deaths in the past decade caused by run-ins with other neighbourhood creatures, mostly raccoons and squirrels.

Still, some dogs and cats—usually strays—do get rabies, so if you are bitten, it is important to have the animal tested. Cats actually pose a greater threat than dogs: cases of feline rabies have outnumbered those in other domestic animals every year since 1988.

This is not to say that you should walk up to strange dogs and start stroking them. Dogs do bite, and they do cause damage. An estimated 2 million people are bitten by mammals (including humans) each year in the United States.

The greatest danger in a bite is not the wound itself but the germs that penetrate the skin. Researcher Tony Brown of the Royal Brisbane Hospital in Australia compared dog, cat and human bites and found that the germiest bites come from humans. (Human "bites" usually happen in fistfights when one person punches another in the face, and the knuckle makes contact with the teeth.) Dogs' mouths have the second largest collection of dangerous germs, and cats come in third. Dogs are also responsible for the largest number of bites.

Yet even though dogs bite more often, and have more germs in their mouths, cat bites are still more deadly. Only 15 percent of dog bites become infected, while half of cat bites do. This is because cat teeth are very sharp. They make a deep puncture wound, much like an injection of bacteria directly into deep tissues.

Cat claws also pose a risk. Each year twenty-two thousand people in the United States are stricken with cat scratch fever. The ailment is caused by bacteria on the cat's claws, often from flea feces. It causes swollen lymph glands and is cured with antibiotics.

Cat feces are a danger too. It can carry toxoplasmosis, which can lead to eye and brain damage.

What You Can Do

Don't send Fluffy away. Just be sure to treat her with care. Never try to pick up a stray cat, especially if it is hissing or arching its back. Even a familiar cat will lash out if it is frightened. Cats get very uneasy when they are cornered.

If your cat is involved in a fight with a neighbour's cat, use caution if you try to break it up. Both cats might turn their aggression on you. Even if your cat is hissing at another cat outside the window, if you try to calm it down by stroking it, you may startle and frighten it. Cats can take up to an hour after being riled to calm down fully. Leave them in peace until they do.

To avoid toxoplasmosis, keep your cat indoors. Pregnant women run the risk of infecting their foetuses. If you're pregnant or think you might be, find someone else to change the kitty box.

Knickknacks

I f your mantle shelf is covered in tchotchkes, doodads and decorative whatsits, watch out! Knickknacks are not as harmless as they may appear. Every year in the United States, an estimated fifteen thousand people are injured by the little things that crowd their mantle shelves, according to the U.S. Consumer Product Safety Commission's National Electronic Injury Surveillance System, which has its own category for "knickknacks, statues, vases and urns."

One of the reasons so many people have dangerous encounters with curios is that many of them are made of ceramics or glass. A snow globe with an image of your hotel in Cancun, Mexico is attractive and festive, but eventually it gets dusty just sitting on the shelf. You reach up to dust it and—*bang*—broken bric-a-brac is all over your floor. Those smithereens are just the right size to give you a nasty cut. Vases, though, are by far the most common offenders.

Here are some actual descriptions of injuries from miniatures, novelties and assorted household objets d'art, as recorded by the NEISS: "Consumer was removing trophies from the top shelf of the display case when the portion of the shelf slipped and came down. The top shelf hit the other three glass shelves and shattered into jagged pieces"; "A female received blisters on her wrist and fingers while adjusting the light bulbs on a mini light sculpture twice"; "Novelty item erupted spontaneously when placed on toilet tank for decorative purposes"; "A 9-year-old male's toy game has a plastic cannon that shoots plastic marbles. A marble shot from the cannon hit a glass vase and shattered it"; "Gum ball glass dome exploded for no reason"; "A boy died of a head injury when a cement statue fell on his head."

What You Can Do
Go to a flea market, sell off all your trinkets and use the money to redecorate your home in a minimalist style.

If you're just too attached to the commemorative glasses you got at your reunion to part with them, be careful where they're kept. One little-known source of home fires is light reflected through glass objects in windows. The glass can act as a magnifying glass and focus sunlight into a tiny beam that burns holes in fabric and wood. The NEISS has reported several cases, including one in which four people were injured in a semi-detached housing fire caused by a glass ornament hanging in a window.

Laundry

Under normal circumstances, doing your laundry is a straight-forward, if tedious, affair. Certainly, washing your clothes outweighs the social hazard of not washing them. Yet the simple act of cleaning clothes somehow creates a unique challenge for the accident prone.

Take, for example, the case of the Moscow, Russia, man who, in October 2003, tried a novel solution to remove a stubborn stain on his trousers. He added a litre of petrol to the detergent. Not smart. The resulting explosion demolished two internal walls and put an end to his kitchen.

A laundry chute claimed the life of a hotel worker in Chicago. No one is exactly sure how the housekeeper ended up in the twenty-storey chute, but after a coworker noticed that no linens were coming down, they investigated and found his body stuck in the wall wrapped in 100 lb/45.36 kg of laundry.

In Norway, a 15-year-old boy became trapped inside a washer for more than an hour after his keys fell in and he climbed in to try to get them. The fire brigade tried all manner of tricks to free him before one member of the team finally came up with the idea of lubricating the boy with liquid detergent. He slipped right out.

These, of course, do not represent the bulk of laundry-related accidents and fatalities, which are numerous. Each year, 12,779

Americans are injured by washers, as are between 4,000 and 5,000 British citizens. Interestingly, almost as many Britons (between 3,200 and 3,500) are injured by clothes baskets.

The most dramatic accidents happen when someone tries to add or remove clothes from a spinning washer and gets pulled into the mechanism. The result can be the loss of a limb and sometimes even death. In the past few years, such cases have occurred in New Jersey, where a 12-year-old's jumper got caught in a machine, strangling him, and in Birmingham, England, where a 4-year-old boy had his arm broken in four places in a washer mix-up.

Accidents are only part of the story. Each year in the United States, about 15,500 fires start in laundry rooms. They usually begin in the dryer. All told, laundry fires cause about $84 million in damage. The washer itself causes about $150 million in water damage in the United States and Canada, thanks to bursting supply hoses.

What You Can Do

Chances are your laundry will not attack. Most of the people that the statistics refer to have minor injuries from slamming fingers in washer lids or tripping and falling over a basket of laundry and landing against the machine.

Still, you don't want to take any chances. Have your machines checked out by a qualified service professional. Most of the time, if a drum spins while the lid is open, it is because safety devices were disconnected or removed during repair and not put back. While you're at it, have him check the supply hoses to the washer and the outtake hoses from the dryer to make sure there is not a lot of lint in there. This is where a fire is most likely to start.

If you decide to go back to beating your clothes on a rock in a stream, be careful that you're not washed away by the current. Rubber-soled shoes help.

Lawn Ornaments

There is a deep, dark secret that the plastic pink-flamingo industry does not want you to know. Every year in the United States 10,677 people are injured by decorative garden equipment. How are so many people hurt by birdbaths, statues of the Virgin Mary and those cutouts that look like a lady bending over in her garden? Newspapers are strangely silent on the subject. Is there a powerful garden gnome lobby at work, or has our blind affection for concrete porch geese prevented us from seeing the carnage before us?

Garden ornamentation may seem like a harmless hobby, but it masks a widespread underworld of crime. Theft of garden statues is an international issue. It may have all started with the Garden Gnome Liberation Front, a group dedicated to returning captive garden gnomes to the woods, which the Front claims is their natural habitat. Over the years the little fellows have been nabbed from countless gardens. In 1997, a northern French court arrested the Front's leader and gave him a suspended gaol sentence and a fine for the theft of roughly 150 gnomes. When a gnome exhibition took place in Paris in 2000, the Front struck again, lifting about twenty gnomes. Also in 2000, about 150 garden gnomes were found superglued to the steps of Australia's central bank in Sydney just as the bank's board was to gather for its monthly policy meeting.

Another serious issue is the illegal transportation of gnomes across international borders. Garden gnomes, you see, date back to the

1800s, when a German named Philipp Griebel crafted the first one. Germans take their gnomes seriously, but in the post-Communist era industrious Poles sensed an opportunity. They went to work making knockoff gnomes at a fraction of the German price. Now gnome-making is a major Polish enterprise. In the city of Nowa Sûl, for example, the 43,000 inhabitants operate 200 gnome workshops, some of them operating three shifts. German makers have tried to protect their trade by banning the import of any figures based on patented German designs. Even so, at least 5 million Polish-made gnomes are believed to have slipped past the authorities and into German gardens. Polish gnome factories, strained to their limit, may be cutting corners when it comes to safety. In 1998, an explosion in a Warsaw gnome factory killed two and injured three others.

That said, gnomes do not top the list when it comes to dangerous garden decorations. In fact, a careful examination of injury reports from the U.S. National Electronic Injury Surveillance System tells the true story, revealing statistics that are inflated by the inclusion of letter boxes in the category of decorative garden equipment. The largest category of garden-ornamentation victims is made up of people who slam their hands in letter box doors, run into letter boxes with their lawn mowers, or stumble into their letter boxes while playing garden games. Birdbaths are the second most dangerous garden decoration. A surprising number of Americans are rushed to hospital after striking their heads on them.

What You Can Do

Do not run across strange lawns in the night. You might trip over a pink flamingo, stub your toe on a concrete duck (or its Australian cousin, the concrete kangaroo), try to stop your fall by grabbing a hanging hummingbird feeder, and end up hitting your head on a nearby birdbath.

Do not be led into criminal activities. Removing lawn statues from other people's gardens gnomes in your possession when crossing European borders. A limit of two gnomes may be taken from Poland to Germany for personal use.

Leave all advanced letter box operations to the trained men and women of the post service.

Left-handedness

When you turned to this page, which hand did you use? Beware—your answer could determine how long you live. Left-handedness has been associated with a vast range of surprising maladies, and it may even be associated with a shorter life span.

The idea that lefties die young is controversial. It stems from psychologist Stanley Coren's 1992 book, *The Left-Hander Syndrome*. In this work, Coren claimed that surveys showed lefties died a full nine years sooner, on average, than their right-handed counterparts. He believed this because he found fewer elderly lefties than righties in his survey. The conclusion: the lefties had died off—most likely because machinery designed for a predominantly right-handed world predisposed them to nasty accidents.

Other researchers disagree. A 1994 study published in the *American Journal of Epidemiology* found no difference in the age at death between righties and lefties. Many scholars who reviewed *The Left-Hander Syndrome* have argued that the reason there are fewer old lefties is that, in the past, lefties were forced to convert to more acceptable right-handed behaviour.

But don't wipe your brow with your left hand and breathe a sigh of relief just yet. Medical literature on the subject of left-handedness does not paint such a rosy picture of life on the left. Doctors have found, for example, that lefties are at greater risk for a stunning array of medical problems, including arm fractures, brain tumours, inflammatory bowel disease, allergies, epilepsy, schizophrenia, depression, drug abuse, bed-wetting, sleeping disorders, autoimmune disease, wall eyes, congenital deafness, back problems, dyslexia, autism, stuttering, mental retardation, asthma and unintentional injury in general. Left-handedness, incidentally, is more common among men than women and slightly more common among homosexual than heterosexual men.

Some left-handedness appears to be the result of trauma in utero when the foetal brain is developing its distinct hemispheres. Researchers have uncovered a strong correlation between multiple births and left-handedness, and between older mothers and left-handedness. If the mother is 40 or older, she is 128 percent likelier to have a lefty than if she gave birth in her 20s. The link between birth trauma and left-handedness can explain some of the other medical problems associated with a leftward preference, like mental retardation and deafness.

What You Can Do
If you're a lefty, there's not really much you can do. Of course, you could train yourself to write with your other hand. Many people have done this throughout history. This won't really change the underlying issue, however, which is the way your brain is wired.

And it's not such a terrible thing to be left-handed. Okay, maybe you're doomed to die young in a terrible industrial accident because the controls were oriented for the majority persuasion. But about 20 percent of the members of Mensa, an organisation for individuals with high IQs, prefer the left. The long list of famous lefties includes Paul McCartney, Albert Schweitzer, Pablo Picasso, Jerry Seinfeld, Marilyn Monroe, M. C. Escher, Leonardo da Vinci, Judy Garland, Cole Porter, H. G. Wells and Jimi Hendrix.

Life

It is perhaps the most deadly condition known to humankind. It is the only thing in this book that is absolutely guaranteed to end in death: being alive.

Consider: The Population Reference Bureau estimated in 2002 that throughout the course of human history somewhere around 106,456,367,669 people had been born. Of those, a mere 6 billion are alive today. In other words, of all the people who have been born, only 5.8 percent are now living, and none of them will get out alive.

What is more, life is most hazardous for children, particularly during the first month of life. A child's risk of death is nearly fifteen times greater in the first month than it is during the rest of his or her first year. Of the 350,000 or so children born each day, almost twelve thousand will die within the first month. Most of these deaths—98 percent—will occur in developing countries.

One of the reasons humans and other animals live shorter lives than, say, trees, is because we have a centralised control system. That is, everything in a person or a personlike organism is controlled by the brain and the central nervous system. No more brain, no more living animal. In trees, the vital functions are decentralised, so big chunks of a tree can die without killing the tree itself. Researchers have discovered bristlecone pine trees as old as 4,600 years. Cypress trees can reach 1,200 years old. Oak trees can make it to age 600.

For similar reasons, tube worm colonies can have life spans of over 1,000 years, though no individual polyp in the colony lives that long. Still, each one lasts a respectable 250 years. People, actually, are not all that different from tube worms. We live much longer as a species than as individuals. Our genes appear to have been programmed by evolution to keep our bodies in prime shape only long enough to reproduce and raise the offspring.

What You Can Do

Nothing, really. You're going to end up dead no matter what. All you can do is make the most of the time you've got. The good news is that the interval between birth and death is getting substantially longer than it was for our forebears. According to the Population Reference Bureau, for much of human history life expectancy at birth averaged only 10 years because of the high infant-mortality rate. Today, in developed countries (where you're likely reading this book), it is nearly 80. Yet even if the rosy predictions of scientists are true and we increase our average life span to 150, after that we will all still end up dead.

Lightning

We say it all the time: You're as likely to have *blank* happen as you are to be struck by lightning. We say it as if being struck by lightning is the rarest, most unlikely thing that could possibly occur. So you may be interested to know that more people are killed by lightning each year than by tornadoes and hurricanes combined. A bolt of lightning can carry up to 1 million volts and can superheat the air to more than 54,032°F/30,000°C. If that's not dangerous, what is?

No one is immune. Two women at a garden party for Queen Elizabeth on the grounds of Buckingham Palace were injured in 1996 when a bolt of lightning struck. In 2003, a New York preacher insisted it was not a comment from God when a tree next to his church was felled by lightning during his sermon. The tree landed on the minister's car.

The most dangerous place in the world when it comes to lightning is Brazil, where around two hundred people a year die from strikes. A study by the National Institute of Space Research has concluded that more than 100 million lightning bolts hit Brazil each year, causing about $200 million/£106,123,315 in annual economic losses, mostly from blackouts and fires.

In the United States, about one hundred people are killed each year, as are about five unlucky British citizens. The real story is not in the death toll, however. Lightning strikes, believe it or not, are not usually fatal. Every year in the United States about five hundred people are injured from being struck by lightning. Storm Data, a group that maintains the only official record of lightning casualties, estimates that lightning deaths are underreported by about 28 percent and injuries by 42 percent. Then there are the wildfires. In the United States, lightning sparks about ten thousand a year.

When people die after acting as a human lightning rod, it is usually not from burns, but from heart failure. The jolt instantly stops the heart, though often it starts again a few moments later. Lightning strike survivors who are burned do not receive the burns from the lightning itself. Most of the current travels over the outside of a person's body too quickly to cause burns. When people are burned, it is from clothing that has caught fire, or from steam caused by vaporised rain, sweat or other fluids. A wristwatch may superheat and burn the skin where it comes in contact with flesh. Moisture in the respiratory tract can vaporise and cause internal burns. Some survivors experience severe ear damage from the shock wave generated by the strike.

Most of the injured are not struck by lightning directly, but are instead hit by a bolt that jumps from or passes through a nearby object. When lightning gets into a human body this way, much of the energy may be dissipated already.

What You Can Do
Change our common expression to "about as likely as you are to be hit by a meteor." There is not a single documented case of a human who has been killed by a meteorite. It's been estimated that a human will be struck by one once every 9,300 years.

Don't worry too much about lightning. It's still not very likely that you'll be hit. The chances of an individual being struck by lightning in the United States are about 1 in 600,000.

Just because it's not raining doesn't mean you can't be struck by lightning. The most dangerous part of the storm is actually the fringes. Lightning can strike within 10 mi/16.09 km of a storm's area of rainfall, and can even reach out and strike from a clear sky.

On average, lightning will hit within 6 to 8 mi/9.66 to 12.87 km of the last strike. There is an easy way to determine how far the last strike was. Light travels faster than sound. Thunder is the sound lightning makes (and you thought it was angels candlepin bowling). When you see a flash, count the seconds until you hear the thunder and divide by five. If thunder takes ten seconds to reach you, the lightning struck 2 mi/3.22 km away. If the count is thirty seconds or less, you should be somewhere safe. Don't go back outside until about thirty minutes after the last thunder is heard.

If you're stuck outside and can't get to shelter, the best bet is to crouch down near small trees or shrubs with taller trees nearby. Minimise contact with the ground and cover your ears with your hands. In a car, the metal casing should protect you, as long as you're not touching the ground. Don't touch the sides of the car.

If you're inside, stay off the phone and don't draw a bath during an electrical storm. Lightning can travel through phone lines and metal pipes.

DANGER

Luggage

The most dangerous thing you face on your overseas trip may be your case. The word "luggage" dates back to the late sixteenth century. It comes from the verb "to lug" and it originally meant "inconveniently heavy baggage." So it's probably not surprising that all this lugging might not be good for your health, or at least your lower back.

The National Electronic Injury Surveillance System estimates that more than thirteen thousand people were injured by bags in 2002. Golfer Phil Mickelson was one high-profile victim. He missed the Canadian Open after he threw his back out picking up his cases.

Carry-on bags alone injure about four thousand airline passengers a year, according to the Federal Aviation Administration. Air hostesses and stewards are hurt while trying to stow bags in overhead bins. Bags also sometimes come crashing down from above, right on people's heads. In a study of 462 falling-baggage reports published in 1998 by the Flight Safety Foundation, Dr Leo Rozmaryn found that bags that fall from bins onto passengers' heads sometimes led to trauma that affected patients months after they deplaned. Signs of "minimal traumatic brain injury" include headache, dizziness, fatigue, irritability, ringing in the ears, reduced concentration and sensitivity to light or noise. Many victims show no symptoms at first. The symptoms may not appear for another forty-eight hours. Yet as much as 20 to 60 percent of patients in Dr Rozmaryn's research had symptoms three months after their injuries.

Even packing can be a problem. Eye specialists have called for a ban on elastic bag straps because they can snap like the giant rubber bands they are and cause eye injuries. The *Medical Journal of Australia* estimates that they cause 170 injuries a year throughout Australia. Not only can they harm the eyes, but when they do, they harm them badly. At Royal Victorian Eye and Ear Hospital in Melbourne, Australia, 28 percent of elastic-strap injuries caused permanent vision loss.

What You Can Do
British inventor Sarteep Kader has come up with a high-tech solution that might take the "lug" out of "luggage." His wheeled bag contains a sensor that reads the infrared signals from a transmitter carried by the owner. It follows the traveller around like an obedient dog. In case you were wondering what happens if two people walk by with electronic bags, the inventor is one step ahead of you (with his bag following three steps behind): preset codes ensure that the bags respond to only one transmitter.

Ask for a window seat. Ninety percent of the bags that fall from overhead bins land on the passenger in the aisle seat.

Finally, pack light. The lighter the bag, the less likely it is to injure your back or cause permanent brain damage if it lands on your head. As an added benefit, you probably will not need elastic straps to keep it closed. A good guideline is, if you have to sit on the bag to get it closed, you're probably taking too many things.

Manhood

R andolph Nesse, a University of Michigan psychiatry lecturer, called it "the single largest demographic factor in early death." What is it? Being a man. In fact, Nesse says, "If you could make male mortality rates the same as female rates, you would do more good than curing cancer."

Nesse and his team studied death rates in twenty countries and found that if men had the same longevity as women, 375,000 lives would be saved each year.

It's not just a human phenomenon. In California, a San Diego Zoo researcher tracked animal longevity and found "all the really old animals are females." The longest lived of all were females that had not had offspring. Among rats and mice, for example, the childless live 5 to 10 percent longer. A study of 375 women in Finland found that giving birth to a boy shortens a mum's life by

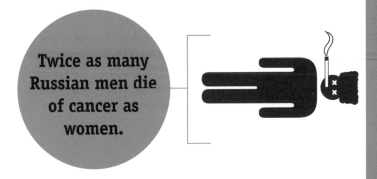

Twice as many Russian men die of cancer as women.

thirty-four weeks, while giving birth to a girl actually lengthens her life span by twenty-three weeks. The researchers attribute this to the higher birth weight of boys, and to the male hormone, testoesterone, which acts as an immunosuppressant, in mothers and in people in general.

Why are men so prone to early death? Parasites may be a factor—or so say a pair of Scottish researchers. Kenneth Wilson and Sarah L. Moore of the University of Stirling say that in species where the males die younger than females, "males suffer a disproportionately high rate of parasitism." They believe that this is because the larger males are more attractive to bloodsuckers, bacteria and all nature of biting things.

It may also be in the chromosomes. Girls have two X chromosomes and boys have an X and a Y. The double X serves as a backup in case of defects. Girls already have protections that boys don't. Then, in the second trimester of pregnancy, the Y chromosome starts telling the tiny male body to start secreting testoesterone, which has a detrimental effect on the immune system. On the other hand, the female hormone, oestrogen, protects the heart, bone, brain and blood vessels.

The good thing about testoesterone is that it gives you a real burst of energy when you need to kill a woolly mammoth. If you happen to live in a world without woolly mammoths, however, you end up pouring that aggression into things like fast driving, sports, fighting and other risky behaviour. Men are four times more likely than women to die violently and three times more likely to die in accidents. Nine out of ten murderers, and eight out of ten victims, are men.

The largest gender gap is in Russia, where a girl born in 1990 can expect to live eleven years longer than a boy. In most developed countries, life expectancy for men and women differ by six to eight years. Part of the problem in Russia is the high rate of smoking among Russian men. Smokers comprise about 30 percent of the Russian population, and more of them are men than women. Twice as many Russian men die of cancer than do women, and 30 percent more men die of circulatory disease. If you're an old age pensioner, and a widower, and you're looking for the best odds on meeting a nice woman, you might consider moving to Russia, where there are one hundred elderly women for every thirty-six elderly men.

What You Can Do

First, find a time machine. Good. Now set the dial back to the Middle Ages. If you're a man, you now have the advantage. Because so many women die in childbirth in your new (old) era, only 39 percent of them reach age 40, compared with 57 percent of men.

Or you could always get a sex change operation. Still, there is no guarantee that it would help. No one is really sure whether a man who is transformed into a female with surgery and hormone therapy actually gains the life expectancy of a born female.

Nine out of ten murderers, and eight out of ten victims, are men.

Mascots

"Ruffy's head came off!" sobbed a child in the crowd. Ruffy, the mascot of the River City Rascals Frontier League baseball team, was having a very bad day. He was lying on the ground as paramedics cut away his fuzzy orange sweater and lifted off his oversize head. "We love you, Ruffy," cried out some of the children in the crowd. It was the 29th birthday of Robert Gerard, the man inside the animal costume. He had been performing his usual stunt, a jump over the pitcher's mound in an all-terrain vehicle. This time, he approached the mound from the back, which had a steeper slope than he was used to, and the four-wheeler tipped and fell on top of him. He crawled out and rose to his knees to show the kids Ruffy was okay, but he quickly realised that Ruffy was *not* okay. He fell back down and was rushed to hospital with a broken right clavicle.

This is not an unusual story. Being a sports mascot is a hazardous occupation. A team at Johns Hopkins University in Baltimore, Maryland, studied forty-eight mascots and reported 179 job-related injuries, including knee problems and ankle sprains. In all, the mascots suffered 2.7 injuries for every one thousand appearances.

Sporting a giant bird's head is not for the weak. The average costume weighs between 21 and 40 lb/9.53 and 18.14 kg. They're also top heavy, which can cause back trouble. In the Baltimore study, 44 percent of the subjects reported that they had chronic back pain.

The giant characters suffer a wide variety of injuries, from falling off benches to being hit with balls and bats to outright violent behaviour by fans.

Erin Blank, a former mascot with the Washington Capitals and Detroit Tigers, told ESPN, "I think it's the Wile E. Coyote factor. It's a big cartoon character, so let's see him smack his face into a cliff. Fans think that's permission to get rough with you."

Injuries are only part of the problem. Those costumes are hot. The temperature inside the costume can be as much as 40 degrees Fahrenheit/22.2 degrees Celsius above the outdoor temperature. A mascot once described it as "doing aerobics in a sauna." More than half of the mascots in the Baltimore study had experienced heat-related illnesses. Half of these had needed intravenous injections of fluids.

You would think with all these drawbacks, the number of crazy people wearing giant animal costumes would decline. In fact, according to International Mascot Corporation, a company based in Edmonton, Canada, that produces about one thousand costumes a year, the demand for mascots continues to grow. As corporations look for new, aggressive ways to market their services, they're looking to spokes-animals to assist them. The group reported a 20 percent surge in mascot sales from 2001 to 2002.

What You Can Do
If you happen to be a mascot, it is important to take breaks, especially in hot weather. And if the weather gets too hot, think about taking the day off. Always drink plenty of fluids, because even while sitting still in the costume, you're going to perspire profusely.

Edward McFarland, the author of the Johns Hopkins University study, suggested creating costumes with more lightweight fabrics.

When asked about the issue of mascots' health by *New Scientist* Magazine, a spokesman for the National Football League Association said, "Maybe the mascots should create a union for themselves." If you see the Phillie Phanatic at the next Philadelphia Phillies baseball game holding a sign reading UNION over his head, you'll know why.

Money

Dirty Money. It's literally true. Legal tender is like a tramway for germs. Made from organic material, it travels around the country and throughout the world passing from hand to hand, pocket to pocket. It's never washed (it tends not to make it through the washer very well), and the average note circulates for eighteen months before it is retired.

A team of researchers from the Medical Center of the Wright-Patterson Air Force Base in Ohio counted bacteria living on sixty-eight dollar notes collected from people at a food shop and a secondary school sporting event. They incubated each note in a nutrient broth and grew any bacteria in a petri dish. Most of the notes—87 percent—contained bacteria. Most of the bacteria was not of a particularly dangerous variety. There were, however, germs that could cause urinary tract infections, sore throats and food poisoning. Two dangerous bugs, *Klebsiella pneumonia* and *Staphylococcus aureus,* also travelled via the currency train. Most at risk are those with weakened immune systems, but these germs, which cause pneumonia and blood infections, could infect even healthy people.

Meanwhile, a study conducted for the U.S. 9th Circuit Court of Appeals concluded that more than three-quarters of the notes in circulation in Los Angeles is tainted with illegal drug residue.

What You Can Do

Get rid of your notes as fast as you can. Send it to me, care of this publisher.

Or you could travel to Japan. In Japan, cleanliness borders on obsession (the Japanese word for "clean", *kirei,* also means beautiful). There you can get your yen from a bank that sanitises its cash by heating it, and you can take it out of your cashpoint machine with a card that is made of plastic impregnated with disinfectant chemicals. Not all experts believe this is a good idea, however. Koichiro Fujita, a professor of parasitology at the Tokyo Medical and Dental University, is the author of the book *Cleanliness Is a Sickness*. He believes that by trying to remove any and all bacteria from the environment, Japanese citizens are weakening their immune systems and losing their ability to cope with germs.

Another option is to launder your notes—literally. We already know the washer is not good for this. Instead, you can follow the example of the Industrial and Commercial Bank of China, which took emergency action in an effort to stop the spread of SARS. They put into effect a policy of holding money for twenty-four hours before recirculating it—long enough for the germs to die. Money is also sterilised by being placed under ultraviolet light for an hour.

Then again, none of these extreme measures is really necessary, say the experts. Although the germs on money have the potential to contaminate people, there are no documented cases that it has. Instead of avoiding or cleaning money, the best protection is to wash your hands regularly.

Music

Sometimes music has charms to soothe the savage beast. Sometimes music is the beast, and I'm not talking about Barry Manilow's "Can't Smile Without You." Making and listening to music, good or bad, can be a hazardous exercise. In the United States, 5,730 people a year are injured by musical instruments, and another 38,956 by recording equipment. In the United Kingdom they're a bit more specific. Stereos hurt 3,530; musical instruments, 1,061; CD players, 915; the wireless, 658; tape recorders, 55; Walkmans (Walkmen?), 55. Musicians' Clinics of Canada has treated more than 6,000 musicians for injuries since its inception in the 1980s.

In 1992, a survey of students at Catholic University's Benjamin T. Rome School of Music found that 76 percent of the students had suffered music-related injuries severe enough to keep them from playing for more than two weeks. Most of these are repetitive stress injuries caused by long rehearsals. But different instruments have their own risks.

When it comes to bodily injury, reports from the U.S. National Electronic Injury Surveillance System reveal that one of the most dangerous "instruments" is, believe it or not, the guitar pick. Apparently guitar players have a habit of swallowing them. The other most deadly instrument is the piano, which causes wrist pain when you play it and back pain when you try to move it.

The piano and the drums are also most likely to lead to fractures and stitches when people fall into them.

In terms of health risks, wind instruments are some of the most deadly. A number of studies have shown that playing a wind instrument increases the pressure on the eyes, which could lead to glaucoma.

The bagpipes have an added danger—fungus and bacteria that grow in the bag.

Most deadly of all? The saxophone. A team of researchers from the South and West Devon Health Authority and the University of Bristol in England analysed biographical information on 813 musicians born between 1882 and 1974. They found that saxophone players were more at risk of death than any other category of musician. The researchers speculated that circular breathing, in which the musician inhales through the nose while inflating the cheeks and neck with air, can increase pressure on the neck and reduce blood flow to the brain, increasing the risk of blood clots.

Rock and pop musicians are often self-taught, and according to the Musicians' Clinics of Canada, they often practise while crouched over on a settee, which can cause back pain and injuries. Electric guitars are heavy, and if worn too long, they can cause nerve compression and blood vessel compression in the neck and shoulder.

NEISS reports reveal even more ways to be jangled out of tune, including:
- "Patient playing with banjo string in mouth, front teeth loose."
- "Hit in mouth with flying cymbal."
- "Running with tuba, tripped."
- "Accordion fell on foot."
- "Poked in eye by violin bow."
- "Abrasion eye—patient who had replaced the strings on his guitar but still had long ends sticking out."

And don't think because you're not a musician you're out of the woods:
- "Playing with a karaoke machine and hit self in face with the microphone."

Finally, a number of studies have shown that musicians are extremely vulnerable to hearing loss. You may be surprised to learn that playing classical music can be more damaging to the ears than rock music. Research has shown that

Instruments of Torture

about 37 percent of rock musicians have hearing loss compared with about 52 percent of classical musicians. This is because classical musicians are seated much closer together when they play.

A study of the Finnish National Opera found that sound exposure levels were an average of 85 decibels (dB). The positions of the players also affect their exposure. Violinists, for example, are more likely to lose hearing in the left than the right ear because of how they hold their instruments. Percussionists and flute players are exposed to about 95 dB, while soloists, with the force of the whole orchestra behind them, are often exposed to sound levels up to 100 dB.

What You Can Do
Don't run with a tuba.

To avoid repetitive strain injuries, warm up with stretches before playing your instrument and take breaks every twenty to thirty minutes. The book *Pumping Nylon* by Scott Tennant provides a host of exercises especially for guitar players. If your hands are starting to hurt, try soaking your arms and hands in cool water for a minute and then in warm water for a minute. Repeat the cycle a couple of times. Massage is also recommended.

If you're suffering from a music-related malady, see your doctor. Many musicians hold off on seeing doctors out of fear that they might be told to give up practice. Without treatment, many problems become worse. If your doctor doesn't understand your particular needs, seek out a doctor with a track record of treating musicians.

To help reduce the risk of hearing loss, elevate your speakers. When a speaker is on the ground, the low frequency bass notes disappear into the floor. Sound engineers often crank up the volume to compensate. Instead, raise the speaker and allow the bass notes to travel farther into the audience at the same volume.

Natural Foods

Warning! The following foods contain chemicals that have been proven to cause cancer in laboratory animals: apples, broccoli, carrots, bread, celery, grapes, lettuce, tomatoes, sweet potatoes, parsley, onions, mangoes.

In 1996, according to the American Cancer Society, there were approximately 555,000 deaths from cancer in the United States. Many health-conscious people try to reduce their odds of developing the disease by avoiding food that contains "chemicals." They're out of luck. There is no such thing. The only difference between processed and organic foods is that processed foods have synthetic chemicals and organic foods get their chemicals from nature. Some of Mother Nature's brews are as potentially deadly as anything cooked up in a food lab.

In fact, according to the American Council on Science and Health (ACSH), some natural foods contain toxins and carcinogens in amounts greater than ten thousand times the levels of synthetic chemicals like pesticides. "It is hard to find any food that does not contain some harmful chemical that either occurs naturally or is produced during cooking or by microbial decomposition," according to the ACSH.

Healthy fruits and vegetables, even when grown without pesticides, still contain cancer-causing nitrates. The National Academy of Sciences estimates that 72 percent of the nitrate exposure to the mouth and esophagus comes from vegetables and only about 9 percent comes from oft-maligned cured meats.

In 1977, nutritionist Dr Richard Hall demonstrated this by examining the menu of a multicourse restaurant lunch. He analysed all the ingredients of each food using the same safety criteria applied to synthetic substances and found that when you eliminated all of the foods that contained ingredients that would not satisfy the criteria, there was only one food left—hearts of palm salad. And this, he noted, remained only because so little was known about its chemical makeup.

What You Can Do
First, what not to do—don't avoid fruits and vegetables. They're an important part of your diet.

Instead, the ACSH suggests that you eat a wide variety of foods, which decreases your chances of getting large doses of any particular carcinogen. Many fruits and vegetables contain compounds that counteract the process initiated by carcinogens. The more variety in your diet, the better your chances of balancing the "good" and "bad" chemicals in your body.

Nursing

It is the most dangerous job in Britain, and perhaps one of the most dangerous jobs in the world. Practitioners are more likely to be attacked on duty than police, security guards, bartenders or cashiers. Every day and night, the nursing sisters of the world must soothe patients who are experiencing the effects of alcohol, drugs or mental illness. Even the most balanced patients can become unruly when they must wait for hours in an understaffed hospital while they are suffering from illness or pain.

Don't let the prim little uniform fool you. Nursing sisters see more violence on average than people who go into the mean streets wearing a badge. Nurses have been thrown down stairs, suffered fractures, had teeth knocked out and been stabbed with syringes and knives. They have even been killed in the line of duty. Figures from Britain's Health and Safety Commission reveal that 34 percent of nurses have been attacked on duty compared with 25 percent of police and security guards. Forty-eight percent of nurses have been threatened with violence. Since most acts of violence in health care settings go unreported, the real totals are probably higher.

Oh sure, doctors get their share of abuse from patients, but it is the Sister who bears the brunt of it. A survey of senior nurses in intensive care units in England and Wales by the Queen Alexandra Hospital found that 77 percent of nurses reported suffering abuse by patients or patients' relatives, while only 38 percent of doctors reported the same. In 1998, the International Council of Nurses found that 94 percent of the 461 nurses it interviewed around the world had experienced verbal abuse in their career, and about 35 percent had left the profession because of it. A survey by the Australian Nurses Federation found that 26 percent of nurses experienced daily violence including intimidation, abusive language and physical assault. Half had been physically assaulted and 13 percent had been attacked with a weapon. In the United States, nurses are three times as likely as those in other professional groups to experience workplace violence.

What You Can Do
Hospitals and legislative bodies around the world are trying to come up with solutions. Some hospitals have introduced security guards and alarms, while others have opted for soothing decor and courses on anger management. Australian hospitals have introduced patient "behaviour contracts." A patient who signs agrees to behave or be discharged. After the killing of a psychiatric nurse in Florida, U.S. organisations have pushed for new legislation to protect hospital employees from workplace violence. Currently there are only voluntary standards.

At Selly Oak Hospital in Birmingham, England, they have had good results by introducing a series of initiatives to cut waiting times for patients. Before the changes, it was not uncommon for patients with minor injuries to wait more than four hours for treatment. As waiting times have come down, so has patient aggression.

If you are a nurse, first of all, thank you for what you do. The experts say to watch out for the following signs that a patient might become abusive: Look for rapid, loud or profane speech, clenched fists, reddened face and agitation. If someone is showing these signs, make sure you have an escape route. Keep a distance of 5 to 7 ft/1.52 to 2.13 m between you and the patient. Don't try to talk to someone who is shouting. Don't react to abusive statements, but clear up misconceptions and acknowledge valid complaints. If you think it's more than you can handle, call for help.

Office Supplies

Want to avoid risk? Take a nice, safe desk job. Just be careful when you get bored and start fiddling with the things on your desk. They might fiddle with you instead. Every year in the United States, about 13,411 people are injured by the things on their desks. If you were to lay all these people down, end to end, they would make a straight line about 14 mi/22.53 km long. You would also prove you had way too much time on your hands.*

Staplers and their staples are some of the biggest hazards. People are also prone to accidental eye pokings with a straight edge, but even such unlikely office supplies as rubbers and paper clips have been known to send people to the casualty ward. Americans buy about 35 million paper clips per day. It is estimated that most of them never end up clipping paper. The experts on the subject (I do not know what type of degree is required) estimate that only 7 million clips are used for their intended purpose. Another 8 or 9 million get lost and end up in hoover bags and dustpans. Another 5 million are untwisted during phone calls. Paper clip experts are apparently not required to study math because they seem to have forgotten about another 14 million clips. The U.S. National Electronic Injury Surveillance System, which tracks hospital admissions, may provide a clue to where they went. The answer is, anywhere they're not supposed to—ears, noses, down the throat.

It seems a fairly large number of office workers spend time cleaning their ears and teeth with various items on their desks. For reasons unknown, they also tend to put things in their mouths, then accidentally swallow them. Here is a representative sampling, from NEISS reports, of how people misuse various office supplies: "Accidentally put correction fluid in eyes, thinking it was eyedrops." "Sat on a letter opener and pierced left buttock." "Accidentally drank a mouthful of computer ink with water." And, um, "Patient put rubber band around penis two days ago. Penile swelling. Pain with urination."

What You Can Do
First of all, the thing with the elastic band—don't do that.

Take special care when stapling. It's a good idea not to hold sharp things like push pins, staples or unwound paper clips in your mouth. You can swallow the loose objects or impale your tongue. If you want a pierced tongue, see a professional.

Don't drink or use as medicine anything that you find near the photocopier.

---

* Of course, this calculation assumes Americans of average height, 5'9"/175.26 cm for men, and 5'4"/162.56 cm for women, and assumes that the ratio of male-to-female desk supply victims is roughly 50/50. Using Japanese subjects, you would only get about 13 mi/20.92 km, as their average heights run slightly lower than Americans'. The Japanese, however, may have a higher or lower incidence of desk supply injury, which would impact the final measurement.

Patient Noncompliance

You have the best doctor in the area, and she gives you wonderful treatment and advice. You stay sick anyway. What's the problem? Well, let's start at the beginning—did you follow that wonderful advice? This might be a factor.

Every year, patients go to their doctors, seek their help, then don't follow their instructions. Patient noncompliance, as the doctors call it, is responsible for 125,000 deaths each year, hundreds of thousands of hospitalisations and millions of lost workdays.

Take these cases from the medical journal *Australian Family Physician*: A 60-year-old man was prescribed the use of a home oxygen delivery system. He was told that he must quit smoking and was warned about the risk of having oxygen near an open flame. While cooking on his gas cooker—wearing his home oxygen device—the patient was badly burned when the nasal cannula he was wearing caught fire. In another case, a 73-year-old patient who had also been given warnings tried to smoke while wearing the oxygen mask. He later graphically described flames streaming from his nose.

Why on Earth would so many people seek the advice of doctors only to disregard it? There are a number of factors. Personality, for example. Alan Christensen, a lecturer of psychology at the University of Iowa, found that people who don't take their meds have a high level of cynical mistrust and suspicion. (One wonders how much this study cost.)

"When you're asking someone to adopt a medical treatment," Christensen told *USA Today*, "you're asking them to change their behavior. Even tablet-taking constitutes a behavior change and physicians tend to underestimate just how difficult it is for most people to modify long-standing patterns of behavior, even when their life depends on it."

Then again, maybe the patients just can't afford to comply. A recent issue of *Health Care News* reported that 22 percent of adults in the United States neglected to fill at least one prescription in 2001 because they couldn't afford it. In lower-income groups, 40 percent reported that they had gone without filling a prescription because they didn't have the money.

Or perhaps they simply don't know *how* to comply. Doctors are far more educated than the average patient, and they often write instructions that are incomprehensible to their patients. The medical journal *Surgery* reviewed more than six hundred medical consent forms. They found that about a quarter of the documents required at least a college education to be understood.

What You Can Do
Some studies have shown good results when patients had follow-up counseling reminding them of the importance of following instructions. Also, if doctors take more time to explain the reasoning behind the instructions, patients with control issues might be more inclined to listen.

Some doctors, however, don't think patient noncompliance is such an issue. In her article in the journal *Social Science and Medicine*, Jenny L. Donovan argues that doctors are underestimating their patients and that patients are simply making their own decisions. They do a personal cost-benefit analysis of each treatment and may come to a different conclusion than the doctor's. "An apparently irrational act of noncompliance (from the doctor's point of view) may be a very rational action when seen from the patient's point of view," she writes.

Penmanship

It's a problem that causes annual losses to business of $200 million/£106,123,315 a year. That's enough to build a seven-storey office complex in Chicago, or to buy everyone in Indonesia a Coke. There is a human cost as well. The American Society of Hospital Pharmacists estimates that this problem results in a death a day. What is it? Sloppy handwriting.

Poor handwriting is most dangerous when it comes from the pen of your doctor. It's no myth: A number of studies have shown that doctors, as a group, have poor handwriting skills. In a study published in the *British Medical Journal*, researchers asked ninety-two doctors, nurses and administrators to write their names, the alphabet and a set of numbers. Then they ran the results through an optical scanner. Nursing sisters had the best results; doctors had almost twice as many errors as nurses and administrators.

Misreading the notes on a medical chart or a prescription pad can be deadly. In 1996, the *Journal of the American Medical Association* reported that the annual number of deaths from hospital errors in the United States is four times the number of deaths from car accidents, and exceeds that from all other accidents combined. Not all of those deaths are attributed to messy handwriting, of course, but many are. The American Society of Hospital Pharmacists estimates that 58 percent of information handwritten onto medical records is illegible.

If you're not a doctor, don't think you get off easy. Chicken scratchings also result in illegible cheques, bookkeeping errors and contractual disagreements. The U.S. Postal Service spends $4 million/£212,246,630 a year to retain a staff of handwriting experts whose jobs are to squint at scribbled addresses and decide where the post needs to go. (At 37¢, almost 11 million first-class stamps could be bought with that money.) Even with their help, envelopes with handwritten addresses commonly baffle optical scanners (which sort 40,000 letters an hour) and are temporarily diverted. A woman in Sunrise, Florida, routinely gets hundreds of personal cheques bound for the Broward County Revenue Collector in Fort Lauderdale because the machine mistakes taxpayers' scribbled Ss for 5s. Another 100 million pieces of scribbled post each year never reach their destinations at all.

If the prospect of a slight delay in processing your post doesn't scare you, consider this: an illegible tax return will catch the attention of the Inland Revenue.

Some education scholars believe bad handwriting leads to poor reading and verbal ability because penmanship exercises these left-side-of-the-brain skills.

Sloppy writing is problematic in other professional arenas, as well. For example, bank robbery: In 2002, in Rochester, New York, a would-be bandit handed a piece of paper to a bank cashier. The cashier couldn't make heads or tails of the penmanship-challenged felon's note and had to pass it to another cashier. By the time they deciphered that the bearer of the note wanted a sack of unmarked bills, it was almost closing time and employees were locking the outer door. The robber was trapped in the entry with her loot, and she was easily apprehended by police.

What You Can Do
Always type your ransom notes.

Practise, practise, practise. Zaner-Bloser, a leading publisher of handwriting materials in the United States, lists the following keys to legibility: shape, size, slant and spacing. Figure out which of these you have trouble with and work on it.

You might also try picking up a quill squib. This old-fashioned instrument, say calligraphers, is more appropriate for cursive writing. The writer could press down harder on the downstrokes, making the actual letters darker. With biros, you end up with more ink in the loops and the joins than on the letters.

Free food is another option—for doctors, that is. The chief of the medical staff at Cedars-Sinai Medical Center in Los Angeles lured his doctors with the promise of free food to a three-hour penmanship course featuring topics such as pen holding, positioning of paper, size of letters and length of strokes.

If all else fails, use your poor handwriting to your advantage. One teacher, writing in the journal *Education*, discovered that as he graded papers his handwriting became increasingly sloppy. When he handed the papers back, the students who had received legible comments glanced at the paper and then put it away, but those who had received the later, messier comments were forced to reread sections of their papers and consult with other students to figure out what he meant. The result was that they spent more time discussing the assignment—not only the poor quality of the teacher's writing, but what they had written as well. From that point forward, the teacher used purposely obscure writing as an educational tool.

HAZARDOUS

PLAYGROUNDS

Playgrounds

Riding the world's longest, fastest, highest roller coaster may be a thrill, but you've gained that adrenaline under false pretenses. You only thought you were pushing the envelope when, in fact, you were as safe as a babe strapped in a safety seat riding in the backseat of a Volvo. More children die each year on playgrounds than have died in the past ten years on amusement rides. Between 1990 and 2003, 147 children died in accidents involving play equipment in the United States. In the same period, there have been only 15 deaths among thrill riders.

While some politicians have made headlines by speaking out about the potential danger of head injury from riding roller coasters after the odd amusement park misadventure, the scientific evidence doesn't support the fears. "It is unlikely that amusement rides cause brain injuries," Dr. Douglas H. Smith, a brain trauma researcher, told *Popular Mechanics*. "Peak head accelerations calculated from roller coaster rides were far below the minimum thresholds for various types of injuries, including bleeding from the brain," he said.

The same cannot be said for climbing frames. The U.S. Consumer Product Safety Commission ranks playground equipment among its most hazardous consumer products. Almost two hundred thousand children are treated in casualty wards each year after a romp in the playground. Most of them have fallen from climbing

157

equipment. Sometimes their clothes get twisted and caught in playground parts. A fall of as little as 3 to 5 in/7.62 to 12.70 cm onto a concrete or Tarmac can generate enough impact force to cause serious injuries or death.

Lately there have been a number of articles complaining that as roller coasters get faster and faster, they're creating higher and more dangerous g-forces. In fact, g-force levels do not correspond with the speed of a coaster. G-forces are created in relation to how tightly the coaster changes direction, and as coasters become faster, the turns become wider. Overall, g-force levels on those scary-looking modern rides are about the same as on the old-fashioned coasters. The top g-force experienced by a modern thrill rider is about 4g.

The Association of Amusement Parks and Attractions estimates that 80 percent of injuries at amusement parks are the result of people ignoring the safety rules. For example, at Waterworld USA in Concord, California, sixty students from a nearby secondary school rushed past a lifeguard in an attempt to set a "record" for the number of people on a single water slide. The slide was designed to handle one person at a time, and it ripped apart and came crashing down under the weight. One student died and 32 were injured. In another case, a boy who ignored warnings not to rock his Ferris wheel seat flipped it over and fell to his death. On a playground, however, there are few safety restraints. A child doesn't need to ignore rules, just misstep.

What You Can Do

If you have enough money, you could replace your garden swing with a roller coaster. The Top Thrill Dragster, the latest addition at Cedar Point, an Ohio theme park that bills itself as the largest amusement ride park in the world, cost only $25 million/£13,265,414.

If you don't have a large enough garden or pocketbook for that, there is another thing you could try. Since the most serious play equipment injuries are from falls, the best thing you can do is make sure you have an impact-absorbing surface underneath. The best surfacing materials are sand, wood chips or ground tyres.

In one out of five playground accidents, the child in question was not adequately supervised. Keep an eye on your kids. (But let them play!)

Think safety:

Install a roller coaster in your backyard
instead of a swing set.

Rubbernecking/ Gawking

"An accident in the northbound lane is slowing traffic. Gawkers are slowing traffic in the southbound lane." They are also putting themselves and others at risk. Distractions are one of the greatest hazards on the road. It is estimated that driver inattention is responsible for a quarter of all car accidents.

One distraction has received most of the attention and blame in recent years—the mobile phone. Of course, speaking on the phone creates a distraction, but it is not the greatest distraction drivers face. Still, around the globe, mobiles maintain a very high profile as a road hazard. In Japan, for example, while mobile phone accidents accounted for less than 1 percent of all traffic accidents in 1997, the National Police Agency called the trend of mobile phone–related accidents "alarming."

A 2003 study of traffic accidents conducted by the Virginia Department of Motor Vehicles and Virginia Commonwealth University detailed the types of distractions that are most likely to cause accidents. Mobile phone use didn't even make the top five. The top hazard, responsible for 16 percent of all distraction-related accidents, was "rubbernecking," aka gawking, gaper's block and spectator delay—slowing and turning to look at an accident in another lane or at the verge of the road.

Traffic flow studies have found that if a crash blocks one lane of a three-lane road, the road's capacity is effectively reduced by half, not one third, because of gawkers. The highway planners who read such studies are so convinced that this is a fact of life, they factor it into road design. After sitting in slow traffic for fifteen to twenty minutes, a driver just *has* to know what got everything so gummed up. So he slows down for a couple of seconds, which causes a chain reaction that can cause delays that outlast the original cause.

Then, as new drivers arrive, they crane their necks to see what happened. They take their eyes off the car in front of them, which has just come to a stop as that driver also tries to see the accident. Meanwhile, the flashing lights of emergency vehicles draw yet more of the drivers' attention.

"There's something called the moth effect," Stephanie Faul, of the AAA Foundation for Traffic Safety, told the *Palm Beach Post*. "No one can prove it exists, but there's plenty of evidence to suggest it does. Drivers are drawn to the light and steer toward it."

Crash! An accident beside the original accident, attracting more gawkers, and more potential accidents.

What You Can Do
The simplest answer is to remember the adage "Curiosity killed the cat" and just drive on. Keep moving. There is nothing to see here.

Many experts suggest law enforcement agencies invest in large screens to hide accidents from passing traffic. Of course the design of the shield would play a major role in the plan's success. As the late traffic reporter Keith Kalland told the *Atlanta Journal-Constitution*, "In this town, they'd put advertising on it, and everybody would stop to look at the advertising."

Safety Devices

After reading about all of the things that can kill you in this book, you may be tempted to go out and buy yourself a house full of safety equipment. Before you do, ask yourself, is it safe?

Often our attempts to guard ourselves against danger come with unforeseen consequences and side effects. Take, for example, safety incentive programmes at work. The programmes offer prizes to employees for a certain number of days without a workplace injury. Many experts believe that the programmes do not really reduce injuries; they simply reduce the reporting of injuries. When the Occupational Safety and Health Administration (OSHA) commissioned a review of safety incentive programmes in 2000, it cited a number of cases of employees hiding injuries in order to reap the rewards. For example, a building site worker refused to go home after being splashed in the eyes with acid because his company was a month away from reaching 3 million hours without a lost-time injury and there was going to be a party. He didn't want to spoil it for everyone.

Engineers often fail to take into account the fact that people change their behaviour when they have safety devices around them. The National Highway Traffic Safety Administration found that cars equipped with antilock brakes saw a decline in some kinds of accidents but an increase in others, perhaps because they relied too heavily on the brakes to save them. Studies have shown that drivers with antilock brakes drive significantly closer to the vehicles in front of them. The administration found no overall benefit in preventing accidents.

Similarly, childproof medicine bottles, introduced in 1972, have resulted in no net savings of life, according to a study by a Harvard Law School professor, W. Kip Viscusi. Viscusi speculated that this was because parents were lulled into a false sense of security by the caps and left medicine in places that were more accessible to children, many of whom figured out how to open them. Some adults also had problems with the caps, so they just left them off completely.

Another potential risk of safety devices is that we often put our resources into high-profile security, while forgetting everyday dangers. Sir Bernard Crossland, a safety expert who led the inquiry into an underground railway fire in London in 1987, questioned the decision to spend $554,790,000/ £300 million on new safety devices like fireproof doors and metal escalators. The money, he said, would be better spent on putting smoke detectors in people's houses. (It was enough to buy a smoke detector for every home in Britain.) House fires kill about five hundred people a year and are most deadly in homes without detectors. The underground fire in 1987 killed thirty-one.

What You Can Do
Don't shun all safety devices. Some are very good. Smoke alarms and highway guardrails have saved countless lives. Life jackets are much more likely to keep you from drowning than they are to cause an accident on their own.

Educate yourself on the true relative risks and benefits of various safety devices. Then make a decision on which you need, and which you don't. No safety device can protect against every possible combination of events.

"A mature society needs to accept the fact that sometimes things will go wrong," wrote Frank Furedi, a sociology professor and the author of several books on risk. "The benefits of taking a risk needs to be balanced against the consequence of native outcomes. But the trick is to manage, not evade risks."

Salons

L ean back, be pampered by the salon staff . . . and put yourself at risk for stroke. A 1992 report in the journal *Neurology*
sounded the alarm about what the press dubbed "beauty parlour
syndrome." Holding the head at a backward tilt over a shampoo
basin can diminish the blood supply to the brain. For people at
risk, this is enough to cause a stroke.

Two doctors at the Department of Pediatrics at the Naval Hospital in
Portsmouth, Virginia, reviewed the records of fifteen children who
were referred to neurology clinics between 1982 and 1992 for
seizures that occurred shortly after hair grooming. They found that
witnesses usually did not think to mention that the child was having
his or her hair brushed when the seizure came on, unless the witnesses were asked specifically about it. Researchers concluded that hair
grooming might precede seizures more often than is reported.

Seizures and strokes are but two of a host of hazards that reside at
the salon. Hairdressing parlours are full of chemicals of all description, permanent-wave solutions, hair dyes, nail enamels, sham-
poos, perfumes and so on. Researchers in Germany studied 2,275
hairdressing apprentices and found that after six weeks of employment 36 percent had developed dermatitis from contact with
chemicals, usually between their fingers. It is such a common
problem among hairdressers that about half of them regard red
hands as normal.

In Sweden, doctors from the Institute of Internal Medicine in Göteborg found that hairdressers suffered from more respiratory problems than a sampling of women from the general population.

Researchers at University Hospital RWTH Aachen in Germany have discovered that artificial nails can cause allergic reactions. The chemicals used in the nails irritate the fingers and anything touched by the fingers, including the face and eyes. Before you shun artificial nails, it's important to note, however, that the study was based on only *two* cases.

In all, the number of complaints of hairdressing injury have increased fivefold in the last ten years—according to David Salinger of the International Association of Trichologists. In case you didn't know, a trichologist is a person who studies the structure, function and diseases of the human hair and scalp. As of 2002, the organisation was receiving about five complaints a week, up from about one a week a decade ago. The complaints include hydrogen peroxide burns, allergic reactions and sloppy practices, such as hairdressers going out to lunch in the middle of a permanent wave.

What You Can Do
Here's a beauty tip courtesy of *Newsweek* magazine: never shave your legs before a pedicure. (The microbes that inhabit salon footbaths have a better chance of getting into your skin if you've recently shaved.)

To prevent dermatitis, doctors recommend wearing gloves while handling water and chemicals and applying moisturiser in the evenings.

Be grateful for the era in which you live. Back in the 1800s, you might have used cosmetics that literally burned the skin or even hair products made of petroleum. As the *British Medical Journal* reported of one tragic accident in 1897: "The unfortunate occurrence of the death of a lady by burning resulting from the ignition of petroleum hairwash at a fashionable hairdresser's affords abundant material for reflection. ... The more volatile kinds of petroleum give off inflammable vapours, even at ordinary temperatures, and that these vapours when mixed with air form explosive mixtures. ... The mere fact of tying up the hair could have generated such an amount of human electricity as to produce the result."

School

Every day the children are rounded up and taken away to dangerous institutions where fully one-quarter of injuries to children in this age group occur. The institutions? Schools.

In the past few years, explosions have rocked numerous schools, killing and maiming young people and teachers. These, however, were not the result of disturbed students. They were caused by science experiments. The explosives included a giant fireball in New Berlin, Wisconsin, that burned 8 students and their teacher; a mixture of potassium chlorate and sulfur that ripped away a counter in Tulsa, Oklahoma, and injured 5 students; an explosion during an experiment involving methyl alcohol in Sydney, Australia, that injured 7 children and their teacher; and a Beersheba, Israel, science lab explosion in which 12 students, a lab technician and a teacher were injured. Over the past four years at least 150 students in the United States have been seriously injured, sometimes with disfiguring burns, in school science labs.

Meanwhile, in technical engineering courses, young people routinely operate machinery that would be illegal for them to use in a work setting. Under U.S. law, children under 18 years of age cannot work with power-driven woodworking tools, circular saws or band saws. Instead, they use them in school. Industrial-arts-class accidents are relatively rare. In a Utah study, about 7 percent of secondary-school injuries could be attributed to these engineering courses. Yet these injuries are some of the most devastating, with lifelong consequences, including severed fingers and thumbs. The authors of the study suggest that adolescents are especially prone to injuries because they experience growth spurts. They are temporarily less coordinated as they adjust to their changing size.

Amongst younger children (primary/elementary school), more than half of school injuries occur on the playground. (See page 157.) As children get older, they spend less time on the playground equipment; instead, they start participating more in organised sports. So by the time they're in secondary school, sport becomes the leading cause of school injury. Both playground and sporting injuries are more prevalent among boys than girls.

Surveys of hospital admission data in Sweden, Canada, New Zealand and the United States all indicate the same major dangers to schoolchildren. Climbing frames and climbing equipment are number one on the list. In a Canadian study, climbing equipment accounted for nearly two-thirds of hospitalisations. Playground falls can result in broken bones, serious injuries and even death. The youngest children, however, are more likely to be hurt on slides. They're also more likely to suffer head injuries than broken bones.

Another of the greatest hazards of school life, it turns out, is other kids. More than 35 percent of injuries in a Swedish study could be attributed to children fighting.

What You Can Do
Urge your fellow citizens to vote for more money for school budgets, or to make safety a higher priority in current budgets. Safety experts attribute many school accidents to outdated and poorly maintained equipment. Science classes often do not have enough in their budgets to supply safety glasses for all the students. They may store chemicals longer than they should because they cannot afford new ones. A small percentage of industrial courses' accidents are traceable to malfunctioning equipment. Other experts point to a lack of proper training of teachers in safety issues, or to a lack of standardised monitoring of safety practices in classrooms.

Proper supervision is also key. Swedish researchers discovered that 66 percent of playground and sports injuries occurred when students were not involved in activities organised by teachers.

There is always home schooling. According to recent estimates, 1 million to 2 million children, representing 2 to 4 percent of all U.S. students, are taught at home.

Screwdrivers

T he workbench is home to such potentially hazardous equipment as the chain saw, power drill, sander and, most insidious of all, the deadly screwdriver. That Phillips head may not look as scary as the axe or the router, but it beats them all when it comes to injuries.

Figures compiled by the Royal Society for the Prevention of Accidents reveal that an estimated 3,823 Britons injure themselves each year with screwdrivers—more than with welding equipment (2,597), axes (2,268), circular saws (2,908) and power drills (3,036), and far more than chain saws (1,116), lathes (128), blowtorches (128) and heating tools like soldering irons and glue guns (43). In fact, the only piece of do-it-yourself equipment that beats out the screwdriver in sheer danger is the hammer. If they had a hammer, apparently, 4,353 Britons would hammer in the morning, hammer in the evening and hammer all over their hands.

So why is it that all but 165 people can safely handle a soldering iron while thousands have trouble turning a screw? Basically, say the experts, if you're firing up a blowtorch or running wood under a jigsaw, you have to be pretty oblivious to be unaware of the dangers. Not so with a screwdriver. One common screwdriver mishap involves a screwdriver that is not quite the right size for the respective screw. A variation on this is using the corner of a flathead screwdriver on a Phillips screw. Either way, the driver can slip off the screw and injure the handyperson's face or hands.

Another way people injure themselves with screwdrivers is by inventing creative uses for them. For example, one woman who could not find a hammer used the plastic handle of her screwdriver to pound a nail into the wall. The handle shattered and plastic shards hit her in the face, blinding her in one eye. In another case, a man used a screwdriver as a lever to pry boards from an old deck. The screwdriver was not up to the task. When it snapped in half, the man lost his balance, breaking two front teeth in the process. In perhaps the strangest case of all, a Smethwick, England, teenager was killed when a screwdriver he was using in a robbery slipped from the church safe he was trying to crack. The young man was holding a screwdriver in the hinge of the safe (which, incidentally, held nothing more than marriage certificates) whilst his friend struck it with a hammer. The screwdriver shot out and lodged in the young man's eye. He died later of a brain hemorrhage.

What You Can Do

Before you pick up that screwdriver, take a deep breath and focus. If you can, send your kids to the neighbour's so you're not distracted by wondering what they're doing in the next room with the cat.

Don't start a project when you're tired, rushed or angry. If your home-improvement task is causing you to utter numerous four-letter words, it's time to take a break and have a cup of tea.

Finally, remember that a screwdriver works best when used as a screwdriver, not as a hammer, a chisel, a key, a scraper or a toothbrush. Especially not a toothbrush.

Self-Employment

I f you're your own boss, you don't have to deal with the stress of shouting managers, gossiping coworkers or even regular schedules. What could possibly go wrong? A lot. In Europe and North America, the self-employed run a greater risk of being killed on the job than their time clock–punching equivalents. One of every five people killed at work in the United States in 1993 was self-employed, according to the Bureau of Labor Statistics census of fatal occupational injuries. This number may not sound that startling until you take into consideration the fact that the self-employed make up only 9 percent of the U.S. workforce. European Union figures show that while the self-employed have fewer accidents than employees, they suffer far more fatalities at work.

"Looking at the trends over the last seventeen years," said Linda Williams, the British Health and Safety Executive's chief inspector of agriculture, "the incident rate for fatal injuries amongst employees has generally declined. However, in the case of the self-employed, we have seen consistently higher rates."

What's going on? First of all, the self-employed do set their own hours, but that doesn't mean they set fewer of them. Studies and surveys in various countries have shown that the self-employed work more hours than those employed by others. A recent study found that self-employed Canadians put in 32 percent more time at work per week than salaried employees. Another Canadian study found that the self-employed work three more hours, on average, than others and that they put in an additional fourteen hours of overtime each week, compared with ten hours for other employees. What is more, the self-employed find it difficult to separate work and nonwork hours. Instead, they work on weekends and take work along on holidays. So the self-employed simply have more time to get themselves killed on the job.

The long hours, the irregular pay packets and the uncertainty lead to stress, and a number of studies have shown a link between self-employment and psychosomatic health problems because of this.

Employees have more access to safety information and training in the workplace. Meanwhile, in countries like the United States, where medical insurance is a benefit of employment, the self-employed often have less access to health care. Depending on where you live, health and safety laws may not cover you if you work for yourself. In Portugal and Ireland, health and safety legislation covers all workers. In Denmark, the United Kingdom and Sweden, it covers most self-employed workers, but not all. In the other European Union nations, health and safety laws do not apply to the self-employed.

Many self-employed people work in dangerous jobs like farming and the building trades. Farming, the industry with the highest rate of fatal injuries, accounts for 13 percent of America's self-employed and only 2 percent of salaried workers.

Finally, the average self-employed worker earns less than her salaried counterpart. This means she can't afford to spend extra money on the kinds of safety equipment and training that an employer might provide.

What You Can Do
Go work for someone else. There is a downside to this, of course. You probably won't be as satisfied with your work. In a recent telephone survey of Canadian workers, more than 68 percent of the self-employed reported high job satisfaction compared with only 47 percent of the regular workforce.

WARNING

Sewing

A grandmother rocking in her chair while knitting a sweater is not most people's idea of an adventurer, but perhaps it should be. Statistically, Granny is more at risk of injuring herself from something in her sewing basket than she would be if she were to strap on crampons and scale a mountain. According to the U.S. Consumer Product Safety Commission's National Electronic Injury Surveillance System, an estimated 4,056 people a year are injured while climbing mountains, while 7,099 are injured by sewing machines and sewing-basket articles.

Sewing involves a lot of scary elements—sharp needles, scissors and pink paisley fabric, to name just three. Even knitting wool can be hazardous: it can become twisted and accidentally choke a person. Buttons can be swallowed. One of the most unusual accidents reported to the NEISS involved a metal button that was kept in a drawer beside a battery. The button completed the circuit of the battery and burned some of the contents of the drawer. Fortunately, no one was injured.

After 1846, when sewing became mechanised with Elias Howe's "lock-stitch machine using double thread," it became even more deadly. Prior to the invention of the sewing machine, seamstresses took their time. They turned out about thirty-five stitches a minute. Sewing machines, meanwhile, could perform three thousand stitches a minute. Now the needle was moving at a breakneck speed, and the act of making a shirt carried the additional hazards of electricity and motors. Injuries from sewing machines have included fingers run over with the fast-moving needles, electric shocks, trips over flexes, appendages pulled into the mechanism that feeds the cloth, and overheated machines that set fabrics on fire.

What You Can Do

First, what not to do. Your mouth is not a good place to hold your extra needles or buttons. The files of the NEISS contain many pages of incidents involving accidental ingestion of sewing items. In one case, doctors at Spain's Hospital General de Castellón performed radiographs on an 85-year-old woman who was suffering abdominal pain and discovered a sewing needle lodged in her liver. She apparently had swallowed it.

Similarly, it is a good idea not to use knitting needles to scratch or clean the inside of your ears. NEISS records reveal that people have a habit of doing this. They tend to injure the eardrum.

If you have concerns about the flame-resistant properties of your knitting wool, avoid doing home tests. A 60-year-old woman learned this lesson the hard way. According to NEISS data, she became worried when she found no fire-resistant label on the yarn she had bought and decided to test it herself by holding it over a lit cigarette. The knitting wool caught fire and burned the woman's hands.

Barbara Gash, a sewing reporter for the *Detroit Free Press*, offers these additional safety tips: use a power strip to avoid tangled flexes, use an ironing board that is stable enough not to fall over, keep your cutting tools sharp (dull ones require extra force that can cause them to slip), keep rotary cutters in protective guards, and be sure that you have adequate lighting in your sewing room.

DANGER

Shaving

Safety razor, schmafety razor! It seems innocuous enough, but there is always a chance that you could end your morning grooming routine with a visit to the casualty ward.

In the old days, real men shaved with a straight razor—a device that bore a striking resemblance to the Grim Reaper's scythe. Slip with one of those and you could slit your jugular. Then again, the risk was sometimes preferable to the risks associated with having a beard. Alexander the Great forbade his soldiers from sporting beards, which he considered nothing but a handle for the enemy to grip as they chopped off your head. Basically, you risked having your throat slit one way or another.

Things changed for the better with King C. Gillette's "safety razor" in 1903. It had replaceable blades that were set at an angle to reduce the likelihood of cutting one's skin. Gillette supplied 3 million razors and 36 million blades to American troops in World War I and the improvements were recognised immediately. Gillette became a very wealthy man.

Women, incidentally, were spared from most of this nicking and cutting because shaving did not come into vogue for the fairer sex until skirts got shorter and arms got barer in the 1920s. Today, however, North American women actually have more acreage to shave than men. They go through razors almost twice as quickly. Interestingly, however, they seriously injure themselves with razors only half as often. About forty thousand men manage to mangle themselves while shaving each year and only twenty thousand women do the same.

What You Can Do
To avoid being one of these people, here are a few shaving tips. Shave first thing in the morning, when the skin is least sensitive, and start by splashing the area to be shorn with warm water. Dull blades inflame your skin, so change your blade or toss your disposable razors out regularly. The folks who sell razors suggest you do this every third shave. Apply moisturising skin cream before you slather on the shaving cream. Massage your skin with a circular motion to make the hairs stand up. Shave downward in the direction of the hair. You get a closer shave going the other way, but it's harder on the skin. Finally, rinse the razor regularly as you shave or the blade will become clogged, which can cause problems.

You can always grow a beard too. Of course, then you face some other risks, like pollutants and bacteria trapped in your facial hair, oh-so-close to your nose. In 1985, a Soviet scientist reported that beards cause a buildup of germs and other nasty things, which the wearers then continuously inhale. In 1994, Chinese scientists reported that men with both moustaches and beards may breathe as much as 50 percent more pollutants than the clean-shaven. The British concur. In 2001, a British employment tribunal ruled that a supermarket was justified in firing a man with a beard because it posed a hygiene risk. The man in question sued for sex discrimination, but lost. "If a bearded lady applied, we might have had to refuse her as well," a spokesperson for the supermarket explained.

Shopping Trolleys

When it comes to getting the adrenaline going, a go-kart beats a shopping trolley every time. When it comes to real danger, however, the shopping trolley wins the race by several laps. According to the U.S. Consumer Product Safety Commission, roughly 10,500 people are treated for go-kart–related injuries each year. Meanwhile, 26,700 people are treated for injuries related to shopping trolleys. Most shopping trolley injuries—84 percent—involve children.

As for the other 16 percent, typical is a story cited by the Royal Society for the Prevention of Accidents: A 54-year-old woman was pushing a heavily loaded shopping trolley when it hit something on the ground. It began to tip, and as she tried to right it, her wrist was twisted. She was later treated in the casualty ward for a sprain, one of the 256 British citizens injured by shopping trolleys each year, and one of 22,533 people in her age group who suffer shopping precinct–related injuries.

Some of the injuries can be traced to poorly maintained trolleys. Most shoppers have had the frustrating experience of trying to steer a trolley with a wobbly wheel. All you are trying to do is push it over to the frozen-food counter. You shove it hard to the right, but it takes off to the left, upsetting a pyramid of specially priced Weetabix: "Clean up on aisle three!"

When the base on a metal shopping trolley gets bent, the wheels can go out of alignment and wobble. Sometimes the wheels pick up stray bits of lint or plastic carrier bags. The wheels get stuck, making the trolleys almost impossible to steer.

Yet even well-maintained trolleys are designed in such a way that they are liable to tip under the right (or wrong) conditions. Trolleys tip when there is a combination of rearward pull in the horizontal direction and downward force on the handle. These forces can come into play when the rear wheels run over an obstruction as small as one-sixteenth of an inch, or a fraction of a centimetre. A spill can also occur when a parent or child leans on the trolley handles. The combination of the horizontal and vertical forces make an angle that is 20 degrees off the vertical in the rearward direction. If there is a child in the seat and he or she leans, the trolley is even more likely to tip.

In the United States, there is a new food shop risk: traffic accidents involving motorised shopping trolleys. These motorised trolleys, with a top speed of 2.5 mph/4.02 kph, are often provided in upscale food shops, especially in areas with large old age pensioner populations. The result has been a rash of lawsuits by people who suffered dog-food-aisle fender benders.

"The keys are sitting in the ignition in some shops, so, theoretically, a blind person, a person on drugs, a younger person, can get in there and create great injury, and it can happen in a second." So argued a Florida personal-injury lawyer who represented a client who claimed a preexisting shoulder injury was aggravated when she was hit by a shopper in a motorised cart. Lawmakers in Florida are working on legislation that would prevent shoppers from suing food shops for the indoor driving behaviour of their customers so that the trolleys, a boon to disabled shoppers, do not become extinct. Some lawyers are even recommending shopping trolley driving tests before customers can use the vehicles.

What You Can Do

"Shopping carts are not designed for the safe transport of children," wrote Dr Gary A. Smith in an article for the American Medical Association's *Archives of Pediatrics and Adolescent Medicine*. Smith has advocated the wholesale redesign of shopping trolleys by widening the wheel base and lowering the centre of gravity. Another possibility would be to provide supervised child minding areas in shops so children can safely play while parents are shopping.

In the off chance that you are not a food shop manager, your options are somewhat more limited. If you choose to use a shopping trolley with a child seat, the experts urge you to try to find one with a child restraint, to look for a newer trolley that is easier to steer, and to avoid leaning on the handle while a child is in the seat.

You shouldn't have to be told, but leave the shopping trolleys at the shop when you're done shopping. Food shops are slow to replace their old trolleys for one good reason—they're expensive, at $40 to $100 each in the United States. (That's £21 to £53.) Add to that the fact that people keep stealing them and you're likely to be using those wobbly trolleys for a long time. In Europe, where shopping trolleys are often kept on the premises through the use of barriers or a coin deposit, theft is not as great an issue as in North America, where the return of trolleys is generally on the honour system. Unfortunately, many Americans have shown dishonour in this regard. According to the Food Marketing Institute in Washington, DC, food shops lose about 11 percent of their trolleys a year. The annual cost to retailers is about $175 million/ £92,857,901.

You shouldn't have to be told, part two: Don't use shopping trolleys as go-karts. A Vancouver, Canada, teen made this mistake and suffered a broken shoulder. She and her friends decided to take a trolley for a downhill ride. As she was racing at 45 mph/72.42 kph she realised that shopping trolleys don't actually have steering. She had an accident.

HAZARDOUS

BEING SHORT

Being Short

A lack of height can cut your life, well, short. In general, tall people earn more, are more respected and live longer. What's more, archaeologists and anthropologists have found evidence that this is true across cultures, and has been for centuries.

A team from the University of Bristol examined the remains of people buried in Northeast England between the 9th century and 1850. They assessed the ages of the dearly departed by examining their teeth and skulls. Next they measured the length of their arm and leg bones. They found that people with longer bones were consistently less at risk of dying before they were age 30.

Researchers are not entirely sure why tall people have an advantage, but they've made some educated guesses. Extra height probably means you had better nutrition in your youth. Then again, it could just be that being short creates added stress. Short people have to fight against a host of stereotypes that put them at a disadvantage. In cultures as diverse as the Chinese, the Mehinaku and Timbira of Brazil, the Trobriand Islanders of the Pacific and the Navajo of North America, height is a sign of status, especially for males.

The trouble begins in youth. Researchers have found that if you show mothers photographs of two 19-month-old boys who are nearly identical in every respect except height, the women will consistently rate the taller one as more capable and responsible.

179

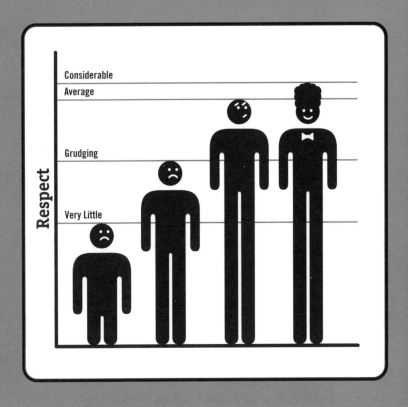

The shortest quarter
of the population earns
about 10 percent less
than the tallest.

Paul Wilson, an Australian psychologist, conducted an experiment in which he introduced the same man to different groups of strangers. Each time he assigned the man a title with a different level of status. For example, he was introduced first as a student, then to another group as a professor. Next the strangers were asked to rate the subject's height. As you might have suspected, when they thought he was a professor they guessed he was a full two inches taller than when they believed he was a student.

This bias has economic consequences. Economists at the University of Pennsylvania determined that the shortest quarter of the population in the United Kingdom and United States earns about 10 percent less than the tallest quarter. With each extra inch of height, wages go up 1.7 percent in England and 1.8 percent in the United States.

The ideal Western height, by the way, appears to be 6'2"/187.96 cm for men. Any taller than that and there is no more social advantage, although there does not appear to be a particular social disadvantage to being, say, 6'10"/208.28 cm.

All of this is good news to the Scandinavians and the Dutch, who are now the tallest people in the world. The Dutch and Norwegians average 5'10½"/178 cm and Swedes measure nearly 5'10"/177 cm. Compare this with teeny, tiny Americans at only just 5'9"/175 cm.

What You Can Do
Choose tall parents. Given that most people do not have this option, the only other suggestion would be to buy shoes with built-in risers or very tall heels. Then again, you might want to see the entry on high heels (page 106). Sorry. Not a lot you can do about this one.

Siblings

I n a confusing and hazardous world, it's comforting to have an older brother or sister to lead the way and protect you from harm.

Sorry—wrong. Having siblings, especially older siblings, puts a child at an increased risk of injury.

Researchers at the Harborview Injury Prevention and Research Center in Seattle, Washington, have conducted a number of studies on injury and siblings. In one study of hospital records, they found that not only did children with older siblings have a greater risk of being injured, but as the number of older siblings increased, so did the risk. The highest risk of all was for kids with three or more older siblings. The closer the children are to each other in age, the more pronounced is the effect. In another study, Harborview researchers found that when one sibling has a relatively serious accident, another sibling is almost 50 percent more likely to have an accident himself or herself within six months, when compared with kids whose siblings haven't had accidents.

Why is this? The experts can only make educated guesses. They believe that the most likely explanation is that accidents happen when families are under stress. The injury of one child creates stress that can make it more likely for another child to be hurt. The first accident may also draw the parent's attention, which could mean the other children have less supervision than normal. Researchers found that the increase in accident risk was greatest in the ten days following the first sibling's injury. After a month, the increased risk had passed.

Of course, older siblings have other ways of causing harm to their little brothers and sisters. A study by researchers at the University of Guelph in Ontario, Canada, found that older siblings have a great impact on how likely their younger siblings are to take risks. In their experiment, they gave the younger child options of different play scenes, some safe-looking, others riskier. After the younger child decided which path he preferred, the older sibling tried to change his mind. The older siblings, it turned out, were very good at persuading the younger ones to take the dicier path. This means that a risk-taking older sibling is likely to draw the younger sibling into daring activities like sledding on ice or, if they've read this book, sitting at a table and trying to open a tin of beans (see page 214). Other studies have shown that when older siblings engage in risky behaviour like smoking or taking drugs, the younger siblings are more likely to do the same.

What You Can Do
Petition your government to institute an official one-child-only policy like they have in China. Then again, before you do this, you should know that some Chinese experts aren't sure this has worked out so well. In 2003, ten experts from the Chinese Academy of Social Sciences recommended that the government revise its birth control policies to allow couples in developed cities to have two children. The number of people aged 60 or older in China is currently 133 million, and by 2059 there will be about 410 million. The experts are concerned that under the current family policy plans there will not be enough young people to take care of them.

A more conservative response was suggested by the authors of the Harborview studies. They suggest using their data to make doctors more aware of the risks to siblings, and recommended providing home visits and educational programmes for families that are at increased risk of further injuries after an injury to one child.

Slips and Falls

If cartoons and comics are to be believed, banana peels are one of the most dangerous things on Earth. People slip on them left and right. While we accept this as a truism, no recent documentation exists to support the theory. The National Electronic Injury Surveillance System, which catalogues all manner of injuries related to consumer products, does not track banana-peel-related falls. "Fruits and vegetables fall under the jurisdiction of the Food and Drug Administration," the agency says. The U.S. Food and Drug Administration, however, has no records of large numbers of people slipping on banana peels. Could it be that the enormous publicity surrounding the dangerous practice of snacking on bananas and leaving the peels on the floor has made our lives safer?

In fact, it may be "banana-cide" that put an end to generations of people going *wooo-aaaa-hhhhh!* The Gros Michel was a variety of banana that was bigger and sweeter than the Cavendish variety we're used to seeing in our North American and European supermarkets. Banana authorities believe that the Gros Michel was the inspiration for the falling-on-a-banana slapstick routine. This tasty but slippery fruit was wiped out by a crop disease in the 1950s or '60s, making it safe for all to walk without fear once again.

Wrong! All you need to slip and fall is a floor and gravity, as twelve thousand Americans will attest. Or would attest if they hadn't died because they slipped and fell. Many of the accident statistics you will find in other chapters—injuries by tables, office supplies, chairs, stereos, drum sets—actually involve people falling down and bashing into them. Almost half of hospital admissions from accidents are caused by falls. Among older people, the proportion increases. Falls are the cause of 64 percent of the admissions of those 65 to 74, 80 percent of patients aged 75 to 84, and 84 percent of patients 85 and older. Thanks to falls and an aging population, older women now outpace young males in admission to hospitals due to injuries. Slips, trips and falls caused about 388,000 lost workdays in 1995.

What You Can Do

If you need more proof that bananas and other slippery things are not to blame: A recent study by the Yale School of Medicine found that slippery showers, loose rugs and other hazards were not responsible for most falls by the elderly living at home. Surprisingly, no relationship was found between potential hazards and the occurrence of falls.

If keeping the floor clean won't work, what is left? If you're stumped, you're not alone. A recent phone survey asked Americans what could be done to prevent various types of accidents. When it came to falling down, only 55 percent of the respondents could think of a countermeasure, compared with 86 percent for drowning and motor vehicle deaths.

So here's one suggestion: falling practice. This is the idea of F. J. Leavitt of Ben-Gurion University in Israel. After studying the available medical literature, he recommended following the example of martial-arts practitioners who perfect the act of falling to prevent injury.

"The ease with which martial artists take even very hard falls suggests the hypothesis that falling practice while relatively young can prevent injury from falls incurred later in life," he wrote.

Perhaps it's time to drop a few banana peels, after all.

Soda/Fizzy Pop

Recently there was a panic in India that occurred as the former prime minister P.V. Narasimha Rao was about to leave his guest house. An explosion was heard and security personnel hustled him back into the building. Local police and bomb squads arrived on the premises and, after an intensive investigation, determined the cause of the blast to be a half-filled fizzy pop bottle that had been left on the lawn. It had exploded due to excessive heat.

Calling in the bomb squad to deal with a Pepsi may seem like an overreaction, but then again, maybe not. When shaken or exposed to heat, a fizzy pop bottle is not that different from a gun—it can propel a bit of metal (the cap) at high speed toward a person and cause serious damage. A fizzy pop explosion can also spread shrapnel (glass) over a large area.

Hot climates are especially likely to produce carbonated-drink bombs. In 1998, a team of doctors at the Department of Radiology at the Chaim Sheba Medical Center in Israel reported a case of two young patients who suffered perforated esophagi (or is it esophagusses?) because high-pressure gas from fizzy drinks was accidentally fired into the mouth. Similar cases were reported in Tel Aviv, where a team from the Assaf Harofeh Medical Centre attended to three children who were admitted after an orange-flavoured drink (which had spoiled) blew up in their mouths. They had tried to open the bottles with their teeth.

Meanwhile, in Ibn Sina Hospital in Kuwait, doctors reported on sixteen cases in a single year of eye injuries from flying bottle caps. In more than half the cases, the drinks had not been shaken. They had simply overheated and blown their tops.

This is not simply a Middle Eastern problem. In the United States, it is estimated that 2,343 people a year suffer bodily harm from glass pop bottles. Nonglass bottles injure almost twice as many—another 4,527 a year. The British chalk up 384 injuries a year from fizzy drinks. In Denmark, injuries from bottles (of all kinds) account for about 14 percent of the total number of patients seen in casualty wards, according to the European Home and Leisure Accident Surveillance System.

What You Can Do
You might consider switching to another tasty beverage. Just be careful what it is. Recently a 15-year-old London girl used her teeth to unscrew the metal cap on a plastic bottle of orange drink that had fermented because it had not been refrigerated. The cap blew off. She recovered, but her tonsils were damaged.

Which leads to safety tip number two: don't open bottles with your teeth.

And safety tip number three: Keep carbonated beverages, and any drink that might ferment (fruit drinks, for example), cool. High temperatures can cause the gases to expand to the point that a bottle can't contain them.

Don't run with pop. Popping pop bottles are the most dramatic fizzy drink injuries, but they're only part of the story. A sizable percentage of bottle injuries are caused by simply falling down and getting cut on glass shards.

Fact that doesn't really fit anywhere else: You probably know that drinking a flaming alcoholic drink can be dangerous, but there is one risk you may not have heard about. If you have a flaming shot, and you try to add additional alcohol from the bottle to the burning drink, the fire can follow the stream of alcohol up and cause the bottle to explode. The burn unit at Augusta Regional Medical Center in Georgia has seen a number of these accidents among barmen. Some victims suffered burns on 10 to 20 percent of their bodies. Save a barman—order a lager.

Sports Spectating

A rmchair sports fans often take credit for a victory as if they actually played the match. ("We won!") It may seem an absurd statement from someone who is safe and sound in an ottoman while athletes are out there putting themselves at risk. The fact is, however, the spectator may not be as safe as you think. Yes, sports fans share the risk. By simply watching the action, they're susceptible to injury and heart attack. How can this be?

The answer: Penalty shots.

Researchers at Birmingham University in England discovered that the 1998 World Cup match between England and Argentina was followed by a surge in heart attacks. The match was a nail-biter for fans, and it got the heart racing—literally. English hospitals saw a rise in admissions by about 25 percent. The team of scholars went on to examine hospital admissions surrounding other World Cup games, and they found no increase. They had to conclude that this particular game, in which England drew with Argentina 2–2 and then lost 3–4 on penalties, was especially traumatic.

Of course, penalty shot–induced heart attacks are just a symptom of a larger problem. Psychological studies have shown that die-hard fans sometimes identify so closely with their team that a loss on the field can lead to depression and a serious loss of self-esteem. The love affair with the team can be as emotionally intense as a love affair with a person, and with the same kinds of ups and downs. Some anthropologists have compared the rush of emotions and hormones during game time with that of a male animal battling over a female.

The ups and downs in men's testoesterone levels can lead to some rowdy behaviour in the stands—football hooligans, screaming "soccer dads", and the like. Even when you put these extremes of behaviour aside, the sheer excitement of the moment can lead to accidents and injuries both in the stands and in front of the television. A study in the *Scottish Medical Journal* listed 151 cases of sports fans reporting for treatment at the Edinburgh Royal Infirmary during the 1998 World Cup games in France, including a fan who had made himself deaf by shouting too loudly at the telly. There was even one fanatic's wife among the "injured." She faked a seizure in order to get her husband away from the television. "Attention-seeking behaviour," wrote the attending doctor. "Husband watching the football."

Often, spectators choose to be in the vicinity of hard objects hurled or struck with great force. Pucks, balls and splintered bits of bats all, at times, fly into the stands.

In 2003, a Virginia baseball fan was struck on the right side of the face with a foul ball, leaving him with an injured eye socket and extensive nerve damage. Ruling on the case, Thurmond v. Prince William Baseball Club, the Supreme Court of Virginia wrote: "When a particular adult spectator of ordinary intelligence is familiar with the game of baseball, that spectator assumes the normal risks of watching a baseball game, including the danger of being hit by a ball batted into an unscreened seating area of the stadium." Don't say you weren't warned.

What You Can Do
Give up sports and take up a healthier hobby, say, canasta. Then again, maybe not. Various psychological studies have shown that sports fans suffer fewer bouts of depression and alienation than nonfans, and have higher feelings of self-worth because they feel they are part of something. A side benefit is that fans are more optimistic about their sex appeal after their team wins. That's the upside of the testoesterone thing.

Perhaps the best solution would be to take a lesson from the athletes themselves. Exercise regularly and warm up before every match.

Stairs

There is a method of transportation that produces more nonfatal injuries each year than motor vehicle accidents. It can produce twice the g-forces of a roller coaster doing a loop. What is this deadly method of locomotion? The staircase. Jumping down a step has an impact of 8g compared with a roller coaster at its most thrill inducing (only 4g). Every year, an estimated 1,091 American stair climbers are killed and 769,400 are injured. (This is similar to the entire city of Charlotte, North Carolina, and the county that surrounds it [less the one thousand departed], suddenly finding itself in casts or on crutches.) In the United Kingdom, errant stepping leads to 230,000 injuries and 497 new members of the choir invisible. (This is as if the entire city of Bolton, England, suddenly found itself in need of stitches, and with 500 fewer residents.) What is more, in a study of Canadian casualty ward patients researchers discovered that stair tumblers were more likely to die than patients admitted for other maladies during the same period.

This is an issue of the greatest importance to national security. Data from the Total Army Injury and Health Outcomes Database reveal that American soldiers are frequently felled by flights of stairs. Falls were responsible for 28,352 hospitalisations of army personnel between 1980 and 1998. Of the falls that took place while soldiers were off duty, 49 percent were caused by treads. It's enough to give even the most balanced person a case of climacophobia (fear of stairs).

What is it about a simple tread that can be so deadly? The answer is, nothing—but the missteps will kill you. An extensive 1995 study of stair use (someone has to do it) revealed that a noticeable misstep occurred every 2,222 treads. "We believe from examining our data and the literature that the strongest pattern for stairway accidents lies in dimensional inconsistency within the stairways," wrote stair researchers P. L. Jackson and H. H. Cohen in the *Journal of Safety Research*. In English, this means that not all the treads are exactly the same size. And while people usually say they "slip" on the stairs, the fact is they fall so fast they don't really know what happened. Generally, people misjudge the distance and plant one of their feet wrong. It only takes one-quarter of an inch of difference—.64 cm—between where the stair is and where you expect it to be to throw you off balance. For some reason, familiarity with the stairs doesn't seem to prevent missteps. The fact that most stair accidents happen at home proves this.

One of the reasons for this is that we walk differently going up than we do going down. Going down stairs, we'd be better off with shorter, broader steps, because as we go down, we balance on one leg, the foot up on its toes, as the other foot reaches down for the tread below. If a high tread forces the forward foot too far down, it can throw off the balance. Going up you want taller treads, because lower treads offer more chances to trip.

What You Can Do
Install escalators in your home. But then again ... (see *Escalators*, page 74.)

Don't drink and step. After home staircases, the most common venue for a stair accident is a bar or restaurant with toilets above or below the main floor.

Put circular stairways in your house. It may seem odd, but you're actually less likely to fall on a circular staircase because you'll pay more attention while navigating it. And if you do trip, you can't fall as far.

Keep your stairway well lit—one study shows that 95 percent of household stairways are too dim.

If you happen to be building a new staircase, experts say the perfect dimensions are 7 in/17.78 cm high with treads 11 in/27.94 cm deep.

Suburban Living

I f you were thinking of moving from the big, bad city to the safety of the suburbs, think again. Recent studies show that some of the sparsely settled outer burbs in the United States are more dangerous than the cities they surround. This is bad news for about half of the nation's population. According to 1999 U.S. Census Bureau figures, one in two Americans now lives in the suburbs.

In 1995, researchers at the University of Virginia compared traffic fatality rates and homicides by strangers. Guess what? You're more at risk from a speeding SUV overtaking than you are from a mugger waiting in a dark alley. Traffic fatalities are about three times more common than homicides in the United States. What is more, most car accidents happen on two-lane roads, not dual carriageways. The same is true in the United Kingdom. According to the Commission for Integrated Transport, there are 20 percent more deaths on rural roads than in built-up areas. And here's a fact that may make you rethink the image of the suburbs as a safe family environment: automobile wrecks are the leading cause of death among people 24 years old and younger, according to the U. S. Government Printing Office's Public Health Reports. One of the most dangerous bits of Tarmac for toddlers, incidentally, is the drive. A 2002 Australian study found that almost 40 percent of children run over and killed by cars in New South Wales were felled on drives, not roads.

Not only does this dependence on cars put you at greater risk for an accident, it also makes you fat. A 2003 study entitled "Relationship Between Urban Sprawl and Physical Activity, Obesity" published in the *American Journal of Public Health* showed that people who live in sprawling housing estates weigh about 6 lb/2.72 kg more than people in more compact communities do.

What You Can Do

Rick Ewing, a lead author on the suburban obesity study, has this rather vague suggestion: "Communities, biomedical scientists, planners, policy makers and others need to identify the mechanisms by which the built environment impacts health and develop appropriate interventions to reduce or eliminate its harmful effects."

What are the appropriate interventions, you ask? Maybe a large-scale public-relations effort is in order to persuade the public to move to town. Just make sure you don't get the folks at the Toronto District Health Council to write the brochures. They define inner cities as "areas generally characterised by above average concentrations of unemployment, full-time workers living on low pay, single parents and the sick and the disabled who are living in poor quality and deteriorating housing conditions."

Howard Franklin, author of the public health report "Urban Sprawl and Public Health," suggests planting more trees and building more footpaths to encourage suburbanites to do more walking. This, combined with better public transportation between urban and suburban areas, could reduce some of the automotive commute and its corresponding dangers.

It's worth noting that the move from the cities to the suburbs is a largely American phenomenon. When you look at the planet as a whole, you see the opposite pattern. The United National Centre for Human Settlements reported in 1996 that nearly half of the world's population now lives in urban areas and that in a few years, for the first time in history, the world's urban population will be greater than its rural population.

Sunbathing

Riding the waves on nothing but a waxed piece of wood, are you crazy? I'll stay on the beach, thank you very much. Slap on a bit of sun creme, put out the beach blanket, and pass a relaxing and safe afternoon. Or is it?

You may not know it now, but in the long run you'd be better off on the surfboard. Surfing, according to Australia's Surfer's Medical Association, is a relatively risk-free sport. Roughly four people are injured surfing for every one thousand surfing days.

Meanwhile, the sun causes skin damage to every human being who dares to venture out into its rays, whether he falls off his beach blanket or not.

Australia, home to some of the world's best surfing beaches, is also the skin cancer capital of the world. Even though Australia has one-third the population of the United Kingdom, thanks to its burning sun and beach-loving culture, it has more cases of melanoma. In 1999, 7,850 cases of malignant melanoma were diagnosed in Australia, compared with 5,990 in Britain. Here's the rub, though: while more Australians contract skin cancer, more Britons die from it. During the same period in Britain, there were 1,600 skin cancer deaths and only 1,000 in Australia. In the past five years, 8,100 Britons have died from malignant melanoma, compared with 4,900 in Australia, and as the incidence of skin cancer has fallen in Australia, it is rising in Britain, doubling every ten to twenty years.

Why? One reason is the SunSmart campaign, which has sought to raise awareness of skin cancer in Australia and elsewhere by making suntans less fashionable. Young people often wear shirts and hats to the beach, and if they see a change in a mole, they are quick to go to the doctor. This early detection means that most melanomas are caught when they are easier to cure.

Melanoma is caused by intense, intermittent exposure to the sun. A fair-skinned woman working in an office in Edinburgh, Scotland, who goes on holiday in the South of France is, therefore, at a fairly high risk.

What You Can Do
The surprising advice—don't rely on sun creme. A number of recent studies have found that people who use sunscreen have higher rates of skin cancer and develop more moles. Philippe Autier of the European Institute of Oncology in Milan, Italy, may have discovered why. His team of researchers found that European adults who used high-protection suncreme, that is, sun creme with a sun protection factor (SPF) of 30 or higher, stayed out in the sun longer and got the same number of sunburns as those who used an SPF 10 formula. Using sunscreen appears to give people a false sense of security. Other studies have shown that most people use too little sunscreen to do them any good.

So slap on the sun creme, just don't rely on it alone to protect you. Keep your shoulders covered, and wear a big, old, floppy hat with a brim. You may not look like an extra from *Baywatch*, but don't worry—with skin cancer–awareness campaigns gaining force across the globe, it will catch on, and for once you'll be ahead of the fashion curve.

Sunny Weather

T he sun is shining. The sky is blue. It is perfect short-sleeved weather. What could be wrong in the world? Well, for one thing, hospital admissions are way up for kids. The staff of the Royal Aberdeen Children's Hospital, which sees more than twenty-thousand children under the age of 14 each year, noticed that more children were showing up on those beautiful, sunny days. When they checked their admission records against weather reports, they learned that they were not imagining things. On average, there were 30 percent more admissions of children in spring and summer than in autumn and winter.

Some American organisations have come to the same conclusion. A 2001 study by the National Safe Kids Campaign stated that nearly half of all injury-related childhood deaths occurred between May and August, with the peak coming in July. The organisation says that about 3 million children each summer are rushed to U.S. casualty wards for serious injuries, and about 2,250 of them die.

The reason is obvious. When the weather is nice, kids go out to play. They get on their bicycles—and ride into busy roads. They play on the swings—and fall off the swings. They climb trees—and so on.

Other researchers cite different statistics and argue that there is no correlation between summer weather and an increase in the overall volume of hospital admissions. Several studies in the medical literature dispute the claim. They do agree, however, that sunny weather has its own set of hazards. As Dr Melissa Stapp of Jefferson Memorial Hospital told the *St. Louis Post-Dispatch*, the patients' afflictions change in pleasant weather.

"It's a different kind of busy," she said. "We see more trauma and accidents."

What You Can Do
You are probably not in a position to affect the global climate. Instead, the British Department of Health is pioneering a project to better predict the weather. Health Weather Forecasts, which were piloted in 2001, give hospitals detailed weather forecasts featuring levels of pollen, radiation, temperature, barometric pressure and precipitation, along with information on illnesses and injuries that may be common in this type of weather. This way hospitals can better prepare for the problems they are likely to face.

In the meantime, medical professionals stress the importance of adequate supervision of children when they go out to play. Just don't get too obsessive about it. As Roger Vincent, spokesperson for the Royal Society for the Prevention of Accidents, told the newspaper *Scotland on Sunday*: "The key is to avoid the tendency to cocoon them away from danger or to simply tell them they can't do something with no explanation. Children need to be given credit and told the specific reason why they should not do something. ... If you sanitise a playground too much, children will not go there and [will] play instead on the old mine workings or building site next door, because there has to be an element of adventure."

Swimming Baths

S plashing away in the clean, cool, deep blue water of the local baths—it's not all rest and relaxation. Every day in the United States, six people drown in swimming baths, most of them children younger than 5. For every drowning victim, there are another four pulled from the water and taken straight to hospital.

Some of the risks of swimming are more obvious than others. Weak swimmers can simply go under. Breathe in a big gulp of water and you can drown. Misjudge the depth and you can strike the bottom with great force.

There are also some lesser-known risks associated with swimming baths. The baths' drains and circulation system have powerful suction forces. Children are fascinated with them, and often stick their hands or feet in their path just to feel the current. If the drain cover is broken, or removed, the force can be significant—perhaps 350 lb/158.76 kg of pressure for an 8-inch/20.32-cm drain with a standard pump. This is enough to suck in hair and hold a person's face underwater until she drowns. It can suck in clothing with the same result. It can pull in whole body parts, and, in the most horrifying cases, it can disembowel a person who sits on a sucking drain.

Meanwhile, some experts question the health impacts of the water itself. Dr Mark Nieuwenhuijsen, a researcher at Imperial College of Science and Technology Medicine in London, England, studied the water in indoor swim baths in the United Kingdom. He found that when chlorine is added to water, it reacts with the organic matter in baths (skin cells and body care products) and forms by-products. The most common are trihalomethanes. Chloroform is a trihalomethane, and has been classed as a potential cancer-causing agent. Trihalomethanes have also been associated with miscarriage and low birth weight. These chemicals can enter the body through the skin, by swallowing the water, or by breathing it off the water's surface as it evaporates. Nieuwenhuijsen concluded that pregnant women who go swimming often could be at risk.

If you're planning an overseas trip, you may want to skip this next paragraph. Researchers from the British Consumers' Association tested the water in eighty baths in popular tourist locations Majorca, Spain, and Corfu, Greece. Only two of them were free of bugs, were properly disinfected, and had water at the recommended level.

"Our results reveal stomach-churning evidence of gross bacterial contamination," wrote editor Paula Yates in the consumer association's *Holiday Which?* magazine. They also found concentrations of chlorine high enough to bleach bathing costumes and liable to irritate the eyes and skin.

What You Can Do
Safety companies have come up with a number of high-tech solutions. The inventions include electric eyes at hotel baths without lifeguards, camera systems that monitor underwater activities, and switches that monitor the vacuum on the inflow side of the swim bath or spa pump.

There are also low-tech and inexpensive remedies: swimmers with long hair can avoid becoming entangled in drains by wearing swim caps.

Better Homes and Gardens magazine offers this water-safety advice: Never leave children unattended at swimming baths. Do not leave toys in the water when you're done, as they may tempt other kids into the water. Invest in swimming lessons. Keep life preservers and a phone near the water. And learn CPR.

Tables

E very year in the United States, 287,933 people—a number greater than the population of the Bahamas or Iceland—are injured after a run-in with a table. In the United Kingdom, another 9,931 suffer table mishaps.

Tables are ever present. They're there when you get up in the middle of the night—and you think they're farther across the room. They're there when you're larking about in the lounge and you trip in their direction. They're in your office when you lean too many books on one end and watch them tip. They're inescapable.

Moving the table outdoors just presents new dangers. In a car/table collision, for example, you know the car is going to have the better end of the deal. Newspaper reports have documented such accidents in Templeton, New Zealand, where a car collided with a picnic table in a berry farm, injuring five; in Biel, Switzerland, where a man mistook the brake for the accelerator and collided with diners on the terrace of a restaurant, injuring three; and in Berlin, Germany, where six people were injured when a car ran into tables at a street-side café. This car actually hit tables at a café on one side of the road, swerved, then hit the tables at the café across the street.

In a collision between a human and a table, however, the human is usually going to come out a bit worse for wear. A quick survey of injuries reported to the U.S. National Electronic Injury Surveillance System (a printout from January through September 2003 alone takes up about a ream of paper) reveals a clear pattern:

- "Fell and hit head on table, lacerated head."
- "Was standing on a chair and fell, hit his face against edge of table."
- "Tripped over cat striking chest on the coffee table at home, fractured ribs."
- "Fell off couch, hit head on corner of coffee table."
- "Wife rearranged furniture, patient fell against table. Facial laceration."

Occasionally tables cause dramatic injuries, as when a person falls into a glass table and smashes it, or as in the case of the Philadelphia primary school student who was killed when he leaned against a folding table, causing it to fall on him. For the most part, however, accidents with tables are caused by poor balance and not quite knowing where the furniture is.

What You Can Do

Eliminate chairs. (See *Chairs*, page 38.) Without chairs, you wouldn't need so many tables.

If you rearrange furniture in your house, be sure the people who share your house know about it.

When moving around the house at night, turn on a light.

If you're especially accident prone, have difficulty walking, or possess poor balance, you might consider round tables instead of those with corners.

Tap Water

T urn on the tap and out flows a veritable river of fresh, clean, life-giving water. But what river did it come from, and what temperature is it when it comes out of the tap? Your tap could be flowing with danger and disease, leaving the person who bathes in it scarred for life and the person who drinks it with a belly full of foreign microorganisms.

Every year in the United States, 44,062 people are burned by hot water. Tap water scalds are often more severe, more disabling, more extensive and require longer hospital stays than other types of burns. Even though many countries have passed laws that limit the temperature of tap water, hotter water is often delivered. U.S. and New Zealand researchers found that more than 25 percent of homes had hot water delivered to the tap at temperatures that were higher than the thermostat setting. New Zealand has a code that seems contradictory. To prevent burns, the maximum temperature in schools and old age homes is 113°F/45°C, and 131°F/55°C in all other buildings. On the other hand, to prevent the growth of *Legionella* bacteria, the law also says that domestic hot water must be stored at a minimum temperature of 140°F/60°C. A tempering valve controls delivery temperatures.

The damage done to water drinkers by contamination is harder to quantify. Sure, lots of icky things get into the water, but we don't know for sure that they can kill you. Take, for example, the water in Dublin, Ireland. In 1997, Dublin residents began to notice fleas, larvae, mites and worms in their tap water. City engineers admitted that these organisms did get into the drinking water through old water mains, but insisted that the water complied completely with national and European Union regulations. In 1993, *Cryptosporidium*, a microbe that comes from animal waste, sickened four hundred thousand Milwaukee, Wisconsin, tap water users and killed more than one hundred. At that time, there were no rules regulating its presence in the water system.

Some of the worst water in Western countries is found in Scotland. A 2002 survey of twenty European cities put Aberdeen and Glasgow at the bottom of the water quality list. More homes there have water showing traces of animal waste than anywhere in western Europe, according to the *Sunday Mail,* which asked Dr Richard Dixon, head of research at Friends of the Earth, why this was.

"The reason given is that [the water] is coming from upland reservoirs and we don't have much control of sheep and cows and fishermen who may need to pee," he said.

What You Can Do
Don't give up drinking water. The experts say most of us do not drink enough. Water is necessary for the proper functioning of kidneys, and it helps regulate temperature and cushion the nervous system. Up to 85 percent of our brain cells are water and a recent study of primary-school kids showed that those who drank water throughout the day were more alert and better at certain tasks.

There is always bottled water. Surveys have shown that Americans and Europeans invest in bottled water for different reasons. Europeans generally say they buy it because it has more healthy minerals. Risk-averse Americans generally say they are afraid of contaminants in their tap water.

Tea

Ah, a warm kettle of tea, nestled under a tea cozy, ready to be savoured and enjoyed. Surely there is nothing remotely dangerous in this picture? Don't be fooled. If you want to know the real story of tea, just listen to this tale about its origins.

Legend has it that in the fifth century a Buddhist monk named Dharuma became sleepy when he was supposed to be meditating. He punished himself by cutting off his eyelids, and where the lids fell, the first tea plants grew. Since that time, tea has tried to hide its true, violent nature. The Americans knew this, and that is why they held the Boston Tea Party. Disguised as American indians so no one would notice they didn't belong on a British ship, the colonists dumped cases of tea into the sea while shouting, "Get this tea and those deadly tea cozies away from us." At least, that's what I remember from the history classes I took as a kid.

Tea cozies, you see, caused close to forty injuries in the United Kingdom in 1999. How can something with a name like "cozy" possibly inflict harm? It usually happens when a child tugs on a cozy and pulls a teapot over. Tea towels caused another 622 home mishaps, and teapots and the tea they contain a whopping 1,097 injuries that year. Figures from the Child Accident Prevention Trust report for the same year reveal that hot liquids were the cause of 70 percent of thermal injuries in children, with hot drinks being the most common cause. A parent brews a cup, turns away for a moment, and the young one reaches for it.

The danger is even greater in China. In case you were wondering how much "all the tea in China" is, the answer is 610,000 tons, or one-quarter of the world's total. Not only do they have a lot of it around, the Chinese brew their tea in a more dangerous fashion. In the West, tea traditionally is served with milk, which lowers its temperature. A team of Asian researchers measured the serving temperatures of tea served in the English fashion and in the Asian fashion and found that a Chinese cup of tea was about 77°F/25°C hotter than English tea. Obviously, spilled Chinese tea produces a more serious burn than the English kind.

What You Can Do

Perhaps teapot safety advocates need a celebrity to bring attention to their cause. I suggest David Duval, the champion golfer. In 1999 (a bad year for tea lovers), he managed to stay safe and sound on a snowboarding trip on the slopes of Idaho, but he had to call in the medics after a run-in with his teapot left him with second-degree burns on his right thumb and forefinger. Apparently, the gas cooker in his new home made the pot's handle hotter than did the electric cooker in his previous home. He became aware of this fact very quickly *after* he tried to pick up the pot.

Avoid drinking tea whilst driving. Especially avoid brewing tea whilst driving. A Christchurch, New Zealand, woman received this fatal lesson. She was trying to brew her cup of tea when her car plunged off a cliff and into a small river. She was found still holding a box of tea bags, her cup wedged against the steering wheel, a flask of hot water beneath her feet.

Teaching

L et's say you run a company that sells income protection or disability assurance (the type of insurance that pays someone when he becomes unable to work). You have to decide which of these people is the greatest risk: a police officer, a building site worker, a firefighter or a teacher. Which do you choose? The teacher, of course. A survey of British insurance-industry figures shows that a nonsmoking, male teacher pays almost $116.43/£64 a month for income-protection insurance worth $36,383/£20,000 a year. For the same type of coverage, a police officer would pay around $80/£44 a month.

As Kevin Carr of insurance broker LifeSearch explained to the *London Daily Mirror*, "While many people might think teachers are not in a dangerous profession, they do make a lot of claims for stress."

A survey of research on the subject published in the journal *Educational Review* found that, typically, about a quarter of schoolteachers rate their jobs as "very or extremely stressful." Of course, teacher stress and burnout are not purely British phenomena. A 1993 Swiss study of 160 secondary school teachers found that amongst the most common reasons teachers gave for leaving the profession were fatigue, nervous tension, frustration and difficulty dealing with problem students.

In a 1998 survey of teachers in inner-city London, England, 91 percent of teachers said students had bullied them. Whilst most of the bullying was verbal, 15 percent said they had been the victims of some form of physical abuse by students. That year the Association of Teachers and Lecturers (ATL), the British union, received 34 reports of assault on teachers; by 2002, the total had risen to 125.

"I haven't been physically assaulted at school," teacher Lesley Ward told the delegates at the 2002 ATL conference. "Apart from being kicked, bitten, hit, scratched and pushed over the last twenty-seven years."

What You Can Do

The professional journal *Educational Review* culled the following suggestions for coping with classroom stress from various published studies: Avoid confrontations. Try to keep problems in perspective. Try to relax after work. Devote more time to your difficult tasks. Recognise your own limitations. Take action to deal with your problems.

Schools can help by minimising red tape and paperwork, offering teachers positive feedback and praise, and making sure teachers are involved in management decisions.

The ATL is taking another approach. Its members are demanding legal prosecution of students and parents who abuse teachers.

Teddy Bears

If you wake up screaming in the middle of the night from nightmares about being attacked by wild bears and clutch your cuddly teddy for comfort, you've got it all back to front. Based on the odds, you have more to fear from Paddington than from a grizzly.

Between 1906 and 1995, eighty-two American deaths by bear attacks have been documented. Eighty-two deaths in eighty-nine years—that's similar to the number of people killed by lightning. When was the last time you heard a news report of a house catching fire when a Kodiak got too close to a nightlight, or of a child choking on a wild bear's clothing?

Meanwhile, toys typically account for over 140,000 injuries and at least twenty-two deaths each year.

Some of the more common types of hazards associated with cuddly toys are its small parts—the buttons, eyes, belts and bows that can come loose and pose a choking hazard—and improperly rooted fur, which can be inhaled by a child.

Yet even these dangers, so often cited by the media, are but a small percentage of actual physical injuries involving cuddly toy animals. Incident reports to the U.S. safety commission include not only accounts of actual injuries, but reports of potential cuddly toy hazards that do not actually result in any injury. For example, a mother discovered her son had swallowed beads that spilled out of a cuddly teddy. She rushed him to hospital, where the doctors noted that, though he'd swallowed a foreign body, he did not have any difficulty breathing. Reports to the U.S. National Electronic Injury Surveillance System also record complaints of toys that could possibly be dangerous—cuddly toys that have loose or small parts. These complaints are listed as "choking hazard, no injury."

Of the incidents recorded by the NEISS in 2002, those that were most likely to result in actual injuries requiring hospital visits involved not swallowing loose pieces of these furry friends, but tripping over ill-placed ones.

- "Fell going down stairs, stepping over a cuddly animal, fell into banister, lumbar strain."
- "Ankle sprain, jumping over a pile of cuddly animals."
- "Fell over cuddly lamb toy at home, landing on mouth, chipping front upper incisor."
- "Tripped over cuddly animal at home, striking forehead against coffee table, contusion face.
- "A large cuddly animal box fell on the patient's head, head injury.
- "Foot sprain sustained when sibling was jumping for cuddly animal and landed on patient's foot, foot sprain."

Hazards associated with cuddly toys

Another way in which teddies outpace real bears is in the disease-spreading department. Chances are that very few Americans ever cuddle up close enough to a black bear to catch cold or the flu. The same cannot be said of teddies. Research by New Zealand's Christchurch School of Medicine published in the British *Journal of General*

BUTTONS, EYES

BELTS

BOWS

Killer

Practice recently revealed that 90 percent of cuddly toys in doctors' offices had moderate to heavy bacterial contamination. Some of the toys carried lice, scabies, herpes viruses and germs that can cause conjunctivitis. The researchers went on to test teddies in other public environments, including libraries and child-minding centres. To their surprise, they found that these toys had similar contamination rates.

What You Can Do

If you needed another excuse to make your youngster tidy up his room, you've got it. A toy on the shelf is much harder to trip over than a toy that is lying at the foot of the stairs. Make sure you heed the age labels on toys. Many parents believe their children are exceptionally bright and well developed for their age, but higher intelligence doesn't necessarily mean that they have the experience to know what or what not to do. Check for small parts, loose fur and ripped seams that can release the contents, but also watch for hard parts like plastic hats and electronic hardware that allow your computerised cuddly parrot to sing. Statistically, kids are just about as likely to be injured by choking as by being hit over the head with a toy a jealous playmate wants for herself.

As for cleanliness, avoid cuddly toys found in waiting rooms. At home, you could try running teddy through the washer, though scientists have found that that's not terribly effective on its own. Even after cleaning a cuddly toy in a washer and dryer, high bacteria counts were present. Don't worry, however—you needn't burn all of your child's fabric companions. You can rid them of most of the dangerous germs by soaking in a diluted mix of bleach and water for thirty minutes before washing and drying them.

LETHAL

The Theatre

What do you call a profession in which more than half of its members are injured in the course of their work? Acting. That is, according to a survey of Broadway performers conducted by researchers at the University of Texas's medical school in Houston. A survey of 313 performers from 23 Broadway companies found that 55.5 percent reported having been injured on the job. The same team of researchers surveyed 269 West End actors, and 46 percent reported that they had been injured at least once on the job.

Exact statistics on the number of thespians and scenery artists injured each year are hard to come by, says Monona Rossol, safety officer of United Scenic Artists Local 829. The Occupational Safety and Health Administration (OSHA) only compiles and publishes statistics on occupations it considers to be "high risk," and theatre is not among them. Many theatre professionals believe this is due more to a lack of reporting than to the inherent safety of the actor's life. The University of Texas researchers, for example, found that most performers stayed out of the system and went to "nonphysician health care providers" when they were injured.

"There have been so many injuries that some theaters' worker's compensation insurance companies have just bailed out on them," Rossol says. "It is my belief that if all of the statistics were reported and collected, professional film, entertainment and theater would be a high-risk industry under OSHA's definition."

The theatre is home to a whole host of hazards. There are emulsions, solvents and special-effects chemicals that can combine in unique and deadly ways. The actors perform on raised platforms with lights in their eyes. Cosmetics cover the face and can lead to infections and allergic reactions. Heavy set pieces, props and other equipment are often moved between scenes in blackouts (that means in the dark).

Drops, as the name suggests, are objects that come down from the ceiling above the actors' heads, and occasionally *on* the actors' heads. Lights and scenery are held by a system of ropes and counterbalances, stage rigging that was once installed and operated by sailors who had learned their craft hoisting sails on the high seas. Modern stagecraft is only slightly less hazardous.

You may be surprised to learn, then, that there are no building codes that cover rigging installations and no nationally accepted standards for the manufacture of rigging components. There are no national standards for regular inspection of the systems, and the people who install them are not required to be licenced.

Consider a few examples of recent theatrical disasters: In 1992 in Seville, Spain, fifteen people were rehearsing on a stage of the Maestranza Theater that was designed to support five or six. It collapsed. One was killed and thirty-six performers were injured.

In 2001, Keith Baxter was starring in *The Woman in Black* at the Minetta Lane Theatre in New York. As he was making his way out, he accidentally fell off the stage and into the audience. He passed out, but quickly regained consciousness and survived with only a few bruises.

In 2003, a technician was testing special effects for the stage version of Disney's animated film *Aladdin* at the Hyperion Theater when he fell 42 ft/12.80 m onto the stage. He was hospitalised but never regained consciousness and was pronounced dead a month later.

What You Can Do
If you run a theatre, be sure to institute regular inspections of your equipment. Make sure the people you have operating the equipment are thoroughly trained.

If you need more information on how to run your theatre safely, a good book on the subject is Monona Rossol's *Stage Fright: Health and Safety in the Theater*.

Tins

According to the United Kingdom's Department of Trade and Industry, about 28,000 people ended up in the hospital in 1994 after run-ins with tins. The most deadly member of the tin can family? The corned beef package with the little key on it. It alone was responsible for about 30 percent of the injuries involving tins. The cost to England's National Health Service from corned beef tin injuries alone is estimated to be $20,859,210/ £12 million. Why do so many people get hurt with tins? The official assessment of the Department of Trade and Industry is that "tins are very sharp."

As you might imagine, most of the accidents involving tins— about 80 percent—occur while opening them, and most of the injuries are to fingers and hands. The reason canned meat is so problematic is that the keys are sometimes lost or the band only opens partially, and once it is open, the meat can still be hard to get out of the two halves of the tin.

Food tins have other, albeit rare, dangers. Under the right conditions—a tiny puncture, some spoilage, and a build up of gases— tins have been known to explode. A woman who was innocently shopping in a Tesco store experienced this phenomenon firsthand in 2001. She had just picked up a tin of cat food when she heard what she thought was a bomb detonating. It was actually a tin of dog food going off. Fortunately, the woman was not injured, though she was coated in the stuff. The food shop offered to pay her dry cleaning and sent her home with two bottles of wine to ease her mental anguish.

At least we can take solace in the fact that tins are not as dangerous as they were in the days before openers. Yes, the tin predates the invention of a device to open it. Until the middle of the nineteenth century, people had to open tins with a hammer and chisel. There are no statistics on how many injuries this led to, but it is probably safe to assume there were many. Then, in 1858, Ezra Warner patented a device that clamped onto the side of the tin. It had a sickle-shaped blade that provided leverage for a second blade that pierced a hole in the top of the metal. The familiar crank-operated opener with the rotating cutting wheel was invented by William Lyman of Connecticut, and made its first appearance in 1870. The second, serrated, wheel was added to the design in 1925.

What You Can Do

The Australian Canned Food Information Service offers the following tin-safety advice: Reject any food tins that are badly dented, especially those with damage to the seams and any with leaks. If the tin's ends are bulging, return it, unopened, to the supplier. The contents might be contaminated.

Low-acid tinned foods can be stored longer—from two to five years—while high-acid foods, like tomatoes and fruit, should be used within twelve to eighteen months to avoid corrosion of the lining.

Wash your tin opener after each use to avoid the risk of contaminating the food with bacteria. Take care of your tin opener to make sure it is clean and sharp. Blunt tin openers are more likely to leave jagged edges on lids, which are more likely to cut you when you remove them.

Toilets

E ach year in the United States, more than 60,800 people are injured while trying to relieve themselves.

You may have heard the urban legends about exploding toilets and crocodiles crawling out of the bowl, but those stories are just that—stories. Toilets tend to harm people in less dramatic ways: People sit down wrong. They miss the seat and fall. Sometimes the seat falls on some part of the anatomy. (For further reading on this subject, see the *Canadian Journal of Urology*, June 2001, "Management of Penile Toilet Seat Injury—Report of Two Cases.")

In Japan, a fad for toilet seats with heating elements has caused special problems. Nearly 40 million of the luxury loos were sold in the past twenty years. About 36 percent of Japanese homes have one. Although the average life span of the product is about seven years, most people never think to replace them. As the hardware ages, the wiring deteriorates, and the seats have been known to cause house fires. If you're a fan of warm toilets, you'll be happy to know that this is still a fairly rare occurrence. Only three fires from 1993 to 1999 were confirmed to have been caused by heated seats.

Scottish researchers also have concerns about defective toilets. William Tullet, Jonathan Wyatt and Gordon McNaughton of Glasgow's Western Infirmary reported on three cases of large

Fun Bathroom Facts

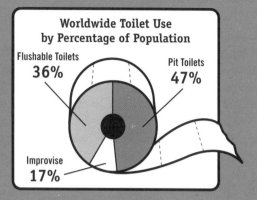

Worldwide Toilet Use by Percentage of Population

Flushable Toilets
36%

Pit Toilets
47%

Improvise
17%

Americans Injured Annually while Going to the Toilet

🚽🚽🚽🚽🚽🚽 = 60,000+

🚽 = 10,000 People

River Pollution in India by Percentage of Contaminant

Other Waste
30%

Human Waste
70%

Japanese Homes with Heated Toilet Seats

36%

patients whose porcelain fixtures collapsed underneath them, causing injuries to their bottoms, and their pride.

What You Can Do
Holding it is not really an option, though many children have tried. A study of children in schools in Sweden and England by doctors at the Sir James Spence Institute of Child Health at the University of Newcastle-upon-Tyne in England found that 62 percent of boys and 35 percent of girls in the United Kingdom avoided using their school toilets because they thought the toilets were dirty and unpleasant, or because the children were afraid of bullying. The authors of the study suggest that this leads to constipation, urinary tract infections and incontinence. Twenty-eight percent of Swedish children were found to have had similar aversions.

If you're large, and your toilet is old, the authors of the Scottish study recommend that you hover "continental style" over the seat instead of sitting on it.

Then again, you may wish to do away with the toilet altogether. Toilets seem like a necessity, but for a large portion of the world's population, they're a luxury. Of the world's 6 billion people, only 1 billion use flushing toilets connected to sewage systems. Another 2.8 billion use pit toilets, and the rest have no formal place at all to get rid of their waste. Of course, there are huge drawbacks to this too. The parasites and bacteria that grow in the waste would cause a health hazard that would far outweigh the benefits. Even today, human waste is a huge health concern. In India, for example, 70 percent of river pollution is a direct result of human waste.

The best bet is to keep the toilet, make sure the seats are kept in good condition, and turn the light on during your nighttime toilet visits.

TVs

A nd you thought bad programming was the only danger involved in owning a television set. Recent studies have linked inactivity due to excessive telly watching with obesity, diabetes and even stunted growth. These are not the only dangers of telly watching, however. Yes, that innocent-looking glowing box can injure, maim and even kill, and it doesn't have to be turned on to do so. The total damage? An estimated 10,224 British and 42,071 U.S. citizens harmed each year.

The same electricity that brings you the pictures of your favourite soap-opera stars—(it's okay, you can admit it)—carries with it a risk of fire. TVs accounted for an average of 621 fire incidents, 3 fatalities and 174 nonfatal injuries per year in England between 1994 and 1998. Adjusted for population, the number of television fires is similar in the United States, but more British citizens are killed when a telly catches fire—280 percent more, in fact. This is most likely because more U.S. than British manufacturers use fire-retardant materials in their TV casings.

The cause of telly fires is most often reported as "fault within the appliance" (87 percent). Does this mean televisions are inherently dangerous, ready and waiting to burst into flame? The experts are skeptical. "The coding and analysis of these general comments is hiding what appears to be a general assumption that a badly damaged telly must have been 'the cause' of the fire. The result is that a significant number of fires may be ascribed to TVs where the TV was not the source," the British Department of Trade and Industry reported.

Another problem with the television is that it is irresistible to children. The U.S. National Pediatric Trauma Registry warns that the number of children injured by falling televisions has more than doubled from the period for 1988 to 1993 and 1994 to 1999. Most of the victims are boys who are hurt when they try to climb furnishings to get to a telly. The authors of the television study believe that the increasing size of screens has worsened the tendencies of TVs to be front heavy.

Children are not the only victims of falling television sets. Janice Pennington, one of the models from the telly game show *The Price is Right*, was injured in 1994 when a television she was gesturing toward fell off a pedestal and hit her on the neck. She was stunned, but her injuries were not serious.

The height record for injury by a falling television may have been set in 1998 when a Brooklyn, New York, man was struck by a television that had fallen from a twelfth-storey window. The 5-in/12.7-cm portable broke his shoulder and gave him a gash on his head.

If you're not hurt by the set itself, pay close attention to the antenna. Quite a few hapless viewers have found themselves in the casualty ward after run-ins with antennae. The injuries range from scratched corneas from adjusting wire antennae a little too close to the face to falls from rooftops while adjusting larger antennae and satellite dishes. In one case, an entire Vietnamese family of five was electrocuted after their antenna fell onto a power line. They had been trying to improve the reception for the World Cup football tournament.

What You Can Do
You could go telly free, but then you'd never find out what happened to the cast of *Big Brother*, and you wouldn't want that.

To avoid the risk of fire, unplug your telly during electrical storms, be careful when dusting not to let any large pieces of lint get into the works, and don't clean the screen while the set is illuminated.

If you still have a television with a rooftop antenna, be very careful if you decide to make adjustments. Be sure that antennae and satellite dishes are far from electrical wires and are not where they are likely to topple if they are coated with ice. If you're still scared of your antenna, consider cable.

If you live in a major city and often find yourself among tall buildings, don't worry. The risk of a television set falling on your head is fairly slim, but you might want to carry a large brolly just in case.

Vacations/Holidays

When city life gets to be too much, city dwellers head to parks, lakes, mountains and tropical islands to enjoy the wonders of nature. That's when they remember why people started building cities in the first place. The greatest wonder of nature is that human beings managed to survive so long in it.

The main danger associated with holidays is that the people who take them are, by definition, not from the area they are visiting. That means they're not accustomed to the area's unique dangers, the weather, the terrain, the animals or the type of physical activity required to explore there. This should make people especially cautious—but hey, they're on holiday. Instead of being at attention, their guards are down.

This is why, for example, most of the people who die snorkelling on Australia's Great Barrier Reef are not Australians, but foreign tourists. Between 1995 and 1999, twenty people died while snorkelling in Queensland waters and all but two were tourists.

"A frequent observation I have made of many visitors is their tendency to have a '911 [999] mentality,'" wrote Ken Phillips, Grand Canyon National Park's search-and-rescue coordinator, in his foreword to the book *Over the Edge: Death in Grand Canyon*. "They often make the assumption that help will always be immediately forthcoming when they place themselves in harm's way."

In 1997, forty-five hundred visitors to the U.S. National Park System needed to be rescued. Fourteen thousand needed emergency medical aid, and three hundred died. (To put this in perspective, 350 million people visit the national parks each year, an area of 84 million acres.)

The parks claim victims in a stunning variety of ways, including falling into bubbling hot springs, snakebites, tumbling off cliffs, drinking contaminated water, dehydrating in desert heat, being crushed by falling rocks and freezing to death on the side of a mountain.

As with many things in life, however, the greatest dangers are not always the most dramatic. CNN recently ran a story warning people of a little-known beach danger: the sand.

"People who are in a recreational environment, such as on the beach, may be focusing their attention on other safety hazards," said Dr Bradley Maron of Brown University in Providence, Rhode Island, "most prominently water safety and drowning. They may be unaware of the hidden risks associated with digging holes in the beach."

Between 1996 and 2002, Dr Maron found that seven people had been killed on New England beaches while trapped in the sand. It took three hundred years to rack up that many shark attack deaths in the same area.

What You Can Do
If you're a pale, suburban office worker whose time outdoors is limited to the walk from your door to the letter box, it's probably not a good idea to jump straight into a hiking or diving holiday. Take the time to get in shape and practise the activity you'll be tackling in your time off.

CNN offers the following tips to avoid sand injuries: always choose a beach with a lifeguard; stay away from holes deeper than your knees; call for emergency help immediately if someone becomes trapped in the sand; and if someone is buried, keep other people away for safety.

Be careful if you put on a grass skirt. They're flammable. A 1983 study by P. Barss and K. Wallace, "Grass-Skirt Burns in Papua New Guinea," published in the *Lancet*, reported that 48 percent of burn cases admitted to Alotau Hospital, Papua New Guinea, over a four-year period were from grass skirts.

Vegetables

A ccording to the British Department of Trade and Industry, 11,632 people are injured each year by veggies.

How exactly are people harming themselves with salad fixings? Are they using them as weapons? Sometimes, as a matter of fact. In recent years, a number of people have been seriously wounded after being hit by flying potatoes fired from homemade potato guns. A number of victims have lost eyes, been blinded or suffered broken bones after a potato attack. A potato gun is a recent fad, and it involves putting a spud in a pipe 28 in/71.12 cm to 5 ft/1.52 m long, then igniting a flammable substance, like hair spray, at one end. It is nearly as dangerous as a real gun, and it can fire the vegetable at 1,000 feet/304.8 metres per second.

The beetroot is another root vegetable of which to be wary. Dr Colin Thomas reported to the BBC on a case involving a patient who came in complaining of blood in his urine, and another complaining of blood in his stool. Both patients underwent numerous medical pokes and prods, and various samples were sent off to labs. They finally discovered it was borscht, not blood, they were seeing.

Vegetables—beans, maize, peas—are also favourite items for children to insert into their noses and ears. Having a nose is pretty much taken for granted by adults, but for your two-year-old, it is still a relatively novel concept. Little Johnny just *has* to figure out how far that hole goes and what would fit in there.

"All casualty ward doctors who see children in their practices will have come across foreign bodies on occasion," wrote Lance Brown in *Pediatric Emergency Medicine Reports*. "Children seem to have boundless imagination when it comes to where they will position a foreign body and what they will use."

Dr Brown led a team of researchers who did an extensive survey of 85 reports in medical literature of foreign bodies in children's various orifices. The average age of the children was 2½, and one of the most common objects was food. If an object is pushed far enough up the nose, it can cause damage to nasal structures. Sometimes a child puts something up there, forgets it, and the spot becomes infected. Medical literature reveals a surprising number of cases of objects that were inserted into the nose and not discovered for some time. The *Ear, Nose and Throat Journal* reported on one case of a metal ring that had been lodged in a child's nose for four years and became embedded into the soft palate before it was discovered. The girl's mother brought her into a specialist because she had chronic bad breath.

But back to vegetables. The fact of the matter is, most vegetable injuries are not strictly caused by the vegetables themselves. The majority occur when people burn themselves while trying to boil them.

What You Can Do
Before you take the lid off the pot to look in on those yummy brussels sprouts, be sure the steam is not going to escape into your face. Take care when chopping carrots and onions. Keep your knives sharp. Although it may seem counterintuitive, a dull knife is more dangerous than a sharp one. You're more likely to put added pressure on a dull one and cause it to slip.

If your child puts maize in her nose, it is best not to go after it yourself. Instead, take her to the doctor. You might accidentally push it farther and cause damage. Bad breath could be a sign of something that has been left inside the nose.

Vegetable missiles can be deadly. If you feel you must keep a potato gun for your own protection, be sure that it is kept out of the reach of children. Using mashed potatoes could reduce the risk of injury, although long-term studies have not yet been conducted to verify this.

Vending Machines

You take a break from work and head to the treat machine in the lobby. You put in a few coins, select B-5 for a package of barbecue-flavored potato crisps with ridges, and watch as the spiral spins. The bag inches forward—and sticks. It is hanging on the edge, teasing you. So you bang the machine a little, and then a lot. Still nothing. If you could just tip the machine forward a little bit ... you could end up with 1,000 lb/453.6 kg of machine on your neck.

At least 35 Canadians have died and 140 others have been injured in such accidents since 1978, according to a Canadian coroner's report. The U.S. Consumer Product Safety Commission blames 37 deaths and 113 injuries between 1978 and 1995 on falling vending machines. Most vending-machine victims are young men—average age 19.8 years, according to the *Journal of Orthopedic Trauma*. Young males are apparently the most likely to rock and beat machines when they don't get their fizzy pop, and they're also the most likely to try to beat the system by tipping the machines to get free food.

One of the most unusual cases of death by vending machine occurred at a U.S. recreation centre's pool. A 10-year-old swimmer, dripping wet, walked up to a bank of three vending machines and dropped a coin into one of them. He began to shake violently, and a friend who tried to help received a shock when touching him. The boy was pronounced dead on arrival at the local hospital. It turned out that the machine had been moved so that it was sitting on top of the flex of another machine. That machine's flex was damaged, and extra voltage was sent into the frame of the machine. The wet boy acted as the earth.

If you manage to get away from a vending machine without being electrocuted or crushed, you are not out of the woods. You still run the risk of illness from the foodstuff.

A recent survey of both drinking water and flavored drinks from coin-operated vending machines in England found that 44 percent of the water samples contained coliform bacteria. Thirty-one flavored drinks were examined; 6 percent contained coliforms. A team of researchers in Taiwan studied 153 food specimens obtained from vending machines. They discovered that most of the food they sampled was unsatisfactory based on the standards for total microbial counts and total coliform counts established by the Department of Public Health. They also found that the sanitation control of vending machines examined was unsatisfactory in approximately 70 percent of the cases.

What You Can Do
The vending industry is doing what industries always do—it's printing warnings. Most North American vending-machine companies have placed warnings on the machines:

TIPPING OR ROCKING MAY CAUSE INJURY OR DEATH.

Those who stock, maintain and host the machines can do their parts as well. The machines should be regularly inspected to make sure that the flexes are not frayed, that the parts are kept clean, and that there is nothing wet on the ground. A moisture-absorbent, felt-topped, rubber-backed floor mat in front of the machine can help reduce slips on wet floors and also offer some protection from electric shock.

For a consumer, here's the best piece of advice: don't steal. Vending-machine spokespersons point out that most of the victims of vending-machine injuries are crushed during the attempted theft of fizzy drinks and chocolate bars. Put into perspective, in 1995, Americans bought 17 billion cans of fizzy pop from vending machines. In that same year, two people were killed by falling machines, both while trying to steal the drinks. So put your coins in the machine.

Vitamins

I f you have a phobia about biting the head off a Fred Flintstone chewable vitamin, you might not be as crazy as your friends think. (Then again, you might be.)

Vitamins are bad for your health? Possibly, if you take too many, or the wrong kind and in the wrong combination. A number of recent studies suggest that in our well-fed world we could be getting too much of a good thing. Diarrhoea, uncontrolled bleeding and nerve damage are but a few of the medical problems that can be caused by an overdose of vitamins.

Take vitamin A, for example. Karl Michaëlsson and his colleagues at University Hospital in Uppsala, Sweden, published the results of their study on vitamin A in the *New England Journal of Medicine* in 2003. They concluded that "vitamin A supplementation and food fortification in many Western countries may need to be reassessed." The researchers found a link between high levels of vitamin A and bone fractures, a result that supported two earlier studies on the subject. They followed the cases of 2,322 men over thirty years and found that those with the highest levels of serum retinol or vitamin A in the blood had the most bone fractures. The men with the most vitamin A were 1.6 times more likely to have fractures, and those with broken hips were 2.5 times more likely to be from the high-vitamin A group. Earlier studies have connected high levels of vitamin A with birth defects and liver problems.

The British Nutrition Foundation in 2001 warned the British public about an "extreme and dangerous fad which has come from the U.S.": vitamin injections. The group warned that overdosing on nonsoluble vitamins is easy to do and can lead to kidney disease, liver damage, jaundice, cramps, nosebleeds, blurred vision and even death. Meanwhile, both the U.S. and British food standards agencies in 2003 proposed banning chromium picolinate, common in diet supplements, amid concerns it could potentially cause cancer.

Even those who do not worry about overdosing on vitamins see a potential danger in their use. John Brewer, head of human performance and sports injury at Lilleshall National Sports Centre in Shropshire, England, told the BBC, "The only danger with vitamin pills is that they could be used as an excuse for a bad diet. People think that taking a few pills gives them an excuse to go out and eat rubbish."

What You Can Do
Dieticians believe there is little need for taking supplements. Instead, people can get all the nutrients they need by eating a well-balanced diet.

In 2000, for the first time in its history, the U.S. National Academy of Sciences set upper limits for safe amounts of vitamins C and E and the mineral selenium. The upper limit of C was set at .07 oz/2,000 mg; of E, .04 oz/1,000 mg; and 400 micrograms for selenium, a portion so small it can't be effectively measured in ounces.

Vitamins A, D, E and K are fat-soluble and can be stored in the body, so you do not need to take as much. Vitamin E can be found in sunflower seeds and nuts. Vitamins A and D are found in fortified milk and cheese. C and B vitamins are water-soluble and need to be replaced each day. They are found in most fruits and vegetables. The U.S. Food and Drug Administration says recommended vitamin C levels can be achieved by eating five servings of fruits and vegetables a day.

Finally, don't try to get your kids to take their vitamins (or medicine for that matter) by pretending they are sweets. When children get the idea that a sweetened, chewable vitamin is a sweet, they want to eat more, more, more. According to the magazine *Pediatrics for Parents*, over 2 percent of all calls received by poison control centres are related to vitamin overdoses. When children down a whole bottle of chewable vitamins, they put themselves at risk for iron toxicity, which could cause heart damage or stomach bleeding.

Walking

Take care when you lace up those shoes, because "Yea, you may be walking through the valley of the shadow of death." The fact is, as you cruise around on your Harley humming "Born to Be Wild," you're much safer than you are on a leisurely stroll. When it comes to methods of locomotion, a simple walk is one of the most likely to end in sudden death. Some 6,000 pedestrians die each year on America's roads. Walking accounts for about 1 out of every 6 traffic-related deaths. Motorcycles, meanwhile, account for only 2,100 deaths. Flying doesn't even come close. In 1996, airlines lost only 342 people (and about 15,000 cases a day). When you add it up, pedestrian accidents end the lives of more people than plane, train and ship accidents combined.

Even nonfatal road accidents are nasty. In a collision between a human body and a car, bet on the car. The typical auto accident victim needs four to six units of blood at hospital, whereas heart bypass surgery requires only one to six units.

This is not strictly a U.S. problem. Here is the annual international body count:

Australia: 2,017	Italy: 3,408	Russia: 11,787
Canada: 404	Japan: 2,783	South Africa: 4,122
China: 7,864	Korea: 6,073	Sri Lanka: 862
France: 5,090	Mexico: 9,500	United Kingdom:
Germany: 5,342	Romania: 1,422	1,799

Why does Russia outpace other nations in pedestrian deaths? During the Soviet period, few people owned personal vehicles. After the collapse of communism, that changed much more quickly than the Russian road grid could. In the words of the *Moscow Times*, "Driving habits have been improvised along the way."

Moscow has strict traffic laws ... on paper. They are not strictly enforced.

But Russia's problems are not that different from the rest of the world's. Even in the most highly motorised countries, roads that were built years ago continue to serve communities that have grown well beyond their initial design capacity. Russian communities are frustrated with local governments that reject their requests to install costly speed bumps. American municipalities face similar budget constraints. Have you ever sat at a red light and wondered just how much that light cost? Of course not, but I'll tell you anyway: Traffic lights cost between $60,000/£31,837 and $250,000/£132,654. Crossing central reservations (those mounds in the middle of dual carriageways that allow you to take a break halfway through) cost between $2,000/£1,061 and $20,000/£10,612. Then again, the average price of medical care for a victim of a pedestrian-car collision is $247,000/£131,062, the cost of one good traffic light.

What You Can Do
The most effective means of reducing pedestrian accidents would be to redesign the roads so that each has a footpath, well-marked zebra crossings and central reservations.

While you wait for your local planning commission to get to work on that, there are a few less ambitious things your city could try. It could, for example, increase the length of time people have to get across the road. Most city planners assume a person can travel 4 feet/1.22 meters per second. This is a bit brisk for most older citizens. A study done on older Americans in Los Angeles found that 27 percent could not make it across the road in the allotted time. In 1994, two women were killed in New York City trying to cross a 60-ft/18.29-m-wide intersection with a walk light that lasted only seven seconds. The Institute for Highway Safety suggests giving pedestrians a three-second head start at zebra crossings before turning vehicles get the green light.

Walking classes. Many schools offer their students instruction in pedestrian safety. Such courses have shown small benefits for half of those participating. Unfortunately, that means they had no benefit for the other half.

Don't walk drunk. An Australian researcher at the 2002 Pedestrian Seminar in Sydney reported that alcohol was involved in about a third of accidents in which a pedestrian was killed. Over half of the pedestrian accidents involving males aged 20 to 60 were alcohol-related.

Remember the lesson from primary school: Look both ways when crossing the road. Look to the left and then to the right, or maybe to the right and then to the left. It depends on what country you're in. This is another challenge for pedestrians. It can happen to anyone who travels to another country and is arrogant enough to think they still know how to cross the street. Even Winston Churchill was hit by a car in New York while looking the wrong way. The bottom line: "Yea, though you walk through the valley of the shadow of death, fear not." Just pay attention.

The Weekend

A ll week you slave away waiting for those two days when you can go out, injure yourself, and wind up in hospital. During the weekend, calls to emergency services increase, as do emergency hospital admissions, car accidents and hospital deaths.

A survey of emergency calls to the London Ambulance Service, which receives about 10,921 calls a week, shows that the largest number come in on Saturdays when doctors' surgeries are closed and normally sedentary people are out playing football full force without warming up first.

Middle-aged office workers go out and try to pick up on the sports they used to play ten or twenty years earlier. They often fail to take into consideration that they have aged, and that they have not been practising, or even doing much with their bodies besides flexing their fingers over a keyboard. They end up with strained muscles, knee and shoulder injuries, and tendonitis from repetitive strain.

Even veterinarians see their share of out-of-shape dogs with weekend sports injuries. Dogs, too, are vulnerable in their knees.

Weekends are hazardous to people throughout the world. A study by the Osaka University Graduate School of Medicine revealed that women are most likely to have heart attacks on Saturday. The researchers speculate that this is because Japanese women face added stress and responsibility on the weekends, compared with the work-week. Studies in Russia and Lithuania have shown an increase in deaths from accidents, violence and alcohol poisoning over the weekend. Researchers have also found a significant increase in heart disease deaths, all of which doctors suspect is caused by binge drinking on weekends.

Americans, too, binge on the weekends. This means more drunk drivers on the road, and more accidents. It also means the diet is out the window. A two-year study of dietary intake conducted by the Department of Nutrition at the University of North Carolina found that the average American consumes 82 more calories per day on weekends than on weekdays, with people aged 19 to 50 consuming an extra 115 calories. The proportion of energy from fat and alcohol also increases.

There is even a category of people who are almost allergic to weekends. Two Dutch researchers have identified what they call "leisure sickness." It could also be called "Okay-I-have-time-to-be-ill-now-itis." It tends to affect people who are perfectionists and who carry a large workload. They work hard all week, and the minute they have a long weekend or holiday, they come down with a terrible flu. If the Dutch study is representative, leisure sickness affects about 3 percent of the population. The researchers speculate that people who are at risk of leisure illnesses have trouble adapting to time off. Relaxing actually causes them stress. Another possibility is that they are so consumed with work that they are not able to read the signs of exhaustion and illness from their bodies until they calm down for a while.

There is also a category of headache sufferers who find themselves with ice packs on their foreheads every Saturday. For migraine sufferers, it is often not stress, but rather the relaxation after having been stressed, that brings on a headache. Thus, weekend headaches.

If you end up in the hospital after a weekend drinking or sporting binge, there is something you should know. Your chances of survival are better if you're admitted to a hospital on a weekday than on a weekend. Two researchers from Sunnybrook and Women's College Health Sciences Centre in Canada tracked all 3.8 million admissions to Ontario's acute-care hospitals over a 10-year period. They found higher mortality rates among twenty-three of the top one hundred causes of death, including pulmonary embolism, kidney failure, certain heart diseases and numerous cancers. A separate study of 158,136 patients admitted to twenty-eight hospitals in the U.S. midwest found that the odds of in-hospital death were 9 percent higher for weekend admissions than for patients admitted midweek. The Canadian researchers blame differences in staffing over the weekends. The people who get stuck with the Saturday-night shift are often less senior, less supervised and have to cope with fewer staff.

What You Can Do

You could change your work schedule around so that you have Wednesdays and Thursdays off, but then you'd just have the same problems on Wednesdays and Thursdays (though at least the first aid you receive might be a bit more thorough). Instead, the best bet is to practise moderation. When you take your dog out for a jog on the weekend, be sure you both are up to the task. Start out with a walk before moving up to a run. Regular exercise during the week will also be a great help. If you do take part in sports or physical activities on the weekend, be sure to warm up.

You know this one already, but binge drinking on the weekend can lead to accidents, illness and embarrassing photographs being passed around the office on Monday.

If you're prone to weekend illnesses, you might try exercising on Friday evening. According to the scientists who identified leisure sickness, this will "facilitate the physiological transition from activity to rest." If you can manage it, an even more effective method is to shift your priorities and relax about work. Make your family and leisure time more of a priority.

Bibliography

"Abolishing Autumn: Genetically Engineered Enzyme Cytokinin Makes Perennials of Annual Plants." *The Economist*, January 13, 1996. **"Abuse of Nurses in Spotlight."** *Africa News Service*, May 15, 2001. **"Action Pledged to Cut Farm Deaths."** *BBC News*, June 6, 1999. **Adams, Cecil.** "Can Trees Live Forever?" *Straight Dope*, April 27, 1990. **"Agency Warns of Vitamins Danger."** *Evening Mail*, May 8, 2003. **"Aging Barbie Dolls May Pose Health Hazard, Researcher Says."** CNN, August 24, 2000. **Ahuja, Anjana.** "The Hand You're Dealt." *Times* (UK), March 13, 2002. **Airport Wildlife Hazard Mitigation Homepage.** *http://wildlife-mitigation.tc.faa.gov/public_html/index.html.* **Ali, K. and J. Spinks.** "No Tea Until Three?" *Injury Prevention*, 2003, vol. 9. **"All Dressed Up Like the Dog's Dinner (Can of Dog Food Explodes at Tesco Store)."** *Eurofood*, March 29, 2001. **Allen, Sandra K. and Robert R. Johnson.** "A Study of Hazards Associated with Playgrounds." *Journal of Environmental Health*, June 1, 1995. **Alliance for Consumer Fire Safety in Europe.** *http://www.acfse.org.* **Allison, Rebecca.** "Women Killed by Lighting Striking the Metal in Bra." *Independent*, October 28, 1999. **Alves, D.W. et al.** "Effect of Lunar Cycle on Temporal Variation in Cardiopulmonary Arrest in Seven Emergency Departments During 11 Years." *European Journal of Emergency Medicine*, September 2003. **American Medical Association**, Science News Update, *http://www.ama-assn.org/sci-pubs/sci-news.* **Aminzadeh, Faranak, et al.** "Utilization of Bathroom Safety Devices, Patterns of Bathing and Toileting, and Bathroom Falls in a Sample of Community Living Older Adults." *Technology & Disability*; 2000, vol. 13, issue 2. **"And Finding Swallowed Coins."** *Child Health Alert*, November 1, 1994. **Anderson, W.P. et al.** "Pet Ownership and Risk Factors for Cardiovascular Disease." *Medical Journal of Australia*, September 7, 1992. **Andreou, G. et al.** "Handedness, Asthma and Allergic Disorders: Is there an association?" Psychology, Health and Medicine, February 2002. **"Animal Bites Can Cause Nasty Infection: Expert."** *Xinhua News Agency*, March 20, 1998. **Appleson, Gail.** "Lightning Strikes Queen Elizabeth's Garden Party." Reuters, July 23, 1996. **Arendt, Y. D. and F. Kershbaumer.** "Injury and Overuse Pattern in Professional Dancers." *Z Orthop Ihre Grenzgeb*, May–June 2003. **Armbrust, Roger.** "Equity Moves on with Production, Disney World Talks." *Back Stage*, August 11, 2000. **Asbell, Bernard.** *What They Know About You.* New York: Random House, 1991. **Association of Emergency Physicians.** *http://www.aep.org/.* **"Asthma and Allergy Update."** *Medical Post*, April 10, 2001. **"At Least Six Injured as Car Runs into Café Terrace in German City."** *Associated Press Worldstream*, June 21, 2003. **"Autopsy Completed on Elevator Accident Victim."** *CBC*, January 23, 2004. **Aydin, P. et al.** "Effect of Wind Instrument Playing on Intraocular Pressure." *Journal of Glaucoma*, August 2000. **Baca, Kelley.** "500 Evacuated From DTC Building After Fan Overheats." *Rocky Mountain News*, June 19, 1999. **Bailey, Ronald.** "Forever Young: The New Scientific Search for Immortality." *Reason*, August 1, 2002. **Bain, Helen.** "Minister Against Cellphone Driver Ban." *Press* (Canterbury, New Zealand), October 12, 1999. **Baker, Robert.** "Evil Under the Scum." *Independent*, September 9, 1999. **Barber, Bethany.** "Garbage Collection Rated One of the Most Dangerous Jobs, Study Says." *Waste Age*, May 1999. **Bardehle, D. et al.** "Home and Leisure Accidents in Europe: Survey and hospital data." *Injury Control and Safety Promotion*, 2001, vol. 8, no. 4. **Barker-Griffith, A. E. et al.** "Potato Gun Ocular Injury." *Ophthalmology*, March 1998. **Barnett, M. J. et al.** "Day of the Week Intensive Care Admission and Patient Outcomes: A Multisite Regional Evaluation." *Medical Care*, June 2002. **Barr, Noreen.** "Living: Fashion Victims: Are Your Clothes Making You Ill?" *Sunday Mercury*, March 18, 2001. **Barron, Alsdair.** "Making Space a Safer Place (European Space Agency)." *European*, September 26, 1996. **Barron, Susannah.** "Style: A Time to Dye: Just When You Thought It Was Safe to Go Back in the Bathroom." *The Guardian*, November 5, 1999. **Barss, P. and K. Wallace.** "Grass-Skirt Burns in Papua New Guinea." *The Lancet*, April 2, 1983. **Bassett, M. and A. H. Arild.** "Hot Surface Temperatures of Domestic Appliances." *Injury Control and Safety Promotion*, September 2002. **"Beards a risk to food safety—British Tribunal."** *Reuters*, March 5, 2001. **Bellandi, Deanna.** "Backpacks' Injuries Detailed in Study." *Associated Press*, January 6, 2003. **BBC News,** *http://news.bbc.co.uk.* **Beresford, Heather.** "Health Zone: Danger at Work—Is Your Job a Health Hazard?" *Mirror* (UK), November 29, 2001. **Berger, Joanne.** "Stand and Decipher." *Family Practice News*, June 1, 2000. **Bergman, A. B. et al.** "Mobilizing for Pedestrian Safety: An Experiment in Community Action." *Injury Prevention*, 2002, vol. 8. **Bergstrom, E. and U. Bjornstig.** "School Injuries. Epidemiology and Clinical Features of 307 Cases Registered at a Hospital During One School Year." *Scandinavian Journal of Primary Health Care*, September 9, 1991. **"Beware Crusty Bagels and Other Sharp Foods."** *Environmental Nutrition*, June 1, 1999. **Bierman, Noah.** "Safety Device Falls on Trash Hauler, Killing Him." *Palm Beach Post*, June 12, 1999. **"Biological Basis for Creativity Linked to Mental Illness."** *Biotech Week*, October 29, 2003. **Birchard, Karen.** "Watching TV Sports Can Be a Health Hazard." *Medical Post*, September 8, 1999. **Blake, John.** "Too Much Protection? Better Safe Than Sorry Has Become a Modern-Day Mantra for Many Parents." *Atlanta Constitution*, June 14, 2001. **Blakemore, Sophie.** "Frustrated Patients' Violence Has Dropped." *Birmingham Post*, July 17, 2003. **Blight, Jayne and Louise Hancock.** "Killeto Heels." *Sunday Mirror* (UK), November 4, 2001. **Bollen, K. A.** "Temporal Variations in Mortality: A Comparison of U.S. Suicides and Motor Vehicle Fatalities, 1972–1976." *Demography*, February 1983. **Booker, Jarrod.** "Car Injures Five at Picnic Table." *Press* (Canterbury, New Zealand), January 5, 2002. **Bowles, Pete.** "Danger Often Falls from the Sky." *Newsday*, May 29, 2003. **"Boxer Shorts Save the Day."** *Evening Mail*, August 4, 2000. **"Boys Shorten Moms' Lives."** Week, May 31, 2002. **Brady, Erik.** "Schools Routinely Limit Risk." *USA Today*, April 26, 2002. **Bremberg, S. and C. Gerber.** "Injuries at School. Influence of Schoolmate Interaction." ACTA Paediatrica Scandinavica, May 1988. **Brisman, J. et al.** "The Incidence of Respiratory Symptoms in Female Swedish Hairdressers." *American Journal of Industrial Medicine*, December 2003. **"Britain: Don't Drink and Fry."** *Associated Press*, August 23, 1999. **British Association for Accident and Emergency Medicine.** *http://www.baem.org.uk/home.html.* **Brook, Judith S. et al.** "Older Sibling Correlates of Younger Sibling Drug Use in the Context of Parent-Child Relations." *Genetic, Social and General Psychology Monographs*, November 1, 1999. **Brooke, James.** "Japan Makes New Pitch to Lure Americans." *New York Times*, September 28, 2003. **Brown, Lance.** "A Literature-Based Approach to the Identification and Management of Pediatric Foreign Bodies." *Pediatric Emergency Medicine Reports*, September 2002. **Brown, Tom.** "Boston Escalator Accident Injures 23." *Reuters*, February 26, 1996. **Buehrer, Jack.** "Myth: Christmas Trees a Fire Hazard." *News-Messenger*, December 17, 2003. **"Bugs in City Tap Water, But It's Safe."** *Mirror* (UK), June 18, 1999. **"Bumps, Bruises and Backaches—Health Hazards of Holidays."** *CNN*, December 25, 1998. **Burke, Michael G.** "Injury from Falling TVs a Significant Problem." *Contemporary Pediatrics*, April 2001. **Burnham, John C.** "Why Did the Infants and Toddlers Die? Shifts in Americans' Ideas of Responsibility for Accidents—From Blaming to Engineering." *Journal Of Social History*, June 1, 1996. **Burrell, Diana.** "Weekend Woes." *Psychology Today*, July 1, 2001. **Byhring, S. and K. Bo.** "Musculoskeletal Injuries in the Norwegian National Ballet: a prospective cohort study." *Scandinavian Journal of Medicine and Science in Sports*, December 2002. **"Candle Danger."** *Press* (Canterbury, New Zealand), December 17, 2001. **Cameron, Amy.** "The Debt Bomb," *Maclean's*, December 10, 2001. **Campbell, Sophie.** "Travel, It's a Hole New World." *Sunday Telegraph* (UK), November 15, 1998. **Canada's Safety Council.** *http://www.safety-council.org/.* **Canadian Association of Emergency Physicians.** *http://www.caep.ca/.* **Canadian Network for Health in the Arts.** *http://web.idirect.com/~cnha/index.html.* **Canned Food Information Service (Australia).** *http://www.cannedfood.org/.* **Carter, Rick.** "Mattel Will Phase Out Petroleum-Based Plastics." *Industrial Maintenance and Plant Operations*, February 1, 2000. **Carroll, Rebecca.** "Yes, We Have Some Bananas, But Only One Variety and That's the Problem." *AP Worldstream*, July 15, 2003. **Carson, Nick.** "Out for a Walk in the Country? Beware Low-Flying Buzzards." *Birmingham Post*, July 24, 2003. **"Ceiling Fan Starts Fire That Leads to Death of Dogs, Cats."** *Baton Rouge Sunday Advocate*, August 22, 1999. **"Cell Phone Figures Disputed."** *United Press International*, May 8, 2001. **Centre de Recherche et d'Information des Organisations de Consommateurs.** *http://www.oivo-crioc.org/fr/.* **Cerabino, Frank.** "Unsafe at Any Speed: Scooters Could Be Public Enemy No. 1." *Palm Beach Post*, March 1, 2002. **Cerhan, J. R. et al.** "Handedness and Mortality Risk in Older Women." *American Journal of Epidemiology*, August 15, 1994. **Chapman, Dan.** "Cell Phones Join Long List of Driving Distractions." *Atlanta Journal-Constitution*, May 3, 2001. **Chapman, S. and S. Morrell.** "Barking Mad? Another Lunatic Hypothesis Bites the Dust." *British Medical Journal*, December 23–30, 2000. **C-Health (Canada),** *http://chealth.canoe.ca.* **Check, Erika.** "Danger: Playing with Fire." *Newsweek*, December 11, 2000. **"Cheerleading Injuries on the Rise."** *All Things Considered*, National Public Radio, March 9, 1996. **Chenet, L. et al.** "Daily Variations in Deaths in Lithuania: The Possible Contribution of Binge Drinking." *International Journal of Epidemiology*, August 2001. **Chi, L. et al.** "Electrical Injuries from Graphite Fishing Rods." *Burns*, December 1996, vol. 22, issue 8. **"China Tea Production Picks Up."** *Xinhua News Agency*, May 18, 1998. **"Chinese Banks Disinfecting Their Cash Amid SARS Fears."** *Associated Press Worldstream*, April 29, 2003. **"Chinese Researchers to Recommend Two Child Policy."** *Kyodo News Service*, September 26, 2003. **Claiborne, William.** "Chicago Faces Up to Falling Facades." *Washington Post*, July 10, 2000. **Clark, Tom.** "Nosocomial Infection in Britain's Hospitals." *BBI Newsletter*, July 2001. **Clavarne, Anthony.** "Do We Need Facial Hair?" *Independent*, September 23, 1996. **Cleveland Clinic Health Information Center.** *http://www.clevelandclinic.org.* **Cohen, Aryeh Dean.** "Local Authorities: Labs Expose Pupils to Hazardous Chemicals." *Jerusalem Post*, January 12, 1998. **Cohen, Jamie.** "Losing Control? Study Finds Sense of Control Affects Heart Health." *ABC News*, September 4, 2002. **Cohl, H. Aaron.** *Are We Scaring Ourselves to Death?* New York: St. Martin's Press, 1997. **"Coin-Throwing Fan's Sentence Quashed."** *BBC News*, April 19, 2001. **"Coins Kill Birds: Zoo Issues a Plea to Public."** *Wisconsin State Journal*, January 26, 2002. **Coleman, Joseph.** "Japan Wakes Up to High Accidental Death Rate for Kids." *Associated Press*, May 26, 1999. **Collman, James P.** *Naturally Dangerous: Surprising Facts About Food, Health, and the Environment.* Sausalito, CA: University Science Books, 2001. **Conan, Neal.** "Interview: McKeel Hagerty Discusses the Dangers of Eating While Driving." *Talk of the Nation*, National Public Radio, August 8, 2002. **Conan, Neal.** "Profile: Extent of Japan's Push for a Germ-Free Environment and Whether It Could Have a Dangerous Result." *Weekly Edition*, National Public Radio, March 18, 2000. **Connor, Steve.** "Pretty Boys Outscore Men with a Strong Jaw." *Independent*, August 27, 1998. **Cooper, Melanie.** "Tall Order." *New Scientist*, June 14, 2001. **Cornish, L. S. et al.** "Automatic Dishwasher Detergent Poisoning: Opportunities for Prevention." *Australia New Zealand Journal of Public Health*, June 1996. **Cosgrove, Christine.** "Pets Contribute to Good Health." *CNN*, February 17, 2000. **Cosio, M. Q. and G. W. Taylor.** "Soda Pop Vending Machine Injuries: An Update." *Journal of Orthopedic Trauma*, 1992, vol. 6, issue 2. **Coughlan, Andy.** "Sea Birds Drop Radioactivity on Land." *New Scientist*, January 4, 2003. **Curtis, Tom.** "Sunny Days Equal Tears Before Bedtime." *Scotland on*

Sunday, March 23, 2003. **Crossland, Bernard.** "Something Must (Not) Be Done." *Economist*, September 13, 2003. **Cutlip, Kimbra.** "Lightning: Serial Killer from the Sky." *Weatherwise*, July 17, 1998. **Dally, Michelle.** "Lessons from the E.R." *Health*, May 2002. **Dane, S. and K. Gumustekin.** "Handedness in Deaf and Normal Children." *International Journal of Neuroscience*, August 2002. **"Danger Jobs."** *Times* (UK), November 28, 2002. **"Danger Lurks in the Office."** *Daily Record*, October 16, 2001. **Davis, Barker.** "Kendall's Injury Not the Unkindest Cut." *Washington Times*, July 17, 2003. **Davis, Fiona.** "Avoiding Disaster." *Stage Directions*, May 2002. **"Deckhand Electrocuted Playing a Computer Game on a Fishing Boat."** *AP Worldstream*, November 29, 2001. **"Deer-Vehicle Collisions are Numerous and Costly. Do Countermeasures Work?"** *Road Management and Engineering Journal*, May 12, 1997. **Del Valle, Christina.** "Killer Heels." *Newsday*, October 6, 1997. **DePaolis, Mark.** "Beauty Is A Fine Thing, but Don't Let It Get in the Way of Your Personal Safety." *Minneapolis Star Tribune*, May 30, 1997. **DePaulo, B. M. et al.** *New Directions in Helping: Vol 2. Help Seeking*. New York: Academic Press, 1983. **Department of Trade and Industry (UK),** 23rd Report of the Home Accidents & Leisure Surveillance System. London, 1999. *http://www.dti.gov.uk/homesafetynetwork/ha_stats.htm*. **Derbyshire, David.** "Painting Is Riskier Than Joining Army." *Daily Telegraph* (UK), August 16, 2002. **Dewar, Heather.** "Tap Water Is Not Always Safe to Drink, Study Finds." *Knight Ridder*, May 9, 1996. **Di Scala, C. et al.** "Causes and Outcomes of Pediatric Injuries Occurring at School." *Journal of School Health*, November 1997.**"Dirty Money Harbors Bacterial Dangers."** *Science News*, June 2, 2001.**Disaster Center, The.** *http://www.disastercenter.com/*. **"Disney Technician Who Fell 42 Feet While Testing Aladdin Special Effects Dies."** *AP Worldstream*, May 19, 2003. **Distasio, Carol.** "Protecting Yourself from Violence in the Workplace." *Nursing*, June 1, 2002. **Dixon, J. J. et al.** "Severe Burns Resulting from an Exploding Teat on a Bottle of Infant Formula Milk Heated in the Microwave Oven." *Burns*, May 1997, vol. 23. **"Do Bras Cause Breast Cancer?"** *Contemporary Women's Issues Database*, April 1, 1997.**Dobson, Roger.** "Health Weather Forecasts to Be Piloted in England." *British Medical Journal*, January 13, 2001. **Donaldson, G. C.** "Cold Related Mortalities and Protection Against Cold in Yakutsk, Eastern Siberia: Observation and Interview Study." *British Medical Journal*, October 10, 1998. **"Don't Ignore Boredom as a Cause."** *USA Today* (Magazine), August 2001. **"Don't Sniff the Compost."** *Waikato Times* (New Zealand), December 7, 2000. **Dorevitch, S. and D. Marder.** "Occupational Hazards of Municipal Solid Waste Workers." *Occupational Medicine*, January–March 2001. **Downey, Charles.** "Officials Warn Against Taking Fido's Pills." *CNN*, August 25, 2000. **Ibid.** "Sweet-Smelling Danger?" *WebMD. http://mywebmd.com/content/Article/14/1668_50139.html*. **Dreyfuss, Ira.** "Golfing Can Make the Back Hurt." *Associated Press*, March 26, 1998. **Driver, Deana.** "Canadian Farm Injuries a Crisis." *Medical Post*, August 8, 2000. **"Drivers Who Listen to Fast Music May Drive Same Way."** *Washington Times*, March 15, 2002. **"DTI: Beware—Your Clothing Could Be the Death of You."** *Telecomworldwire*, February 19, 1997. **Dugan, Kevin.** E-mail correspondence with author, December 2002. **Duke, James.** "Death by Pharmaceuticals?" *Better Nutrition*, June 2001. **Dumas, Bob.** "Troubled Waters: Suction Entrapment Is an Emotional Issue." *Pool and Spa News*, October 24, 2003. **Dymski, Gary.** "Prevent Laundry Room Floods, Fires." *Newsday*, January 21, 2003. **"E Features—Lifespans."** *The Sacramento Zoo. http://www.saczoo.com/3_kids/8_lifespans/_lifespans_zooanimals.htm*. **Easterbrook, Gregg.** *The Progress Paradox: How Life Gets Better While People Feel Worse*. New York: Random House, 2003. **Ebersole, Rene.** "Thrills and Spills." *Current Science*, October 26, 2001. **Edelman, Susan.** "Old Glass Poses Threat." *Record*, November 11, 1993. **Efrati, Y. et al.** "Oral Blast Injury Caused by an Accident." *Annals of Otology, Rhinology and Laryngology*, July 1993, vol. 102. **Egan, Danielle.** "A Furry Flurry." *Canadian Business*, March 4, 2002. **Eisenberg, Jennifer.** "Russian Women Widen Gap With Men." *WE/Mbi*, January 23, 1994. **Eisenberg, P. et al.** "Lunar Phases Are Not Related to the Occurrence of Acute Myocardial Infarction and Sudden Cardiac Death." *Resuscitation*, February 2003. **"Elderly Driver Smashes into Restaurant Diners, Injuring Three."** *Associated Press Worldstream*, July 18, 2003. **"Elevator Death in Hong Kong."** *Associated Press*, January 3, 2002. **"Elevator Surfing Deadly Game for Kids."** *Cincinnati Post*, July 5, 1996. **"Employment: Better Protection for Self-Employed Workers."** *European Report*, October 30, 2002. **Englehardt, J. D. et al.** "Analytical Predictive Bayesian Assessment of Occupational Injury Risk: Municipal Solid Waste Collectors." *Risk Analysis*, October 2003. **English, Paul.** "You've Had Your Chips." *Daily Record*, January 11, 2003. **"Escalator accident."** *Daily News* (Taranaki, New Zealand), September 21, 2002. **Escoffery, C. T. and S. E. Shirley.** "Fatal Head Trauma From Tree Related Injuries." *Medical Science Law*, October 2001. **European Consumer Safety Association.** *http://www.ecosa.org/*. **Evans, Rhodri.** "Poll Hammers Home DIY Safety." *Western Mail* (Cardiff, Wales), August 22, 2003. **Fagan, A. A. and J. M. Najman.** "Association Between Early Childhood Aggression and Internalizing Behavior for Sibling Pairs." *Journal of the American Academy of Child and Adolescent Psychiatry*, September 2003. **"Falling Table Kills Five Year Old."** *Associated Press*, February, 1, 2001. **"Family Sues Coke Over Man's Death."** *Toronto Star*, July 12, 2001. **Farabee, Charles R.** "Butch." *Death, Daring and Disaster: Search and Rescue in the National Parks*. Lanham, MD: Roberts Rinehart Publishers, 1998. **"Fed: Elderly Dominate Snorkeling Fatalities."** *AAP General News* (Australia), June 17, 1999. **"Fed: Falling Coconuts a Health Hazard in Pacific."** *AAP General News* (Australia), February 4, 2001. **Feldman, W. et al.** "Prospective Study of School Injuries: Incidence, Types, Related Factors and Initial Management." *Canadian Medical Association Journal*, December 15, 1983. **Feris, Melanie-Ann.** "It's Murder on the Runways at South Africa's Airports." *Cape Argus* (South Africa), September 1, 2003. **Fernandez, Bob.** "Agency Finds Health, Safety Violations at U.S. Mint's Philadelphia Plant." *Knight Ridder*, February 20, 2002. **"Finland Leads Western Europe in Accidental Injury and Death."** *Helsingin Sanomat* (International Edition), September 25, 2000. **"Firemen Free Trapped Teen from Washing Machine with Liquid Soap."** *AP Worldstream*, September 5, 2003. **"Five Caught in Mall Escalator Mishap."** *Hong Kong Standard*, January 11, 1999. **"Five Killed in Vietnam While Adjusting TV Antenna."** *Associated Press*, July 6, 1998. **Fleishman, Sandra.** "Swing Time." *Newsday*, June 20, 2001. **Fletcher, David.** "Nursing Is Most Dangerous Job." *Daily Telegraph* (UK), December 8, 1997. **"Flu Death Toll Rises to 26 in Russia."** *Itar-Tass*, February 12, 1997. **"Focus: Lightning Strikes Cause Fear Under Brazilian Skies."** *Kyodo World News Service*, February 2, 2001. **Foley, Michael J.** "Case of the Lethal Candy Machine." *Electrical Construction and Maintenance*, January 1, 2002. **Folkenberg, Judy.** "Pet Ownership—Risky Business?" *FDA Consumer*, April 1, 1990. **Foreman, Judy.** "Pet Talk: Pets Bring Disease Risk as Well as Pleasure." *Minneapolis Star Tribune*, May 28, 2000. **Fox, Mark.** "DIY Shows Should Have Health Warnings On Them." *Mail on Sunday* (UK), March 18, 2001. **Fradkin, A. J. et al.** "Warm Up Practices of Golfers: Are They Adequate?" *British Journal of Sports Medicine*, April 2001. **Fragar, L. J. and R. C. Franklin.** "The Health and Safety of Australia's Farming Community." *Farm Health and Safety Joint Research Venture*, 2000. **Franklin, Howard.** "Urban Sprawl and Public Health." *Public Health Reports*, May 1, 2002. **Franzese, Christine B.** "Delayed Diagnosis of a Pediatric Airway Foreign Body: Case Report and Review of the Literature." *Ear, Nose & Throat Journal*, September 2002. **French, David.** *Everything Is Bad for You*. Naperville, IL: Sourcebooks, Inc., 2002. **Fukunishi, K. et al.** "Characteristics of Bath-Related Burns in Japan." *Burns*, May 1999. **"Full Moon Not Linked to Behavior."** *Nutrition Health Review*, September 22, 1989. **Furedi, Frank.** *Culture of Fear*. London: Continuum, 1997. **Ibid.** "You Can't Ban Accidents." *Spiked*, August 24, 2001. **"Garden Gnome Liberation Front Strikes Paris Show."** *CNN.com*, April 13, 2000. **"Garden Gnomes Meet Ignominious Fate at Aussie Bank."** *Reuters*, July 31, 2000. **"Garden Grenade."** *Dominion* (Wellington, New Zealand), June 25, 2002. **Gash, Barbara.** "Here's to Safe Sewing." *Detroit Free Press*, November 11, 2001. **Gergen, K. et al.** "Obligation, Donor Resources, and Reactions to Aid in Three Cultures." *Journal of Personality and Social Psychology*, vol. 31, 1975. **"Geri Warned Over Vitamin Jabs."** *BBC News*, May 16, 2001. **Gibson, Lydia.** "How Safe Is Your House?" *Professional Builder*, February 1998. **Gillette, Becky.** "A Burning Dilemma." *E. The Environmental Magazine*, November 1998. **Glassner, Barry.** *The Culture of Fear: Why Americans Are Afraid of the Wrong Things*. New York: Basic Books, 1999. **Ibid.** "It's Hard to Tell, but Teen Violence is on the Decline." *Palm Beach Post*, August 14, 1999. **Golden, N. H.** "Osteoporosis Prevention: A Pediatric Challenge." *Archives of Pediatrics & Adolescent Medicine*, 2000, vol. 154, issue 6. **"Golf Ball Epilepsy."** *Australian Broadcasting Company*, January 26, 2000. **Gordon, Richard.** *Great Medical Disasters*. New York: Barnes & Noble Books, 1988. **Graedon, Joe and Teresa Graedon.** "The Perils of Eating Poppy Seeds." *Buffalo News*, July 7, 1998. **Graham, C. J. et al.** "Left-Handedness as a Risk Factor for Unintentional Injury in Children." *Pediatrics*, December 1993. **Graham, Lawrence.** "Stage Rigging 101." *Sound and Video Contractor*, October 1, 2002. **Green, Caroline.** "Property: Accidents will Happen." *Independent on Sunday*, May 24, 1998. **Grein, Robert.** "No Smoke Without Fire: Aggro Fear as Yobs Turn Screw." *Daily Record*, April 23, 1998. **Grice, Ayesha.** "Full Moon Madness." *Essence*, August 1, 1993. **Griego, R. D. et al.** "Dog, Cat and Human Bites: A Review." *Journal of the American Academy of Dermatology*, December 1995. **Grimes, David.** "Attack of the Killer Bagels." *Sarasota Herald-Tribune*, February 9, 2003. **Groves, Bob.** "NOW WHAT!!??" *Record* (Bergen County, NJ), March 1, 1993. **Guest, Ted and Richard J. Newman.** "Product Paranoia." *U.S. News and World Report*, February 24, 1992. **Guide to Working with Controlled Products in Visual Arts.** Ottawa, Canada: University of Ottawa, June 2003. **Guthrie, Patricia.** "Ouch! That's Going to Hurt." *Atlanta Journal-Constitution*, June 13, 2000. **Habib, Marlene.** "Weighing the Consequences." *Toronto Star*, September 22, 2000. **Haines, P. S. et al.** "Weekend Eating in the United States Is Linked with Greater Energy, Fat and Alcohol Intake." *Obesity Research*, August 2003. **"Hair Dyes and Cancer."** *Health News and Review*, 1993. **Hamilton, Linda.** "Dance Camp RX for Overworked Bodies." *Dance Magazine*, July 2000. **Harder, B.** "Antibiotics Fed to Animals Drift in Air." *Science News*, July 5, 2003. **Harper, Jennifer.** "Not to Put Too Fine a Point on It, but Let's Be Legible." *Washington Times*, January 21, 1998. **Harré, Niki et al.** "New Zealand Children's Involvement in Home Activities that Carry a Burn or Scald Risk." *Injury Prevention*, 1998, vol. 4. **Harris, Alan.** "Carnival Yob Blinds Ashley." *Coventry Evening Telegraph*, June 13, 2001. **Harris, Catherine.** "Drive Behind Ban on Cellphone Use in Cars." *Press* (Canterbury, New Zealand), March 16, 2001. **Harris, Francis.** "International: Germans Battle on the Gnome Front." *Sunday Telegraph* (UK), July 5, 1998. **Harrison, Angela.** "Is Fear Stopping Playground Fun?" *BBC News*, September 26, 2003. **"Harry Hurt by Slamming Door."** *Evening Telegraph* (UK), April 7, 2001. **Hartston, William.** "At Long Last, the Safe Tea Cosy." *Independent*, April 5, 1996. **Hatcher, S.** "Debt and Deliberate Self-Poisoning." *British Journal of Psychiatry*, January 1994. **Haubrich, William S.** *Medical Meanings: A Glossary of Word Origins*. Philadelphia: American College of Physicians, 1997. **Havel, Václav.** "Cities Rated Safer Than Suburbs." *Futurist*, July 1, 1995. **Havender, William R. and Roger Columbe** "Does Nature Know Best? Natural Carcinogens and Anticarcinogens in America's Food." *American Council on Science and Health Booklets*, December 1996. **Hawkins, Kenneth.** "Spark from Fan Started Fire." *Sarasota Herald-Tribune*, May 10, 2001. **Hayes, Jack.** "Blowing Away the Ceiling Fan Myths." *Saturday Evening Post*, September 1, 1987. **"Head Injury Risks from Overhead Luggage."** *Air Safe Journal*, September 7, 1999. **Health and Food** (Belgium). *http://www.healthandfood.be/indexhffr.html*. **"Health: Forget Vitamin Pills—Eat Your Greens."** *BBC News*, June 9, 1998. **Heath, S. E. and M. Champion.** "Human Health Concerns from Pet Ownership after a Tornado." *Prehospital Disaster Medicine*, January–March 1996. **Heath, S. E. et al.** "Human and Pet-Related Risk Factors for Household Evacuation Failure During a Natural Disaster." *American Journal of Epidemiology*, April 1, 2001. **"Heel Warning on Rail Crossings."** *Dominion* (New Zealand), August 17, 2001. **Henderson, Evan.** "The Buzzzz on Ssssummer Safety." *Daily News* (Los Angeles), May 28, 2001. **Henderson, Mark.** "Scientists Close in on Cause of Troubled Genius." *Times* (UK), June 16, 2003. **Hendrickson, Robert.** *QPB Encyclopedia of Word and Phrase Origins*. New York: Facts on File, 1997. **Herman, Steve.** "Candle Power." *Global Cosmetic Industry*, February 2003. **Hetts, Suzanne and Daniel Estep.** "Tread Softly When Dealing with Cats." *Denver Rocky Mountain News*, April 8, 2002. **Heubusch, Kevin.** "Standing Tall (Average Height of Americans)." *American Demographics*, April 1, 1997. **"Hidden Dangers of Dog Stroking."**

BBC News, April 24, 2003. **"High Vitamin Doses 'May Harm'."** *BBC News,* April 12, 2000. **Hijar, M. et al.** "Pedestrian Traffic Injuries in Mexico: A Country Update." *Injury Control and Safety Promotion,* May/June 2003. **Hindell, Juliet.** "Japan's War on Germs and Smells." *BBC News,* May 30, 1999. **Hintikka, J. et al.** "Debt and Suicidal Behaviour in the Finnish General Population." *ACTA Psychiatrica Scandinavica,* December 1998. **"Holiday Dinner Menu: Naturally Occurring Mutagens and Carcinogens Found in Foods and Beverages."** *American Council on Science and Health Booklets,* November 1998. **Holm, Erik.** "Good Heavens! A Bolt from Above Shakes a Preacher While He's Preaching." *Newsday,* June 23, 2003. **Holmes, Miata.** "UNC Study Names Cheerleading One of the Most Dangerous Sports for Women." *University Wire,* April 30, 1999. **"Honeybees Make Traffic Hazardous Near Milwaukee."** *CNN,* December 1, 1998. **Horwitz, Simi.** "The First Couple of Theatrical Insurance Take a Look Back." *Back Stage,* September 26, 2003. **"Hot Teapot is Hazard for Duval."** *Minneapolis Star Tribune,* June 12, 1999. **"How People Die at Work."** *Newsday,* October 2, 1993. **"How to Clean."** *Consumer Reports,* 1996, vol. 61, issue 1. **Howatt, Glenn.** "Teaching Wheelchair Safety Involves Rolling Along Through Cyberspace." *Minneapolis Star Tribune,* April 23, 1996. **Hruby, Patrick.** "The Seedier Side of Fur and Fun." *Espn.com,* February 10, 2003. **Human Mortality Database.** *http://www.mortality.org.* **Hummel, Rick.** "Edmonds is Sidelined After Freak Accident." *St. Louis Post-Dispatch,* September 11, 2000. **Hunter, P. R. and S. H. Burge.** "Bacteriological Quality of Drinks from Vending Machines." **Journal of Hygiene** (London), December 1986. **"Hurting Like Crazy,"** *The People,* September 29, 2002. **Husarska, Anna.** "Gnomenklatura (an Encounter with German Customs Along the German-Polish Border)." *New Republic,* November 21, 1994. **Hyde, Justin.** "Hands-Free Phone Talk Can Distract Drivers—Study." *Reuters,* August 16, 2001. **"Industrial Dust Explosions Prove Deadly: An Estimated Two to Three Dust Explosions Occur in Manufacturing Facilities in the United States Each Day."** *Occupational Hazards,* May 2003. **Ing, Lisa.** "Youthful Ballerinas Face Regimen Said to Pose Health Risks; Schools Solicitous of Dancers' Well-Being." *Washington Times,* August 9, 2000. **Ingram, Jay.** "New Insight into Madness and Great Art." *Toronto Star,* October 19, 2003. **Inskip, P. D. et al.** "Handedness and Risk of Brain Tumors in Adults." *Cancer Epidemiology, Biomarkers & Prevention,* March 2003. **"Installing Ceiling Fans."** *Do it Yourself Retailing,* May 1, 2001. **"Interested in Bra Art."** *Business Daily* (Philippines), May 18, 1998. **"It's a Plane—No, It's a Bird—Ouch! Falcon Attacks Reporter."** *Wisconsin State Journal,* June 29, 2000. **Iwamoto, J. and T. Takeda.** "Stress Fractures in Athletes: Review of 196 Cases." *Journal of Orthopaedic Science,* 2003. **Izon, Lucy.** "Sleep in Underground City in Turkey." *Toronto Star,* June 27, 1998. **Jacoby, Melissa.** "Does Indebtedness Influence Health? A Preliminary Inquiry." *Journal of Law, Medicine and Ethics,* Winter 2002. **Jamal, Muhammad.** "Job Stress, Satisfaction and Mental Health: An Empirical Examination of Self-Employed and Non-Self Employed Canadians." *Journal of Small Business Management,* October 1, 1997. **"Japan: Fatal Car Accident Blamed on High-Heel Boots."** *AAP General News* (Australia), November 2, 1999. **"Japanese Police Say Phoning and Driving Kills."** *Reuters,* March 14, 1997. **"Japan's Vaccination of Schoolchildren Cut Flu Deaths Sharply."** *Kyodo World News Service,* March 22, 2001. **Jaret, Peter.** "Death by Dust." *Health,* June 2002. **Ibid.** "Why Tiny Particles Pose Big Problems." *National Wildlife,* February/March 2001. **Jayasundera, T. et al.** "Golf-Related Ocular Injuries." *Clinical Experimental Ophthalmology,* April 2003. **Jaye, C. et al.** "Barriers to Safe Hot Tap Water: Results from a National Study of New Zealand Plumbers." *Injury Prevention,* 2001, vol. 7. **Jenkins, M. G. et al.** "Violence and Verbal Abuse Against Staff in Accident and Emergency Departments: A Survey of Consultants in the UK and the Republic of Ireland." *Journal of Accidental Emergency Medicine,* July 1998. **"Jet Lag: A Cancer Sleeper?"** *Science News,* September 19, 1988. **Johns Hopkins University.** "Pool Danger Checklist." *Better Homes and Gardens,* June 1, 1999. **Johnston, B. D.** "Transient Elevation in Risk of Injury in Siblings Following Injury Encounters." *Journal of Pediatrics,* January 2003. **Jones, Anya.** "Urban Sprawl May Lead to Obesity." *Philadelphia Tribune,* August 29, 2003. **Jones-Bay, Hassaun Ali.** "Hands On: How to Avoid and Treat Guitar-Related Injuries." *Acoustic Guitar,* August 1993. **Jonsson, Patrik.** "Lab Safety—Beyond Goggles." *Christian Science Monitor,* January 28, 2003. **Jury, Louise.** "Hidden Dangers of the Wendy House." *Independent,* May 23, 1998. **Kaharit, K. et al.** "Assessment of Hearing and Hearing Disorders in Rock/Jazz Musicians." *International Journal of Audiology,* July 2003. **Kalajian, Douglas.** "It's a Stretch to Claim You're No Rubbernecker." *Palm Beach Post,* January 9, 1999. **Katcher, Murray L.** "Tap Water Scald Prevention: It's Time for a Worldwide Effort." *Injury Prevention,* 1998, vol. 4. **"Keep Alert to Holiday Hazards."** *Child Health Alert,* December 1, 1994. **Kellan, Ann.** "Dogs, Like People, Suffer from Weekend Sport Injuries." *CNN.com,* October 24, 2000. **Kendall, Paul.** "The Luggage That Can Wheel Itself to Check-In." *Daily Mail* (London), August 9, 2001. **Kendzior, Russell J.** Telephone interview by author, February 26, 2003. **Kensho, Skyler.** "Gain without Pain." *Men's Health,* May 1, 2002. **Kershaw, Sarah.** "Concrete Falls from School." *Newsday,* February 5, 1998. **Kesich, Gregory.** "Settlement Ends Suit over Death in Elevator." *Portland Press Herald,* January 7, 2003. **Kinjo, K. et al.** "Variation During the Week in the Incidence of Acute Myocardial Infarction: Increased Risk for Japanese Women on Saturdays." *Heart,* April, 2003. **Kita, Joe.** "Beat the Odds." *Men's Health,* April 1, 1995. **Knight, Stacey.** "Injuries Sustained by Students in Shop Class." *Pediatrics,* July 2000. **Knight, Will.** "Heavy Geese Threaten Aircraft Safety." *New Scientist,* December 17, 2001. **Knowsley, Jo.** "Store to Check Doors After Shopper Dies." *Sunday Telegraph* (UK), June 28, 1998. **Kozlowski, James C.** "Lack of Safety Information and Training Faulted in Cheerleading Injury." *Parks and Recreation,* June 2001. **Krautwurst, Terry.** "The Truth About Mistletoe: There's More to this Traditional Holiday Plant than Love and Kisses." *Mother Earth News,* December 1, 2002. **Kunle, Olorundare.** "Road Accidents Are Caused by Distractions, Not GSM." *Africa News Service,* May 9, 2002. **Kurukulasuriya, Lasanda.** "At Debt's Door: Lasanda Kurukulasuriya Reports on an Agrarian Crisis That Is Driving Sri Lankan Farmers to Suicide." *New Internationalist,* January–February 2001. **Kynaston, J. A. et al.** "The Hazards of Automatic-Dishwasher Detergent." *Medical Journal of Australia,* July 3, 1989. **Kyriacou, Chris.** "Teacher Stress: Directions for Future Research." *Educational Review,* February 2001. **"Label Backers Deserve a Pop."** *Wisconsin State Journal,* January 4, 1996. **Labreche, F. et al.** "Characterization of Chemical Exposures in Hairdressing Salons." *Applied Occupational Environmental Hygiene,* December 2003. **Lacey, Stephen.** "A Brave Front." *Sydney Morning Herald,* December 26, 2002. **Lackey, Patrick.** "Safety in Numbers Suburban Living Can Kill or Maim You." *Virginia Pilot,* May 7, 1999. **Landers, Ann.** "Designer of Vending Machines Upholds Industry in Accidents." *St. Louis Post-Dispatch,* November 5, 1998. **Landers, Susan J.** "CDC Asks Physicians to Come Clean." *American Medical News,* November 18, 2002. **Langley, J. D. et al.** "Unintentional Injuries to Students at School." *Journal of Paediatric Child Health,* December 26, 1990. **Lantin, Barbara.** "Catching Cold? It Could be the Death of You." *Daily Telegraph* (UK), February 25, 2002. **Larson, Ruth.** "Gender Gap Dooms Men to Shorter Life Spans." *Insight on the News,* June 7, 1999. **Latinen, H. M. et al.** "Sound Exposure Among the Finnish National Opera Personnel." *Applied Occupational Environmental Hygiene,* March 18, 2003. **Laudan, Larry.** *Danger Ahead: The Risks You Really Face on Life's Highway.* New York: John Wiley and Sons, Inc., 1997. **Ibid.** "It's Not the Toys, Stupid. (Toys Are Not a Major Cause of Children's Injuries)." *Consumers' Research Magazine,* February 1, 1997. **"Laundryman Dies in Mishap with Machine."** *Boston Herald,* March 26, 2003. **Laurance, Jeremy.** "Skin Cancer Kills More Britons than Australians." *Independent,* March 28, 2003. **Lawrence, Anne.** E-mail correspondence with author, October 6–7, 2003. **Laws, Marcus J.** "Daniel Barry, 17, of Denton, Texas, lost his sight after being shot in the face with a potato gun." *KRT Photos,* May 23, 2003. **Lawson, Tracey.** "Hotel Swimming Pools Branded Health Hazard." *Scotsman,* January 6, 2004. **Leavitt, F. J.** "Can Martial Arts Falling Techniques Prevent Injuries?" *Injury Prevention,* 2003, vol. 9. **Ledford, Joey.** "Rubbernecking Is the Price We Pay for Being Human." *Atlanta Journal-Constitution,* September 19, 1999. **Lee, Laura.** *The Pocket Encyclopedia of Aggravation.* New York: Black Dog & Leventhal, 2001. **Lefkowitz, Melanie and Stephanie Saul.** "Repairman Killed in Elevator-Shaft Accident." *Newsday,* December 13, 2002. **Lessell, S.** "Handedness and Esotropia." *Archives of Ophthalmology,* October 1986. **Leth, P. M. et al.** "Fatal Accidents in House Fires." *Ugeskr Laeger,* June 1, 1998. **Lieberman, Janice et al.** "Escalator Accidents." *Good Morning America,* ABC Network, February 25, 1999. **"Lightning Kills Two Utah Campers,"** *Associated Press,* July 20, 2003. **Lillington, Catherine.** "Inquest Told of Screwdriver Death." *Evening Mail,* April 23, 2001. **Lillis, K. A. and D. M. Jaffe.** "Playground Injuries in Children." *Pediatric Emergency Care,* April 13, 1997. **Ling, T. C. and I. H. Coulson.** "What do Trainee Hairdressers Know about Hand Dermatitis?" *Contact Dermatitis,* October 2002. **Lironi, Brian and Steve McKenzie.** "Scotland's Water Scandal Special Report: Dirtier Than Athens; The Hidden Dangers; Tap Water Tests Put Scotland Last in Europe." *Sunday Mail,* March 24, 2002. **Lopez, Pablo.** "Safety Devices Post Threats." *Fresno Bee,* January 12, 2004. **Lowy, Joan.** "Sprawl Brings Drivers, Deer Too Close." *Washington Times,* April 1, 2001. **Lu, Vanessa.** "Weekend Woes of Hospitals." *Toronto Star,* August 30, 2001. **Lucy, William H.** "Watch Out: It's Dangerous in Exurbia. (Suburbs More Dangerous Than Cities)." *Planning,* November 1, 2000. **Luetters, C. M. et al.** "Left-Handedness a Risk Factor for Fractures." *Osteoporosis International,* November 2003. **Lutz, John Cloud.** "Nude Family Values." *Time,* June 30, 2003. **Lynch, J. et al.** "Survey of Abuse and Violence by Patients and Relatives Towards Intensive Care Staff." *Anaesthesia,* September 2003. **"Macho Image Costly."** *Dominion* (Wellington, New Zealand), August 25, 2000. **MacIntyre, B. H.** "The Dangerous Kitchen." *Ugeskr Laeger,* July 1997. **Macgregor, D. M.** "Golf Related Head Injuries in Children." *Emergency Medical Journal,* November 2002. **Mackay, Caitlin.** "Home's Hidden Danger." *Mirror* (UK), August 28, 2002. **"Malfunctioning Elevator Kills Man."** *CNN,* August 18, 2003. **Maltin, Liza Jane.** "Button Eyes, Cuddly Fur, and Stuffed with . . . Germs." *WebMD, www.webmd.com,* February 5, 2002. **"Man Attacked by Sparrow."** *Press* (Canterbury, New Zealand), January 19, 1999. **"Man Installing Ceiling Fan Electrocuted."** *St. Petersburg Times,* March 10, 2002. **"Man Trapped in Bed."** *Mercury* (Australia), March 26, 2003. **"Many Sting Deaths Can Be Prevented."** *Medical Observer Weekly,* July 4, 2003. **Marandino, Cristin.** "Stay in the Game." *Vegetarian Times,* May 2000. **Marder, Amy.** "Preventing Rabies: Best-Bet Protection from the New Epidemic." *Prevention,* May 1, 1994. **Markowitz, Arnold.** "Fishing Safety: Finding a Port in a Storm of Lightning." *Waterfront News,* July 2003. **Marks, Kathy.** "The Complete Guide to Australian Beaches." *Independent,* December 21, 2002. **Marlowe, Tammy.** "Sweater Snag Causes Accident." *Winnipeg Sun,* August 3, 2003. **Marshall, Anthony.** "Common Dangers in Bathrooms Should Grab Your Attention." *Hotel and Motel Management,* July 3, 2000. **Ibid.** "Swimming Pool Safety Devices." *Hotel and Motel Management,* November 19, 2001. **Mason, Betsy.** "Men Die Young—Even if Old." *New Scientist,* July 25, 2002. **Massey, Ray.** "Country Roads Are the Most Deadly." *Daily Mail,* May 4, 2001. **Matthews, Owen.** "Don't Look Up! Icicles Are Falling." *Moscow Times,* November 18, 1995. **McCafferty, Keith.** "When Tackle Attacks." *Field and Stream,* May 2001. **McCann, Michael and Gail Barazani, Editors.** *Health Hazards in the Arts and Crafts.* Washington, DC: Society for Occupational and Environmental Health, 1980. **McClam, Erin.** "U.S. Life Expectancy Reaches High." *Associated Press,* October 10, 2001. **McConnaughey, Janet.** "Lots of Bugs in Dog and Cat Bites." *AP Online,* January 14, 1999. **McGain, Forbes et al.** "Wasp Sting Mortality in Australia." *Medical Journal of Australia,* 2000. **McGivern, Mark.** "Nice Little Burner." *Daily Record,* June 28, 2001. **McKenney, Christy.** "Sloppy Handwriting Diverts County Checks to Sunrise, FL, Woman." *Sun-Sentinel* (South Florida), January 29, 2003. **McMillan, Matt.** "VA Study: Eyes on the Road; Rubbernecking Riskier Than Using Cell Phone." *The Washington Post,* March 18, 2003. **"Medical Research,"** *The Press* (Canterbury, New Zealand), February 5, 2002. **Meechan, Mary.** "Achoo!" *Better Homes and Gardens,* December 1997. **Meier, Peg.** "At a London Museum, a Lecture on Why Tea Has Gone to Pot." *Minneapolis Star Tribune,* July 16, 1995. **Meikle, James.** "Cold Stations and Bus Stops Blamed for Winter Deaths." *Guardian,* January 11, 2002. **Mellor, John P.** "Danger Lurks in Unlikely Places." *Birmingham Post,* April 16, 2001. **Mencimer, Stephanie.** "Tuna Lips, Guitar Nipples and Other Musical Maladies." *Washington Post,* March 25, 2003. **"Men's Style: Tips For A Close Shave."** *Birmingham Post,* October 10, 2001. **Merseyside Fire Service.** *http://www.merseyfire.gov.uk.* **Metzgar, Carl R.** "Steps, or Hazard Enhancers." *Pit &*

Quarry, August 1996. **Meyerovitch J. et al.** "Pneumatic Rupture of the Esophagus Caused by Carbonated Drinks." Pediatric Radiology, 1988, vol. 18. *Michigan Lawsuit Abuse Watch. http://www.mlaw.org/.* **"Mickelson Will Skip Canadian Open with Back Injury."** *AP Worldstream*, August 29, 2002. **Miller, Ian.** "Invasion of the Dangerous Tea Cosies." *The Mirror* (UK), June 7, 2001. **Minerd, Jeff.** "Protecting Pedestrians." *Futurist*, August 1, 1999. **Moffett, Dan.** "Gladiators of the Street: Garbage Men Battle Hazards Galore." *Palm Beach Post*, April 11, 1999. **Ibid.** "State's Most Dangerous Job: Trash Man." *Palm Beach Post*, February 25, 1999. **"Money Back: Pooch Nearly Dies After Ingesting Dime, Two Pennies."** *Grand Rapids Press*, August 28, 2003. **"Moon Madness a Myth?"** *Spectrum: The Wholistic News Magazine*, January/February 1990. **"More Electric Wheelchair Users Involved in Accidents."** *Kyodo News Service*, January 15, 2004. **Morgan, Sarah and Lori Parry.** "Quantum Sufficit. Just Enough." *American Family Physician*, April 1, 2002. **Morris, D. L. et al.** "Inflammatory Bowel Disease and Laterality: Is Left Handedness a Risk?" *Gut*, August 2001. **Morrison, Dan.** "Brooklyn Man Injured by Falling TV Set." *Newsday*, March 7, 1998. **Morrongiello, B. A. and M. D. Bradley.** "Sibling Power: Influence of Older Siblings' Persuasive Appeals on Younger Siblings' Judgements About Risk Taking Behaviours." *Injury Prevention*, March 1997. **Morrow, Ed.** *The Grim Reaper's Book of Days: A Cautionary Record of Famous, Infamous, and Unconventional Exits.* New York: Carol Publishing, 1992. **Morse, John.** "Shopping Carts Can Be a Danger to Children." *Ryan Engineering. http://www.ryanengineering.com.* **Morson, Berny.** "Keep Rollin', Rollin', Rollin', Though the Carts Are Stolen." *Denver Rocky Mountain News*, August 1, 2001. **Moses, Melinda.** "Well at Work, Sick on Vacation." *New Straits Times*, August 13, 2003. **"Mountaineering Team Clears 2 Tons of Garbage from Everest."** *Japan Policy and Politics*, June 3, 2002. **Moyle, Elaine.** "Parents Warned of Platform Shoe Perils." *Toronto Sun*, November 5, 1999. **"MRSA Superbug Carried by Pets."** *BBC News*, December 14, 2003. **Muir, Hazel.** "Penalty Shoot-Outs are a Health Hazard." *New Scientist*, December 19, 2002. **Mulford, J. S. et al.** "Coconut Palm-Related Injuries in the Pacific Islands." *Australia New Zealand Journal of Surgery*, January 2001. **Muller, Karen.** E-mail correspondence with author, August 20, 2003. **Munro, Alistair.** "Countryside Danger Kills 30 Brits a Year." *Daily Record*, August 18, 2000. **Murphy, Jamie Hannifin.** "Dodging Celestial Garbage." *Time*, May 21, 1984. **Murray, Paula.** "Farm Horrors." *Daily Record*, June 20, 2003. **Muse, Melinda.** *I'm Afraid, You're Afraid: 448 Things to Fear and Why.* New York: Hyperion, 2000. **Musicians Clinics of Canada.** *http://www.musiciansclinics.com.* **Nagourney, Eric.** "A Few Drinks of Soda Too Many." *New York Times*, May 13, 2003. **Nandy, Madhurima.** "Ceiling Fan Crashes Down on Student." *Midday Mumbai* (India), January 7, 2004. **Napoli, Maryann.** "Hospital-Borne Infections Can Be Reduced." *Healthfacts*, June 2001. **Narain, Jaya.** "The First-Aid Lessons that Saved My Brother from Choking to Death." *Daily Mail*, April 2, 2002. **Nathens, A. B. et al.** "Effect of an Older Sibling and Birth Interval on the Risk of Childhood Injury." *Injury Prevention*, September 2000. **National Association of EMS Physicians.** *http://www.naemsp.org.* **National Candle Association.** *http://www.candles.org.* **National Center for Health Statistics.** *http://www.cdc.gov/nchs/.* **National Electronic Injury Surveillance System,** *U.S. Consumer Product Safety Commission. http://www.cpsc.gov/library/neiss.html.* **Nattero, G. et al.** "Psychological Aspects of Weekend Headache Sufferers in Comparison with Migraine Patients." *Headache*, February 1989. **Nelms, P. K. et al.** "Time to B Cereus About Hot Chocolate." *Public Health Report*, May–June 1997. **Nelson, Rick.** "Ten Appliances that Shook the World." *Minneapolis Star Tribune*, April 18, 2002. **Nicholson, David.** "Home Safety: Simple Household Tools Can Cause Accidents." *St. Louis Post-Dispatch*, February 23, 1993. **Nielsen, K. K. et al.** "Bottle Injuries in Denmark 1991–1995." *Ugeskr Laeger*, May 1998. **Nilsson, C. et al.** "The Injury Panorama in a Swedish Professional Ballet Company." *Knee Surgery, Sports Traumatology, Arthroscopy*, July 2001. **Nissinen, M. et al.** "Left Handedness and Risk of Thoracic Hyperkyphosis in Prepubertal Schoolchildren." *International Journal of Epidemiology*, December 1995. **"No Damage to Elevator Doors: Police."** *CBC*, January 26, 2004. **North, Rosemarie.** "Violence on the Rise, Say Staff." *Waikato Times* (New Zealand), May 22, 2001. **Nriagu, J. O. and M. J. Kinm.** "Emissions of Lead and Zinc from Candles with Metal-Core Wicks." *Science of the Total Environment*, April 24, 2000. **"NSW: Drunk Walking a Major Safety Threat, Leading Researcher Warns."** *AAP General News* (Australia), May 24, 2002. **"NSW: Driveways More Dangerous Than Roads for Toddlers."** *AAP General News* (Australia), September 16, 2002. **"NSW: Nurses Subjected to Daily Violence: Survey."** *AAP General News* (Australia), July 2, 2002. **"NSW: Parents Warned: Recliner Chairs Pose Risk to Small Children."** *AAP General News* (Australia), December 03, 2001. **"NSW: School Fire Injures Seven Students, Teacher."** *AAP General News* (Australia), March 11, 1999. **"NSW: Show Dogs Killed by Bee Stings."** *AAP General News* (Australia), March 13, 2000. **"NSW: When the Quest for the Perfect Coiffe Goes Wrong."** *AAP General News* (Australia), February 25, 2002. **"NSW: Woman Dies from Bee Stings, Daughter Seriously Ill."** *AAP General News* (Australia), March 2, 2000. **Nunez, James.** "Are Vitamins Healthy for Society?" *University Wire*, February 14, 2001. **"Nurse's Death Prompts Call for Protection."** *Nursing*, July 1, 2001. **Ode, Kim.** "Take Playground Stats with a Grain of Sand." *Minneapolis Star Tribune*, June 20, 2000. **Oglesbay, Floyd B.** "The Flammable Fabrics Problem." *Injury Prevention*, 1998, vol. 4. **Ogilvie-Harris, D. J. et al.** "The Foot in Ballet Dancers: the Importance of Second Toe Length." *Foot Ankle International*, March 1995. **Ogut, Faith.** "A Metal Ring That Had Been Lodged in a Child's Nasopharynx for Four Years." *Ear, Nose & Throat Journal*, August 2001. **"One in Three Workers Fear Assault."** *BBC News*, November 2, 2002. **O'Neil, Sean.** "A Striking Mystery: Lightning Can Kill, Maim, or Leave Some Unharmed." *Washington Post*, July 29, 2003. **Ooman, A. et al.** "A Novel Trigger for Acute Coronary Syndromes: The Effect of Lunar Cycles on the Incidence and In-Hospital Prognosis of Acute Coronary Syndromes—a Three Year Prospective Study." *Journal of the Indian Medical Association*, April 2003. **"OSH: Many Accidents Not Reported."** *Daily News* (Taranaki, New Zealand), October 3, 2002. **Othman, Rahmat.** "Two Pupils Hurt When Fan Crashes in Class." *New Straits Times*, October 4, 2000. **Owen, Cathy et al.** "Lunar Cycles and Violent Behavior." *Australian and New Zealand Journal of Psychiatry*, August, 1998. **Padawer, Ruth.** "Man Is Burned in Yard." *Record* (Bergen County, NJ) January 19, 1991. **Palfreyman, Louise.** "Our Health: When Changing Rooms Ends in ER." *Sunday Mercury* (Birmingham, England), April 11, 1999. **Parcells, C. et al.** "Mismatch of Classroom Furniture and Student Body Dimensions: Empirical Findings and Health Implications." *Journal of Adolescent Health*, April 1999. **Parker, Tom.** *In One Day.* Boston: Houghton Mifflin, 1984. **Parsons, Tom.** "Sensible Packing Tips Ease Worries." *Knight Ridder*, June 11, 2001. **Pedestrian Council of Australia.** *http://www.walk.com.au/pedcouncil/homepage.html.* **Perkin, Joan.** "Sewing Machines: Liberation or Drudgery for Women?" *History Today*, December 1, 2002. **Perlman, Shirley.** "Door Safety Not Automatic. Family Seeks $2M in Woman's Death." *Newsday*, August 7, 2002. **Personick, Martin E. et al.** "Self-Employed Individuals Fatally Injured at Work." *Monthly Labor Review*, August 1, 1995. **Pervin, Kauser and Anthony Turner.** "A Study of Bullying of Teachers by Pupils in an Inner London School." *Pastoral Care in Education*, December 1998. **"Pet Blamed for Aerosol Fireball."** *Sunday Mercury* (Birmingham, England), January 28, 2001. **Peterson, Scott.** "The Cold War that Moscow Always Manages to Win." *Christian Science Monitor*, January 24, 2001. **Petheram, Judith.** "Growing Dangers." *Nelson Mail* (Nelson, New Zealand) June 28, 2002. **"Pets Boost Children's School Attendance."** *BBC News*, June 14, 2002. **Pickus, E. J. et al.** "Burns and Injuries Resulting from the Use of Gel Candles." *Journal of Burn Care Rehabilitation*, May–June 2000. **Pinker, Susan.** "The Truth About Falling Coconuts." *Canadian Medical Association Journal*, March 19, 2002. **"Playing Sax Can Be Risky, Researchers Say."** *Minneapolis Star Tribune*, December 29, 1999. **"Police Name Polish Woman Killed in Elevator Accident."** *AP Worldstream*, March 14, 2004. **Population Reference Bureau.** *www.prb.org.* **Potts, J. R.** "Ceiling Fan Injuries: The Townsville Experience." *Medical Journal of Australia*, February 1, 1999. **Poulsen, O. M. et al.** "Collection of Domestic Waste. Review of Occupational Health Problems and Their Possible Causes." *Science of Total Environment*, August 18, 1995. **Pountney, Michelle.** "Winning Idea Just Dropped in His Lap." *News.com.au*, May 27, 2003. **"Power-Chair Safety."** *Paraplegia News*, April 1, 2003. **Prasso, Sheridan.** "Up Front: 9 to 5: Bored to Death at Work—Literally." *Business Week*, July 1, 2002. **"Prosecute Violent Pupils and Parents."** *Education* (UK), March 29, 2002. **"Woman Injured by Flying Potato."** *AAP General News* (Australia), January 1, 2000. **Queensland Poisons Information Centre.** *http://www.health.qld.gov.au/PoisonsInformationCentre/homepage.htm.* **Quirk, Barbara.** "Cane, Crutch More 'Macho' Than a Walker." *Wisconsin State Journal*, October 17, 2000. **Rackl, Lorilyn.** "Artists at Risk: How Could Painting, Sculpting, Dancing or Playing Music Be Hazardous to Your Health?" *Chicago Daily Herald*, October 23, 2000. **Ragg, Michael et al.** "Analysis of Serious Injuries Caused by Stairway Falls." *Emergency Medicine*, 2000, vol. 12. **Raloff, J.** "Dusty Workplace May Cause Change of Heart." *Science News*, September 15, 2001. **Ibid.** "How Inhaled Dust Harms the Lungs." *Science News*, January 31, 1998. **Raloff, Janet.** "Beware Bathtub Wines." *Science News*, May 5, 2001. **Ibid.** "Newer Pennies Pose a Special Toddler Risk." *Science News*, December 5, 1998. **"Rate of Fatal Accidents to Self-Employed in Agriculture Growing Warns HSE."** *M2 Presswire*, July 1, 2003. **"Really Bad Driving (Golf Ball Hits a Florida School Bus and Shatters the Windshield)."** *Golf Digest*, May 2003. **Recer, Paul.** "Study Links Parasites, Life Spans." *Associated Press*, September 19, 2002. **Redfearn, Suz.** "Picking a Bone with Vitamin A." *Washington Post*, February 4, 2003. **"Ref Injured in Bruges Clash."** *BBC Sport*, June 21, 2000. **Reich, Rebecca.** "Playground Issue Highlights Traffic Concern." *Moscow Times*, July 15, 2003. **Reilly, Kevan.** "Classed as High Risk: Teachers Take a Caning on Insurance." *Mirror* (UK), August 6, 2003. **Rennicke, Jeff.** "Face Your Fears (encountering grizzly bears while hiking)." *Backpacker*, February 1, 1995. **Richards, A. M. and P. A. Arnstein.** "Treatment of Tea Burns in Asian Children." *Burns*, November 1996. **Richardson, Pete.** "Rearranging Rooms; Students Left with Pigsty After Carol Team Visit." *Daily Record* (Glasgow, Scotland), October 21, 2000. **Riddington, L. J. et al.** "Eye Injuries Caused by Elasticated 'Octopus' Straps." *Medical Journal of Australia*, November 17, 1997. *Rieko, Goto et al.* "Thermal Burn of the Pharynx and Larynx After Swallowing Hot Milk." *Auris Nasus Larynx*, July 2002. **Riley, Jamie.** "The Lung Association Will Study Leaf Burning." *St. Louis Post-Dispatch*, November 3, 1997. **Riley, Marianna.** "Not Quite Write. Handwriting Experts Lament Poor Penmanship." *St. Louis Post-Dispatch*, January 23, 1997. **"Robber Done in by Bad Handwriting."** *Associated Press*, April 3, 2002. **Roberts, Stephen E.** "Hazardous Occupations in Great Britain." *The Lancet*, August 17, 2002. **Roca, Bernardino.** "A Sewing Needle in the Liver (Case Report)." *Southern Medical Journal*, June 1, 2003. **Romania Factbook 2003**. *http://www.factbook.net.* **Rose, V., D. Moloney, A. Fleming.** "The Bra-Strap Injury: Should Men Have Lessons?" *British Journal of Plastic Surgery*, 2002, vol. 55. **Rosenthal, Donna.** "When Birds Become Missiles." *International Wildlife*, November 1998. **Ross, Brian et al.** "Toys in Trouble?" *20/20*, ABC Network, November 13, 1998. **Ross, Philip E.** "Safety May Be Hazardous to Your Health." *Forbes*, September 6, 1999. **Rossol, Monona.** E-mail correspondence with author, January 18, 2003. **Ibid.** *Stage Fright: Health and Safety in the Theater.* New York: Allworth Press, 1991. **Royster, J. D. et al.** "Sound Exposures and Hearing Thresholds of Symphony Orchestra Musicians." *Journal of the Acoustic Society of America*, June 1991. **Rowland, D. and Roberts, I.** "Potential Public Health Importance of the Oven Ready Chip." *Injury Prevention*, 2002, vol. 8. **Rowland, Rhonda.** "Sand Can Turn from Castle to Trap." *CNN*, July 5, 2002. **Royal Society for the Prevention of Accidents.** *http://www.rospa.com.* **Roys, M. S.** "Serious Stair Injuries Can Be Prevented by Improved Stair Design." *Applied Ergonomics*, April 2001. **Ruben, Paul.** "Scared to Death." *Popular Mechanics*, August 2003. **Rupp, Diana.** "Fish Catches Man." *Sports Afield*, October 1996. **Ryan, Caroline.** "Major Effort to Crack Flu." *BBC News*, February 18, 2002. **"SA: Farm Safety Scheme Being Planned."** *AAP General News* (Australia), February 28, 2000. **"SA: Two Bee Sting Deaths in a Day Prompt Allergy Warnings."** *AAP General News* (Australia), January 31, 2001. **"Safety Board Says Dust Caused Fatal N.C. Blast."** *Occupational Hazards*, July 2003. **Salinas, Mike.** "Woman Thespian Okay After Tumble." *Back Stage*, June 29, 2001. **Salleh, Anna.** "Birdstrikes in Australia Soaring." *Australian Broadcasting Corporation*, April 7, 2003. **Salmon, Lisa.** "Health Issues: Good Health On Tap." *The News Letter* (Belfast, Northern Ireland), July 24, 2002.

"The Satisfaction of Self-Employment." *Worklife Report,* September 22, 1997. **Saul, Stephanie and Joshua Robin.** "Rising Concern Over Elevators." *Newsday,* October 28, 2002. **Sawer, Patrick.** "Official: It Pays to be Tall as a Teenager." *Evening Standard* (London), April 25, 2002. **Schaff, Rachelle Vander.** "Children's Health: Don't Stick That There!" *Parenting,* April 1, 2000. **Schatzman, Dennis.** "Most Paper Money Has Drug Residue Stuck to It." *Los Angeles Sentinel,* November 23, 1994. **"School Accident Claims 21 Lives in Northern China."** *Xinhua News Agency,* September 24, 2002. **Schremp, Valerie.** "Rascals' Mascot Breaks His Collarbone While Performing Stunt During Game." *St. Louis Post-Dispatch,* August 16, 1999. **Schuman, J. S. et al.** "Increased Intraocular Pressure and Visual Field Defects in High-Resistance Wind Instrument Players." *Ophthalmology,* January 2000. **Schwanitz, H. J. and W. Uter.** "Interdigital Dermatits: Sentinel Skin Damage in Hairdressers." *British Journal of Dermatology,* 2000. **"Sea Fishing Claims 70 Lives Daily."** *Xinhua News Agency,* January 25, 2001. **Seeger, Nancy.** *An Introductory Guide to the Safe Use of Materials.* Chicago, IL: Art Institute of Chicago, 1984. **Seligman, Daniel.** "Twenty Days that Shook the World, The Southpaw Sorrows, Betting on Criminals and Other Matters." *Fortune,* January 16, 1989. **Senier, L. et al.** "Hospitalizations for Fall-Related Injuries Among Active-Duty Army Soldiers, 1980–1998." *Work,* 2002, vol. 18, issue 2. **"Severe Flu Season Coming."** *News in Science* (Australia), April 16, 1999. **Sharp, Deborah.** "When Lightning Strikes." *USA Today,* August 9, 1994. **"Sheep Push Farmer off Cliff in Rush for Hay."** *Press* (Canterbury, New Zealand), January 30, 1999. **"Shell Blast Rocks Scrapyard, School."** *American Metal Market,* December 12, 2002. **Sherr, Lynn et al.** "Ups and Downs of Elevators." *20/20,* ABC Network, May 29, 1998. **Shetland, Tom Morton.** "Fresh in From Far Out. Macho Attitudes Prevent Use of Safety Equipment in Scotland's Fishing Industry." *New Statesman,* December 20, 1999. **Shinoda-Tagawa, T. and D. E. Clark.** "Trends in Hospitalization After Injury: Older Women Are Displacing Young Men." *Injury Prevention,* September 2003. **"Short Guys Finish Last."** *Economist,* December 23, 1995. **Shukla, Hema.** "Hindu Priest Attempts to Give Ganges a New Lease on Life." *Associated Press,* May 16, 1998. **Simeone, Lisa.** "Interview: Dr. Stephen Zawistowski Talks About Holiday Hazards for Pets." *Weekend Edition,* National Public Radio, December 23, 2001. **Simons, Paul.** "Health Zone: Bolts from the Blue." *Mirror* (UK), October 4, 2001. **Simplicio, Joseph.** "The Use of Illegible Handwriting as an Effective Teaching Tool." *Education,* 1996, vol. 116, issue 3. **"Size Does Matter: Flight Attendants Propose that Luggage Measure Up to an Industry Standard."** *World Airline News,* December 18, 1998. **"Skyscrapers Rain Terror on New York."** *Independent on Sunday,* January 4, 1998. **Sloan, Gene.** "Horseplay Can Override Amusement Park Safety Steps." *USA Today,* June 17, 1997. **Smiley, Alison.** "How Auto Safety Devices Bring New Risks." *Consumer's Research,* March 1, 2001. **Smith, Ian.** "Personal Time/ Your Health: A Dangerous Mix Anesthesiologists Warn Patients to Stop Taking Herbal Supplements Before Surgery." *Time,* October 9, 2000. **Smith, Scott.** "Golf Course Safety: Getting the Shaft." *Golf Digest,* July 2000. **Ibid.** "Saving Lives on the Golf Course: Join the Battle Against Golf's Deadliest Enemy—Sudden Cardiac Arrest." *Golf Digest,* October 1999. **Smith, Stephen.** "Cheerleading Becoming Riskier." *Toronto Star,* November 16, 2002. **"Soc: Henry Injured by Coin Thrown from Stand."** *AAP Sports News* (Australia), March 26, 2003. **Spaite, D. W.** "Banning Alcohol in a Major College Stadium: Impact on the Incidence and Patterns of Injury and Illness." *Journal of American College Health,* November 1990. **Spang, S. et al.** "Eye Injuries Caused by Opening or Explosion of Beverage Bottles." *Ophthalmologe,* February 1995, vol. 92. **Spitz D. J. and W. U. Spitz.** "Killer Pop Machines." *Journal of Forensic Science,* March 1990. **Springen, Karen.** "Perilous Parlors." *Newsweek,* August 19, 2002. **"Squirrel Knocks 'Seed Head' for Six."** *Evening Telegraph* (UK), November 27, 2001. **"Stain Removal Attempt Wrecks Residence."** *CNN.com,* October 13, 2003. **"Standing Tall Against Slips and Falls."** *Occupational Hazards,* April 1, 1998. **Stein, Joel.** "Something Evil in the Ear Canal." *Time,* March 26, 2001. **Stephens, Edward.** "Canine Killers in the Car." *Evening Mail,* March 5, 2003. **Still, J.** "An Unusual Mechanism of Burn Injury Due to Flaming Drinks." *American Surgeon,* March 1997. **Stoppard, Miriam.** "Dr. Miriam Stoppard's Health Focus Today." *The Mirror* (UK), March 7, 2002. **Strauss, Gary.** "Open at Your Own Risk." *USA Today,* July 13, 2001. **"Study on Workplace Violence Shows Healthcare Positions Are the Riskiest."** *Pittsburgh Post-Gazette,* February 16, 1998. **"Study Shows Maximum Life Span is Changing."** *Oakland Post,* October 4, 2000. **Stuttaford, Thomas.** "Hot and Bothered; Body and Mind." *Times* (UK), January 2, 1997. **"Suburbia (1950s)."** *American Decades CD-ROM.* Gale Research, 1998. Reproduced in History Resource Center. Farmington Hills, MI: Gale Group. *http://galenet.galegroup.com/servlet/HistRC/.* **Sullivan, R. Lee.** "Snob Water: Most Designer Water Has About the Same Minerals and Purity as San Antonio Tap Water." *Forbes,* August 14, 1995. **"Sunscreen Keeps People Out in Sun Longer—Study."** *Reuters,* August 4, 1999. **"Supermarket Fined Over Glass Accident."** *Birmingham Post,* November 28, 2002. **Surfers Medical Association** (Australia). *http://www.damoon.net/sma/SMAhealth.html.* **Syal, Rajeev.** "DIY Programmes Blamed for 27 pc Rise in Injuries." *Daily Telegraph* (UK), January 7, 2001. **"Syncope and Seizures Due to Hair Grooming."** *American Family Physician,* October 1, 1993. **Talbot, Jillian.** "Sports Physician Gets to Grips with Injuries." *Dominion* (Wellington, New Zealand), December 19, 2001. **Tanner, Lindsey.** "U.S. Flu Deaths Up Sharply Since 1970s." *Associated Press,* January 8, 2003. **Tarr, Joel A.** "Managing Danger in the Home Environment." *Journal of Social History,* June 1, 1996. **Tasker, Georgia.** "The Toe-Away Zone and Other Gardening Dangers." *Knight Ridder,* August 1, 2002. **"Teenager Regrets Potato Gun Incident."** *Nelson Mail* (Nelson, New Zealand), October 27, 2000. **Teitz, C. C. and R. F. Kilcoyne.** "Premature Osteoarthritis in Professional Dancers." *Clinical Journal of Sports Medicine,* October 1998. **Tenner, Edward.** "How the Chair Conquered the World." *Wilson Quarterly,* March 22, 1997. **Tezel, Adnan et al.** "The Effect of Right or Left-Handedness on Oral Hygiene." *International Journal of Neuroscience,* 2001. **Thakur, C. P. and D. Sharma.** "Full Moon and Crime." *British Medical Journal,* December 22, 1994. **Thomas, Colin.** "The Hidden Dangers of Beetroot." *BBC News,* February 18, 2000. **"Those Reports of Bagel Injuries Have Only a Crumb of Truth."** *International Herald Tribune,* June 3, 1996. **"Tight Neckties Linked to Glaucoma Risk."** *Reuters,* July 28, 2003. **Tilles, Denise.** "Danger Zone." *Opera News,* April 16, 1994. **"Tin Levels Down in Canned Foods."** *Eurofood,* September 12, 2002. **Todd, Joan Ferlo.** "When Bed Isn't Safe Haven." *Nursing,* December 1, 2002. **Todd, Susan and Jim Lockwood.** "Tempting Bagel Made Bear Swipe." *Star-Ledger* (Newark, NJ), July 3, 2001. **Torelli, P. et al.** "Weekend Headache: A Possible Role of Work and Life-Style." *Headache,* June 1999. **"Tot Breaks Arm in Washing Machine."** *Birmingham Evening Mail,* October 1, 1998. **Toth, Sara.** "Prevention Is Key to Staying Out of Hospital, ER Staff Says." *St. Louis Post-Dispatch,* April 25, 2002. **"Traveling in Wheelchairs—Increased Risk?"** *Paraplegia News,* March 1, 2001. **Tung, M. Y. et al.** "Golf Buggy Related Head Injuries." *Singapore Medical Journal,* October 2000. **Turnberg, W. L. and F. Frost.** "Survey of Occupational Exposure of Waste Industry Workers to Infectious Waste in Washington State." *American Journal of Public Health,* October 1990. **"Two Die in Polish Garden Gnome Factory Blast."** *Reuters,* May 14, 1998. **"UK Government: Whitehead Welcomes New Fire Deaths Low."** *PressWire,* February 20, 2002. **"UK Suffers Most Cold Weather Deaths in Europe."** *BBC News,* January 11, 2002. **"U.S. Children Swallow 3,000 Coins in 1996."** *Medical Post,* May 26, 1998. **U.S. Consumer Product Safety Commission. U.S. Department of Labor, Bureau of Labor Statistics.** *http://www.bls.gov.* **U.S. Environmental Protection Agency.** *http://www.epa.gov.* **Utton, Tim.** "Why a Full Moon Makes Us Want to Have a Party." *Daily Mail,* November 20, 2002. **VanFlein, Thomas.** "Allocation of Fault and Products Liability: A Comment of Safety Products and Human Error." *Alaska Law Review,* June 1, 2002. **Victor, C. R. et al.** "Who Calls 999 And Why? A Survey of the Emergency Workload of the London Ambulance Service." *Journal of Accidental Emergency Medicine,* May 1999. **Viestenz, Arne and Michael Küchle.** "Eye Contusions Caused by a Bottle Cap: A Retrospective Study Based on the Erlangen Ocular Contusion Register." *Ophthalmologue,* February 2002, vol. 99. **Ibid.** "Ocular Contusion Caused by Elastic Cords: A Retrospective Analysis Using the Erlangen Ocular Contusion Registry." *Clinical & Experimental Ophthalmology,* 2002, vol. 30. **Vingerhoets, A. J. et al.** "Leisure Sickness: A Pilot Study on Its Prevalence, Phenomenology and Background." *Psychoterapy-Psychsomoatics,* November–December, 2002. **Vigoda, Arlene.** "OUCH, OUCH, OUCH." *USA Today,* October 27, 1994. **"La Vitamine A Met Les Os en Danger."** *Health and Food,* February 14, 2003. **"Vitamin A Seen as Risk in Fractures."** *Newsday,* January 23, 2003. **"Vitamin Overdoses."** *Pediatrics for Parents,* February 1, 1994. **Walker, E. P.** E-mail correspondence with author, October 10, 2003. **Wallis, Anna.** "Dairy Work Most Dangerous On-Farm Activity." *Evening Standard* (Manawatu, New Zealand), October 17, 2000. **Walsh, James.** *True Odds: How Risk Affects Your Everyday Life.* Los Angeles, CA: Silver Lake Publishing, 1998. **Wang, H. and Y. Nie.** "Municipal Solid Waste Characteristics and Management in China." *Journal of the Air and Waste Management Association,* February 2001. **"Warning: Hanukkah Menorah Poses Fire Hazard."** *Consumer Reports,* December 2003. **"Warning Over Candle Danger."** *Evening Mail,* December 19, 2000. **Warren, Ellen.** "Could It Be that Old Books Are Really, Uh, Mind-Altering?" *Chicago Tribune,* September 21, 1996. **"Washing Machine Boy Recovering."** *Birmingham Post,* October 27, 1998. **Wasylenki, Donald.** "Inner City Health." *Canadian Medical Association Journal,* January 23, 2001. **Wasson, S. J. et al.** "Lead in Candle Emissions." *Science of the Total Environment,* September 16, 2002. **Watanabe-Suzuki, K. et al.** "Traumatic Basal Subarachnoid Haemorrhage Caused by the Impact of a Golf Ball: A Case Report." *Medical Science Law,* April 2003. **Weaver, Jefferson Hane.** *What Are the Odds?* Amherst, NY: Prometheus Books, 2001. **Wehrfritz, George et al.** "Death by Conformity: Mental Health in Japanese Workers." *Newsweek,* August 20, 2001. **"Weigh the Risks, Lighten the Load."** *Girls' Life,* August–September 2002. **Welsh Injuries Prevention Network.** *http://www.capic.org.uk.* **Westcott, Sarah.** "Pool Danger to Pregnant Women." *News Letter* (Belfast, Northern Ireland), April 4, 2002. **"When One Sibling Is Injured, Another Is At Risk—For a While."** *Child Health Alert,* April 2003. **"When the Mercury Falls: Autumn Leaves Taint River with Poison."** *Science News,* March 9, 2002. **Whittlesey, Lee H.** *Death in Yellowstone: Accidents and Foolhardiness in the First National Park.* Boulder, CO: The Court Wayne Press, 1995. **"Why Flu Can Kill."** *BBC News,* December 6, 2002. **Wilstein, Steve.** "Harvard Study Links Fans, Binge Drinking." *Associated Press,* December 12, 2002. **Winfield, Armand.** "Fifty Years of Plastics." *Plastics Engineering,* May 1, 1992. **Witze, Alexandra.** "Lefties Apparently Unfazed by Evolution." *Dallas Morning News,* October 10, 2003. **Wolkomir, Richard.** "An Architect Who Takes Stairways One Step at a Time." *Smithsonian,* June, 1993. **"Woman, 31, Dies After Falling Into Dishwasher."** *Evening News* (Edinburgh, Scotland), May 28, 2003. **"Woman Dies When Caught in Subway Escalator."** *Associated Press,* November 27, 1998. **"Woman Electrocuted After Placing Key Card in Hotel Room Door."** *Minneapolis Star Tribune,* June 28, 1995. **Wood, Gaby.** "Dream Doll: From Feminist Bugbear to Forbidden Cultural Artifact, This Contentious Toy Was, in Fact, Designed by a Working Mother for Her Daughter." *New Statesman,* April 15, 2002. **World Against Toys Causing Harm, Inc.** *http://www.toysafety.org.* **Wright, P. et al.** "Left-Handedness Increases Injury Risk in Adolescent Girls." *Perceptual Motor Skills,* June 1996. **Wright, Peter.** "Angler Overboard." *Motor Boating & Sailing,* July 1997. **Wu, J. S. et al.** "Microbiological Examination of Foods Sold via Vending Machines." *Zhonghua Min Guo Wei Sheng Wu Ji Mian Yi Xue Za Zhi* (Abstract), May 1985. **Wyshak G.** "Teenaged Girls, Carbonated Beverage Consumption, and Bone Fractures." *Archives of Pediatrics & Adolescent Medicine,* 2000, vol. 154, issue 6. **Yeager, Robert C.** "Walking into Danger." *Ladies Home Journal,* November 1, 1995. **Young, Emma.** "Cycle of Violence." *New Scientist,* December 22, 2000. **Ibid.** "Occupational Hazard." *New Scientist,* May 30, 2001. **Yoo, R. T. et al.** "Corneal Injury from Explosion of Microwaved Eggs." *American Journal of Ophthalmology.* March 1998, vol. 125. **Zablocki, Elaine.** "Keep Weight Training Injury-Free: Don't Be a Dumbbell." *WebMD,* August 27, 2001. **Zanen, A. L. and A. P. Rietveld.** "Inhalation Trauma Due to Overheating in a Microwave Oven." *Thorax,* March 1993. **Zebrowitz, L. A. et al.** "Bright, Bad Babyfaced Boys: Appearance Stereotypes Do Not Always Yield Self-Fulfilling Prophecy Effects." *Journal of Personality and Social Psychology,* November 1998. **Zolotov, Andrei.** "The Dangers of Riding the Escalator." *Moscow Times,* April 5, 2002.